The Torments of Love

AMPLE

NARRATION FAI-

cte par *Quezinstra*, en regrettant
la mort de son compagnon *Guene-*
lic, & de sa Dame *Helisenne*
apres leurs deplorables fins
ce qui se declarera auec
decoration du stille
poëtique.

The Torments of Love

Hélisenne de Crenne
(Marguerite Briet)

Edited and with an introduction by Lisa Neal

Translated by Lisa Neal and Steven Rendall

University of Minnesota Press

Minneapolis / London

Published by the University of Minnesota Press
111 Third Avenue South, Suite 290, Minneapolis, MN 55401-2520
Printed in the United States of America on acid-free paper

Library of Congress Cataloging-in-Publication Data

Crenne, Hélisenne de.
    [Angoysses douloureuses qui procedent d'amours. English]
    The torments of love / Hélisenne de Crenne (Marguerite Briet) ;
edited, with an introduction by Lisa Neal ; translated by Lisa Neal
and Steven Rendall.
      p. cm.
    Includes bibliographical references.
    ISBN 0-8166-2788-6 (hc)
    ISBN 0-8166-2789-4 (pbk)
    I. Neal, Lisa. II. Rendall, Steven. III. Title.
PQ1607.C65A813   1996
843'.3—dc20
                                     95-41011

Contents

Acknowledgments

Work on this book was facilitated by a travel grant from the National Endowment for the Humanities and research grants from the University of Puget Sound. Fellowships held at the NEH Institute on Translation Theory conducted by Marilyn Gaddis Rose and Joanna Bankier in 1993 also made a valuable contribution to this work. We would like to thank our daughter, Josephine Dow Neal, for her patience and good cheer throughout this project.

Introduction

In 1538 a Parisian publisher, Denis Janot, printed a volume titled *Les Angoysses douloureuses qui procedent d'amours* (translated here as *The Torments of Love*). Before 1560 no fewer than eight complete editions of this work appeared, and between 1538 and 1541, Hélisenne de Crenne published three other works, two of which present variations on the basic plot of *The Torments of Love*, one in an epistolary format, and the other as an allegory.[1] Hélisenne clearly enjoyed a certain literary success in the first half of the sixteenth century. However, from then until the early years of the twentieth century, relatively little interest was shown in her works. They were neither reprinted nor, so far as we can determine, read.

Interest in Hélisenne was rekindled in 1908, when Gustave Reynier devoted a chapter to her in his study of the early French novel *Le Roman sentimental avant l'Astrée* and identified *Les Angoysses* as "the first sentimental novel" in French, a distinction that has since been often reiterated by historians of French literature (120).[2] More recently, her work has attracted considerable attention from critics interested in French women's writing. Discussion of *The Torments of Love* has been hampered, however, by the unavailability of a modern edition of the complete text of the novel, for despite the importance now accorded to Hélisenne, the two modern editions of this work, both published in 1968, reprint only Part One. Consequently, most studies of *The Torments of Love* deal only with this first part, emphasizing, for instance, its intent—self-defensive, apologetic or scornful (Larsen, Nash)—or the symbolism of the gaze and its appropriation by the female narrator (Winn, Cottrell). The privilege critics have granted the first part of the novel appears to be closely linked to the assumption that it is in some sense autobiographical.[3] We do not know whether early readers of this account of a married woman's infatuation with a younger man were aware that "Hélisenne de Crenne" was a pseudonym adopted by Marguerite Briet, a member of the lesser aristocracy born in Abbeville, in Picardy, around 1510 (Loviot, Saulnier). The name of the novel's female protagonist is the first name of the author as it is given on the title page (reminding us perhaps of Proust's "Marcel," since the heroine's last name is never mentioned), and "Crenne" bears a close re-

Introduction

semblance to the name of the estate from which Marguerite's husband, Philippe Fournel, lord of Crasnes (or Craonne), took his name. It is therefore possible that many of the author's contemporaries assumed the text was an autobiographical account of real events, and certainly many modern readers have made the same assumption.

Whether, and to what extent, this assumption is justified remains one of the most important questions facing anyone who seeks to understand Marguerite Briet's text.[4] It is especially crucial in assessing the significance of the second and third parts of the narrative, which are not so clearly autobiographical, since they are not spoken in the first person by the female narrator. In Part Two, the lover Guenelic recounts his own adventures, though the title and preface of this part indicate that Hélisenne in fact is speaking, "in the person of Guenelic." The "full and ample narrative" (Part Three, chapters 11-12), on the other hand, is narrated in the first person by Guenelic's companion, Quezinstra. Given this obvious difference between the narrative voice of Part One and the narrative voices in the subsequent parts of the work, it is perhaps not surprising that few readers have seen them as forming an integral whole.

This perception is reinforced by Paule Demats's suggestion that the author may have circulated the first part of the novel in manuscript in order, as Tom Conley puts it, "to criticize her cruel husband and unworthy lover and to exonerate herself from public blame" (325).[5] If Part One was originally conceived as an apologia complete in itself, then its success may have encouraged the author to write the subsequent "fictional" parts. This hypothesis is plausible and cannot be ruled out, but it is seriously weakened, not only by the fact that no manuscript copy or separately published edition of this part has ever been discovered, but also by the ambiguous portrayal of the main characters and of their marital conflict, a point to which I will return.

Some details in the life of Marguerite Briet also suggest that the novel is autobiographical. Like her heroine, the author did in fact legally separate from her husband and may have been sequestered by him as well;[6] she held properties in her name (a fact referred to in the novel); and a number of place-names in the book are palindromes of places important in her life ("Eliveba" for "Abbeville," "Hennerc" for "Crenne"). Perhaps the most intriguing fact uncovered in the archives is that Briet's last will and testament left a pension to a certain Christophe Le Manyer, "for good and pleasant services." It is tempting to speculate that he may have been the model for the lover in the novel, but we know nothing further about him.

Even a reader unfamiliar with the life of Marguerite Briet may be inclined to imagine that this novel is a self-defensive autobiographical account—though somewhat displaced—of the author's own travails. After all, as we have seen, the first name of the author on the title page and that of the first-person narrator-protagonist are identical. A well-known contemporary theorist of autobiography, Philippe Lejeune, has seen in this nominal identity the fundamental article of the "autobiographical contract," which assures the reader that the narrative following is an account of verifiable facts relating to the author's life.

Furthermore, the apologetic agenda announced in the preface to Part One encourages readers to expect an autobiographical narrative on the model of Saint Augustine's *Confessions*, recounting the author's youthful folly and eventual conversion to Christian virtue. In *The Torments of Love*, the female narrator sometimes seems to express two distinct points of view, a situation that has been understood according to this model, as if the narrator were relating a past (painful) experience from the point of view of the (enlightened) present. In the following passage, past and present voices are juxtaposed:

> And I said to myself: "It is foolish to be so timid . . . I want to have the delectable pleasure of seeing my beloved. I shall nourish love secretly in my heart without divulging it to anyone . . ." and thus I began to drive reason away, whereby sensuality won the day.

However, the view of the narrative as autobiographical and self-defensive encounters a number of serious problems. First of all, if we pursue the narrative to the end, we learn that the heroine dies before its completion, and we are thus forced to reconsider the assumption that she is telling her own story. Even before her death—when she is escaping with Guenelic and Quezinstra from her husband's henchmen—it is unclear who is telling the story, since, under these circumstances, she would have had no opportunity to write anything.

Second, the narrator's ethical stance seems to shift repeatedly. In the Epistle to Readers that begins Part One the narrator's tone leads the reader to conclude that the book's purpose is to warn women of the dangers of yielding to illicit passions:

> O dear ladies, when I consider that in seeing how I was caught, you will be able to avoid love's dangerous snares by resisting them from the outset, and not persisting in amorous thoughts, I beg you to try to avoid idleness, and to busy yourselves with some honorable activity.

This passage seems to define a clear ethical stance for the narrator and a clear notion of the audience addressed. As we read through Part One, however, we are often struck by passages in which the narrator seems to lose sight of the cautionary goal of the work; she takes relish in her love for Guenelic, especially in the activity of writing and reading about it, which she calls a "delightful occupation": "In this solitude, I took delight in reading my beloved's letter; afterward, I looked over the copy of my own, examining in detail all the terms of each of them"; "I immediately began the present work, thinking it would be a very happy labor for me." While these passages might be seen as describing a perspective later abandoned, others suggest that the narrator continues to view her work as a means of satisfying her desire rather than as a condemnation of adulterous love. Thus she expresses her hope that the written account of her passion may serve to persuade Guenelic of her devotion to him and thereby convince him to liberate her from the tower to which she has been banished:

> It seemed to me that if [the book] could be delivered into the hands of my beloved, that could cause my sufferings to come to an end and give rise to a joyful life. . . . If I am granted the felicity of having it fall into my beloved's hands, I beg him not to deprive me of my hoped for and expected delight.

At this point we realize that the narrator has expressed at least two mutually exclusive reasons for writing her story: to warn women about love and discourage them from falling prey to passion, and to inform her lover of her devotion to him in the hope of perpetuating her own passion. To complicate matters further, the narrator seeks understanding and forgiveness for her moral weaknesses from her female readers, while nonetheless admitting that she experiences great pleasure from writing and reading about her illicit love.

How is the reader to sort out the contradictions among the explicit goals of the narrator-protagonist? One might be inclined to draw a distinction between the female voices in the prefaces and in the body of the work, that is, between what seems a primary, authorial narrator and a secondary, character narrator. Both voices are heard throughout the novel, however, and often it cannot be determined which one is speaking. For instance, in the following passage, Hélisenne describes the feelings that move her when she writes about her great love for Guenelic:

> The recent memory of [diverse and fantastic images] makes my hand so weak it trembles and several times I stopped writing and broke my quill. But since this might cause me to be thought pusillanimous, I shall try to write them down.

What, precisely, is the nature of the feelings described here? Is it remorse or passions revisited?

The distinct moral and cognitive perspectives we noticed in Part One persist in later sections of the novel. On one hand, Hélisenne seems to be preoccupied with her sensual desire; she is both imprudent and impatient. From the moment she is sequestered, all her energy is devoted to writing an account of her love in the hope of making contact (and then making off) with Guenelic. Just a day before her death, upon leaving the castle with her lover, she makes it clear that she intends to renounce her marriage vows and instructs the maid to inform her husband that he should find himself another wife. Shortly afterward, a noticeably different voice speaks in the high moral tone characteristic of the early warnings to the "Dear Ladies." Her last words to Guenelic espouse the tenets of Neoplatonic love; she considers her death a blessing since she has been prevented from committing the sin of adultery, and she exhorts Guenelic to change his behavior and lead a good life. Her speech reads like a series of maxims: "As much as you have loved the body, henceforth be a lover of the soul." "There is no travail so great that it cannot be moderated by prudence, nor any pain so acute that it cannot be broken by patience."

There is no single or simple way to qualify the character, narrator, and implied author designated by the name Hélisenne. At one moment obsessed, at another remorseful, and then feigning remorse but being obsessed, she incarnates and maintains difference.[7] She is restrained reason and pure passion as she oscillates between moral stances; she is female and male as she shifts from one writing voice to another; and she is public and private as she addresses her innermost thoughts to her readers, her lover, and also to herself. Such shifts of the Hélisenne voices have led one critic to propose that the juxtaposition of the past and present voices contributes to the novel's suspense, and another to posit an elaborate evolution in this character's persona (Bergal, Wood). Yet it is not possible to restrict any given voice to a fixed temporal zone, nor can we discern the kind of linear evolution within the speaking voice we might expect in an autobiography: passionate and impulsive in youth, patient and wise in old age (Roy Pascal).

All this raises questions about the narrator's reliability in the sense defined by modern theorists of narrative: the coincidence of the narrator's perspective with that of the implied author. As we have seen, in *The Torments of Love* it is virtually impossible to determine which of the moral perspectives and goals espoused by the narrator should be attributed to the implied author. It seems clear that the narrator of an autobiography—at least, a "nonfictional" autobiography—cannot be unreliable in this way. Hélisenne's unreliability as a narrator thus provides a compelling reason to question the notion that Part One is an autobiographical account.

But Hélisenne is not only an unreliable narrator; as a character, she repeatedly deceives not only her husband and her counselors, but even her lover. There are many examples of her lies, dissimulation, and lack of piety: "On the spot, I quickly invented a clever lie"; "I began to deny everything, for I had become bold and audacious"; "I . . . quickly found, through diligent feminine reflection, some clever lie"; "I pretended that I wished to reform . . . nonetheless I did not repent having been captured by love." Hélisenne's irreverent attitude is amply illustrated in the description of a confession her husband encourages her to make in order to "unburden [her] heart":

> Being in this temple without feeling any devotion, I began to premeditate my confession to this monk, and I said to myself: "Oh Lord . . . I am neither contrite nor repentant. . . . And so it seems to me folly to divulge it to this old man who has grown all cold, impotent, and useless for nature's purposes. . . . If I were to believe him, I should have only pain and torment, without receiving any pleasure of delight. . . . But when all is considered . . . he cannot force me to follow his advice, and so I shall take pleasure in talking about the man I love more ardently than any lover was ever loved by his lady."

The characterization of the female protagonist as deceptive and unrepentant (though ever faithful to love) tends to undermine the thesis that Briet intended the work as an apologia of her own actions. If she had truly wished to defend her honor publicly, is it reasonable to suppose that she would depict herself as an impious woman who, in the absence of her lover, derives pleasure from recounting her passion? It might, of course, be considered one of Briet's great achievements that she managed to move beyond flat, stereotypical characters and maintain a complex tension between two quite different ethical attitudes throughout a long novel. Her Hélisenne reflects the contradictions that characterized a woman's situation in her society: on the one hand, she is passionate and unrepentant; on the other, virtuous and moralizing.

Just as critics have tended to overlook the unsavory aspects of Hélisenne's conduct in the story, so too they have largely ignored the complexity of the husband and reduced him to a caricature of the jealous, malevolent spouse. He is described, for instance, as a "cantankerous, jealous, sadistic husband who resents his wife's beauty" (Mustacchi and Archambault, 2).[8] The tendency of modern readers to perceive the husband as an ogre is no doubt largely determined by the violence to which he resorts in dealing with his wife: he strikes her on three occasions, once knocking out her teeth. In our justifiable desire to denounce the husband's acts of cruelty, however, we may have overlooked another achievement of the author: she presents the husband as a nuanced and complex character who defies facile categorization.

The husband detects signs of his wife's amorous obsession from the outset. "He was clear-sighted enough to be sure I had been captured," Hélisenne writes, adding that his reaction is to show her "more fondness than usual." At first, he conveys his perception to her with no recrimination: "My love, that young man there is looking at you very hard, he keeps his eyes fixed on you. I know he is in love, for I know what love is." He assures her that if she were to overcome her infatuation and return to a more decent way of life, he would not hold her in any less esteem. As we know, Hélisenne does not abandon her passion; though she never actually commits adultery, she repeatedly makes promises to her husband that she immediately breaks. Faced with such obstinacy, the husband nonetheless continues to excuse her, saying that the "first impulses of love are not under our control," and to declare his abiding love for her: "I love you so much that it would be difficult and (I think) impossible for me to try to turn you away from your love." The husband does on occasion use harsh words, calling her "False woman!" and "wicked woman," but his most threatening words are directed not at Hélisenne but at her lover, whom the husband promises to kill should she ever kiss him. Knowing this, Hélisenne nonetheless tells Guenelic that her husband suspects nothing, thereby encouraging him to be more bold than he might be were he fully conscious of the danger involved, and showing herself to be as unscrupulous with respect to her lover as she is to her husband.

The husband then attempts to end his wife's infatuation by threatening to separate from her if she continues to compromise herself by being seen with Guenelic in public. A surprising aspect of this "threat" is the husband's assurance that, in the case of a legal separation, he would not lay claim to her property and fiefdoms. In making such a promise, the husband shows a sense of fairness—the properties came from her family but he would have rights to them as her husband—and also moral principle insofar as he does "not want to profit from the wealth of a lascivious woman."

These admonitions and supplications on the part of the husband occur before he commits any act of violence. The first blow Hélisenne receives from her husband occurs immediately after he reads a letter from her to Guenelic, in other words, when the proof of his wife's infidelity seems irrefutable (though she denies her letter is an expression of her own sentiments). Before the second and third blows, the husband attempts to gain control of himself by leaving the scene: "not being able to endure such lapses into immodest looks, [he] was compelled to leave," and "he had left, not being able to endure the violent rage that seized him."

In both instances Hélisenne expresses thoughts that suggest she does not view herself as a victim of wanton aggression: first, she admits her transgressions and broken promises and she later claims her husband loves her "more than any man ever loved a woman." It is true that we could interpret her sense of guilt and lack of anger at her husband as symptoms of a kind of battered-wife syndrome or, put in different terms, as an example of a female subscribing to the male point of view. In this vein, Robert Cottrell concludes that "she internalizes the male imago as the super-ego and thus participates in her own degradation" (12). It should be noted, however, that Hélisenne's reaction would not have surprised her contemporaries, who were well aware of men's legal right to discipline and even imprison their wives and children for suspected transgressions. Given the fact that her sixteenth-century readers were not apt to blame a man for beating an adulterous or deceptive wife, it is all the more surprising that Briet went to such lengths to portray the husband's compassionate side, as if she were attempting to exonerate him in the reader's eyes. For example, Briet devotes a long passage to a description of the husband's compassion for his wife when she falls ill from her emotional anguish:

> My husband, seeing me in this misfortune, was diligent in sending for doctors and physicians who . . . prepared several medicines for me intended to help me; they did hardly anything for me, because I was as tortured by passions of the soul as by corporeal illness. Seeing this, my husband was thrown into a great sadness, for although I had greatly erred, his original love was so deeply anchored and alive in his heart that it was not in his power to avoid its influence. Thus, to incline the divine goodness to aid my salvation, there was no place dedicated to the name of God that my husband did not visit and where he did not offer sacrifices.

Thus, the complex characterizations of the husband and wife tend to undermine the notion that Part One was conceived as an apologia; they also have important implications for our understanding of the novel's raison d'être and its place in literary history and feminist literature. If Briet is a "champion of women's rights" (Robbins-Herring), it is not in any simple sense; in terms of its characterizations, *The Torments of Love* seems to reinforce images of woman as lascivious and deceitful that appear all too frequently in medieval and Renaissance misogynistic writings.

A second implication of Briet's characterizations concerns the criticism of her novel as incoherent, a criticism based on perceived shifts in the character of Guenelic, an issue to which I will return. Those who see the novel as incoherent often argue that it shifts from one genre to another, that Part One is characterized by a very personal expression of inner turmoil while the subsequent parts contain a series of formulaic chivalric adventures. Thus Henri Coulet, in a section devoted to *The Torments of Love* in his well-known history of the French novel, expresses the commonly held view that Part One is the only significant part because it is the only one that is based on the real-life experience of the author: "The account Hélisenne gives is as engaging and personal (based on personal memories) as Guenelic's is conventional . . . The second part is of hardly any interest to us today" (105). Implicit in this view is the assumption that the subsequent parts are an unfortunate addition.[9] Coulet is following here the line of criticism first formulated by Gustave Reynier. After qualifying Briet's novel in its entirety as "not very coherent," Reynier suggests that it be truncated after Part One:

> [The novel] was popular for quite some time, and it undoubtedly would have been for longer if some intelligent editor had separated the sentimental part from the chivalrous and didactic parts, which had perhaps at first complemented the whole but later weighed it down and made it seem antiquated, thereby hiding what is sincere, passionate and truly modern in the book. (122)

Such views authorize a reading of the novel as originally or essentially autobiographical, and justify neglecting those parts of the text that might suggest otherwise.

The critique of the novel as incoherent is not, however, completely without foundation, if by incoherence one refers to an apparent shift in narrative voice and in focus (from Hélisenne speaking about herself in the first person to Hélisenne narrating Guenelic's tale in "his" first person; and from emphasizing the female character's psychology to the heroic actions of Guenelic and Quezinstra). Indeed, Briet herself alludes in the Epilogue to these shifts, and this suggests that she regarded them as worthy of attention; at least they were not an oversight on her part. The "full and ample narrative" dramatizes the way in which the book is divided against itself, and it makes explicit two questions that have been implicit throughout the work: What kind of story is this? For whom is it written?

This fantastic account of the afterlife of the lovers is related by Quezinstra, who accompanies the bodies of Guenelic and Hélisenne to the underworld when Mercury transports them there. The manuscript of Hélisenne's book, *The Torments of Love*, is discovered next to her body, and Mercury, assuming it to be a cautionary tale, offers it to Minerva, the goddess of wisdom. This goddess, "born from the brain of thundering Jupiter," seems to him the appropriate recipient, for she is chaste and wise and, as Mercury points out, she loves to read. Venus strongly objects, saying: "O Mercury . . . you have deprived me of this book, which ought to be dedicated to my divinity, since you know it deals with matters of love and sensuality." Then Minerva replies that because the book deals with warlike matters usually conducted under her protection, the book is rightfully hers. This complicates matters further, for now Venus maintains that, on that ground, the book should go to Mars, "under whose power warlike acts are conducted." The conflict between the goddesses of wisdom and love thus parallels the difference between the narrator's voices, one calling for wisdom and chastity, and the other abandoning herself to desire. The Venus-Mars dichotomy also anticipates one of the questions that, as we have seen, dominates critical debate on the book—is the book a sentimental novel or a chivalric romance?—without offering a definitive answer to it.

As I mentioned, certain critics argue that the work is incoherent because the change in Guenelic—from an immature and impatient young man to a knight embodying chivalric values—is, in a word, implausible. The epistle prefatory to Part Two does at first appear to significantly alter details that had been established earlier in the novel. For example, the female narrator claims that Guenelic is not of a social class inferior to her own (as he was said to be in Part One), nor did he ever behave badly (as had been amply illustrated in Part One). Hélisenne assures her readers that Guenelic had been slandered in the past and that "now" he is "praiseworthy through his deeds":

> I have remembered that on several occasions I wrote in my Torments about Guenelic's importunities and the accusations against him, wherefore, I believe, some readers may find it strange that after I had depreciated him in this way, he should have been able afterward to endure so many travails in order to find his lady. . . . For that reason, you might think Guenelic's love not very great. Nevertheless, if you have recently read my writings, and consider them carefully, you will see that I was never certain the reports I heard were true. Hence I believe, and you should also assume, that bearers of false tales imputed such crimes to him.

The claim that Guenelic was the victim of "bearers of false tales" encounters a problem when we recall that these gossipmongers do not appear in Part One until after Hélisenne has witnessed Guenelic's treachery at first hand. But rather than proving the novel incoherent or supporting the claim that Part One was written or published separately, the "false" defense of Guenelic by the narrator can just as easily be seen as reinforcing the image established in Part One of an impassioned Hélisenne who will go to any lengths to maintain her love, including lying about his caste or deeds in order to make him appear her social and moral equal.

Other aspects of Part One reappear in the epistle prefatory to Part Two—the multiple ethical stances and characterizations—leading the attentive reader to perceive a certain consistency from one section to another despite changes in focus and voice. First, the narrator's explicit goals for writing her book are parallel to those of Part One; they reflect the two main ethical stances present throughout the first section and are just as incompatible. The audience has been broadened to include men,[10] but the novel is still presented on one level as a cautionary and exemplary tale:

> Having shown you, benevolent readers, the vehement passions that sensual love can cause in the tender and delicate hearts of women in love, I have conceived the desire to narrate and recite to you the calamities and extreme miseries young men may suffer as a result of indiscreet love . . . I have no doubt that the present work will not only stir modern gentlemen to martial activity, but will in the future stimulate our posterity to be true imitators of this art.

On another level, the narrator belies her personal interests in writing the tale: to redeem Guenelic in the eyes of readers so he appears a lover worthy of her, and, as the narrator explained in Part One, to convince Guenelic of the ardor of her love.

Despite this element of consistency with Part One, the question remains: is the tale recounted in the subsequent parts so transformed into a series of knightly adventures that the reader loses sight of the sentimental aspects that characterized Part One? In response, M. J. Baker has compared Briet's work to traditional chivalric romances and concluded that *The Torments of Love* does not fit under this rubric since it continues to subordinate plot to characterization, and accords to love more importance than it receives in chivalric tales, in which the woman is generally considered a "prize," chastity is treated lightly, and love is rarely tragic. Baker concludes that the work is "of interest to the study of the novel precisely because of its significant departures from novels of chivalry."

The generic affinities of the parts of the novel following Part One are closely linked to the question of characterization, insofar as critics claiming the novel shifts from one genre to another tend to base their conclusion in part on the character of Guenelic, and in particular on the changes in his attitudes and actions as he evolves from an Adonis figure into a heroic knight (Reynier, 119-20). And yet one should question whether this character actually changes; if he does not fulfill the role of a chivalric lover, Parts Two and Three could not be categorized in any simple sense as "chivalric romances." Indeed, I would agree with Baker that although the novel does include detailed accounts of heroic feats and battles, Guenelic is far from incarnating values traditionally associated with chivalry. Rather than showing courage in the face of danger, he periodically slips into melancholy and often fails to act at decisive moments. Put simply, sentiment still governs Guenelic's behavior, just as it did in Part One.

Guenelic, the unheroic knight and despairing lover, relies less on his good deeds than on his good looks. For example, in chapter 13 of Part Two, he is taken prisoner by enemies who mistake him for his more valorous cohort. The enemy leader's brother is much impressed with Guenelic's great beauty and pleads for clemency for him:

> He [Guenelic] possesses such natural beauty that I have taken a singular pleasure in looking at him, wherefore I should be greatly saddened by his death.

At first glance, we may recognize in this passage the conceit of the "gaze" so familiar in Petrarchan love poetry of the Renaissance: to gaze is to desire. But what is particularly interesting is that the *object of the gaze is male,* and that the male-as-desired object is a theme prevalent in Part One. Thus, in words resembling those used by the enemy leader's brother to express his pleasure at looking at Guenelic, Hélisenne had expressed her reaction to gazing at the young man:

> I was inwardly astonished to find myself thus led to gaze at this young man; this had never happened to me with other men . . . I desired no pleasure other than this one.[11]

In Part Two, as in Part One, Guenelic plays the role of object of desire that is traditionally played by the female. Just as the emotional aspect of the characters, so important in Part One, is never completely absent from subsequent parts, so too the theme of the gaze runs through the entire novel.

The nature of the relationships among the main characters also remains similar throughout the book. The interaction between Guenelic and Quezinstra is not unlike that of Hélisenne and her husband insofar as the young, handsome Guenelic, like the beautiful Hélisenne, struggles with a seemingly irrepressible emotion while Quezinstra, like the husband, attempts to awaken his friend to the true nature of his folly. Although Quezinstra and the husband represent the force of reason and social responsibility (as does one of the voices of the female narrator), neither is immune to strong emotions. As we have seen, the husband is particularly prone to strong reactions in his dealings with Hélisenne. His emotions cause him to be anxious and tormented, and do not always spur him to violence. "He was struck by anguishing pain because of the excessive love he had for [Hélisenne], of which he was unable to divest himself, and which had the power to restrain the anger which tortured his poor heart, and to convert it into compassion." Likewise, Quezinstra is prone to bouts of anxiety—for example, during Guenelic's captivity in the aforementioned episode. Quezinstra was "so anxious that he could not in any way be consoled until he was sure [Guenelic was] out of danger"; he awaited his friend's release from captivity with "more desire than the ladies of Greece awaited the arrival of their husbands."

Insofar as the principal characters all grapple, throughout the novel, with the force of passion and with the desire to maintain (or redeem) their reputations, we cannot classify certain parts of the novel as strictly sentimental and others as chivalric. By the same token, many of the themes and devices that characterize the first, allegedly "autobiographical" part of the novel are in fact repeated in other forms in subsequent parts, and thus it does not seem prudent to distinguish among the parts on that basis. What we can conclude, however, is that Briet was able to create multidimensional figures engaged in complex relations with one another and also to maintain common themes across several hundred pages. We should note here that *The Torments of Love* is exceptional in the history of French narrative forms in the sense that it is a long, continuous story written at a time when short novellas were proliferating (Jeanneret, 85-86). Briet's novel calls for a reading that follows a single diegetic movement over hundreds of pages. This may be as truly a "modern" aspect of the novel as its focus on the characters' emotions.

The Torments of Love also uses narrative framing and embedding in a way that establishes constantly changing relationships among the different parts of the narrative.[12] What is unusual in Briet's use of framing is, first, the way in which readers are provided with unknown facts about the conditions under which the story is being told, and must therefore "reframe" or reinterpret the entire preceding narrative. This distinguishes Briet's use of the framing device from what might be considered a more traditional use, for example, in Marguerite de Navarre's *Heptameron*, where framed narratives are identified before they begin and the reader knows at all times who is speaking and under what circumstances. In *The Torments of Love*, it is more difficult to determine the circumstances under which the story is narrated, for the delayed frames are rarely identified as such. The frames require readers repeatedly to reconsider the assumptions on which they have been operating, and thus to alter their conception not only of the local context but of the narrative as a whole. Some of the most significant instances of reframing occur in later parts of the novel, and once again this suggests the importance of reading the text in its entirety.

The first example of such reframing occurs near the end of Part One. Up to this point there have been numerous indications leading us to think that Hélisenne's love is but a memory (and a bad one at that) and that her new objective is to serve as a moral exemplar. Assimilating it to the Augustinian model, we naturally assume the text was written years after the end of the infatuation:

> Now, would to God I had the Trojan Cassandra's powers . . . I should have saved myself the endless regrets which daily pullulate in my sad heart; but I believe it was divine predestination, because I know I shall serve as an example to others.

Statements like this one, expressing regret and repentance about what seems to be a love long past, must be rethought and reframed when the activity of writing is resituated temporally or described differently. One such description occurs when the narrator is telling how her husband discovered her writings: "I didn't think of hiding my writings, in which were set forth and amply declared all the good and bad fortune that had befallen me since Cupid had won domination and mastery over me." This suggests that what we have been reading was not written in retrospect but is rather the result of an ongoing process, a kind of personal diary Hélisenne kept as her love story unfolded. The difference between the two narrative instances is significant, for the account appears to be, on one hand, an autobiographical confession written years after the events described and, on the other, a more immediate and thus more fluctuating record of the narrator-protagonist's sentiments as they were experienced at the time.

This second frame, the "book-as-diary," lasts a mere fifteen pages before a new frame is set in place, when we discover that the diarylike account no longer exists; it was destroyed by her husband during one of his rages. We then recognize that we are *not* reading this account after all, but instead a rewritten version that Hélisenne decided to compose once she was imprisoned; in other words, we return to our first assumption that the book was written after the end of the love affair and that this frame encompasses all that precedes it. And yet if we believe that Hélisenne intends this later, reconstituted story to be read by Guenelic, the interjections of high moral tone associated with the addresses to the "Dear Ladies" seem counterproductive. This may lead us to doubt that the book we have been reading is in fact the book the character wrote.

The next frame differs from the others in that it is, or appears to be, announced at the beginning of Part Two and frames what follows: the narrative in which the speaking voice belongs to Hélisenne *qua* medium, ventriloquist, or scribe of Guenelic's voice (as indicated at the beginning of Parts Two and Three and, in editions after 1538, in the titles as well to these parts: "Composed by lady Hélisenne speaking in the person of her beloved Guenelic"). His account of the quest for his lady is thus embedded within Hélisenne's narrative, as if she were reporting his speech, as if the whole of Part Two and much of Part Three should be enclosed within quotation marks. The absent narrator makes her presence known only on the title pages and in the prefaces to Parts Two and Three, and in letters and dialogues between Guenelic and Hélisenne in Part Three.

In one of these letters Hélisenne informs Guenelic that her guardian at the prison tower, her husband's "perverse" sister, "had been shown a book about [her] torments." The book in question must be the rewritten account of Hélisenne's love for Guenelic and also may contain some description of her anguish as a prisoner, but it certainly does not include the adventures of Guenelic, since at the time she wrote the letter Hélisenne had not yet had any further contact with him. We cannot determine whether Hélisenne lost possession of her book when the sister-in-law saw it, nor is it clear exactly when this event took place. At this juncture, it is nonetheless possible to imagine that the story of Hélisenne's love for Guenelic is being told after the sister-in-law's discovery, though this would not affect the temporal point from which Guenelic's story is narrated: sometime after his visit to the castle. The episode of the sister-in-law's reading of Hélisenne's account demonstrates the extent to which the narrator's attempts to write a book become events in and of themselves that are recounted in the context of more encompassing frames. As readers become aware of the successive acts of rewriting, they must often alter their perception of the narrative frame, sometimes returning to a previous assumption about the conditions of the book's composition.

The repeated references to the writing of the book bring to mind another unusual aspect of Marguerite Briet's use of the framing device: it forces readers to be aware of the narrator as a woman writer who composes as a response to, and in spite of, social constraints.[13] Indeed, at every point when Hélisenne is confined by her husband, she writes something, perhaps as much to reread as to communicate with her beloved. The resulting book becomes something of a character in its own right as the novel progresses, one that survives the anger of her husband, who burns it, the vindictiveness of the sister-in-law, and the demise of the author herself. Each mention of the book, and the activity of producing it, reinforce in readers' minds the image of a woman whose main activity is *writing*.

As we have seen, the book figures prominently in the "full and ample narrative," a section that also presents the final framing effect of the novel. It is Quezinstra who explains how the book came to be completed and printed. Although it is much shorter than the preceding parts, the "full and ample narrative" constitutes the most comprehensive frame in the sense that both Hélisenne's narrative of her own torments (rewritten once or twice) and her impersonated narrative of Guenelic's adventures are now embedded in Quezinstra's account of the afterlife of the lovers and of their stories. This delayed frame that retrospectively reframes all the preceding narratives also serves to draw attention to the book as an entity transcending the death of its author. There is no suggestion that Quezinstra wrote, or rewrote, any portion of the novel, not even the final chapters of Part Three in which he witnesses both deaths. Instead, he assumes a role that was to become familiar in eighteenth-century literature, that of an "editor" whose contribution to the narrative is chiefly to attest to its authenticity and to explain how it appeared in print.

At each juncture where a new frame is put in place, the reader becomes aware of the process of telling the story, the identity of the storyteller, the conditions under which the story and the storytelling take place, how the information the story contains was learned and how the text itself came to be published—all things that tend to disrupt the text by interposing themselves between the reader and any vicarious experience of another person's life. But they also unify the text insofar as the reader, after finishing the book, is apt to perceive it as an integral whole, rather like a set of Chinese boxes: one fits within another that fits in another and so on. Of course, in the case of Chinese boxes, we know immediately what the object is upon opening it, and this knowledge is not put in question. In *The Torments of Love*, on the other hand, the delayed frames make us progressively rethink and modify our initial assumptions. This aspect alone of Briet's use of framing—its retroactivity—should distinguish her as a literary innovator.

And yet, despite Briet's innovative characterizations and narrative structures, she has often been criticized for the derivative nature of her writing.[14] There is no doubt that certain elements of plot and phrasing can be traced to other works, in particular to Boccaccio's *Fiammetta*, a psychological romance whose heroine may have been a real woman; Caviceo's *Peregrino*, a tale of fantastic adventure; and Jean Lemaire de Belges's *Les Illustrations de Gaule et Singularitez de Troie*, a prose collection of legends and tales from antiquity.[15] This criticism seems to be related to the perception of *The Torments of Love*, again, as an autobiographical account of experiences that are, by definition, lived. Borrowing ideas and words is deemed incompatible with a sincere personal account that is not influenced by literary models—that is, in a word, "artless." To again quote Henri Coulet: "Hélisenne clearly takes her inspiration from

Boccaccio's *Fiammetta*, but Boccaccio created *Fiammetta* whereas Hélisenne is recalling personal experience" (105).

In considering this criticism of Briet's practice of borrowing, it is important to bear in mind that sixteenth-century notions about creativity and originality differed from our own. Many Renaissance writers borrowed freely from the writings of the ancients and of their contemporaries; Caviceo himself drew heavily on Boccaccio, who in turn drew on Virgil and Ovid. One index of the degree to which this was considered a nonissue in Briet's time is the lack of typographical marks to set off quotations, a convention that was not established until well into the seventeenth century. It therefore seems somewhat odd that Briet is criticized for having borrowed from her literary predecessors. (Paule Demats, in her edition of Part One of *The Torments of Love*, goes so far as to italicize phrases and words also found in the works of Boccaccio, Caviceo, and Jean Lemaire de Belges.)

Second, the intertextual nature of Briet's work opens the possibility that the novel is not a mimetic representation of the author's life but rather a work created in the imagination of its author whose memories concern the details not of her past life but rather of her past reading. Hélisenne herself puts into question the autobiographical nature of *The Torments of Love* in Part One when she claims to write about events she denies having experienced personally. One such declaration occurs when her husband has just discovered the letter in Hélisenne's hand containing incriminating evidence against her. Hélisenne retorts, "with loud moans and exclamations . . . 'Alas! my love, what moves you to be so cruel because of the letter you found, which was composed *only as an exercise and to avoid idleness?*' " (my emphasis).[16] Later, in the Epistle that begins Part Two, the fact that the book is a creative exercise, a first-person fictional narrative, is explicitly indicated: the female narrator announces that she will henceforth tell in the first person a story that contains not her own experiences but rather those of men: "the battles fought by Quezinstra and Guenelic, while wandering over the earch in search of the aforesaid lady." If Parts Two, Three, and the "full and ample narrative" are clearly presented as a first-person fictional narrative, one might well wonder why Part One should not also be seen as such.[17]

Briet's creative independence as a writer is also forcefully stated in another of her works: *The Personal and Invective Letters* (*Les Epîtres familieres et invectives*, 1539). This epistolary novel comprising a correspondence among various fictitious characters—Hélisenne, her husband, and friends—contains references to the basic plot of Part One of *The Torments of Love*. The husband accuses his wife of infidelity, just as in the earlier novel, but here he claims his suspicions were confirmed when he read a book she wrote entitled, not surprisingly, *The Torments of Love*.

The husband, like any naive reader, obviously assumes that the text is an autobiography and that he can reliably infer from it what his wife has done in fact. Hélisenne tries to dispel from his mind the notion that the events and emotions recounted in her book were personally experienced by her, and in so doing, she strongly asserts her autonomy as a writer:

> Your heart's hasty judgment has led you to imagine that my [*Torments of Love*] (which I had composed, in fact, only to pass the time) were intended to immortalize an illicit love. You believe, moreover, that I really experienced the lasciviousness about which I wrote. I am surprised you should imagine this to be the case . . . In a matter like this one I find that my opinion rather conforms to the generally accepted one. I shall, therefore, speak of love (not because I have learned this through experience, but because literature has taught me to understand). (Mustacchi and Archambault, 81, 84)

This passage is of crucial importance. First, we should note that Briet claims her right to base her writing on literary precedents, to join the world community of writers, as it were. The author's frequent allusions to works of antiquity as well as to those of her contemporaries suggest that she saw herself as a member of a literary tradition.[18] They also indicate the broad range of her reading and her awareness of the main humanistic issues of her day, including the ongoing debate concerning women known as the "Querelle des Femmes."[19] It is somewhat ironic that modern scholarship on Briet has criticized the derivative nature of her writing rather than seeing her appropriation and rewriting of earlier, authorial, works as typical of Renaissance rewriting of earlier texts and as an indication of her efforts to legitimate herself as a learned writer within the tradition.

A second, even more important point to be made about this passage is that the letter writer asserts her right to compose *fiction*, just as the character Hélisenne does when she announces in the epistle prefatory to Part Two of *The Torments of Love* that she will henceforth use the first person to tell another person's story. In these and other cases, Briet claims her right to speak as another, to write stories not based on her own experience as a woman, and to derive pleasure from reading her own stories. These assertions should lead us to reevaluate the role Briet plays in the history of women's writing. Her work cannot be regarded as simply testimonial; it affirms the woman author's right to create and enjoy fiction. Constance Jordan, one of the few critics to recognize the importance of Briet's stance on this issue, suggests that such an affirmation is "potentially revolutionary," and adds, "I know of no other instance in the feminist literature of this century in which a writer has insisted particularly on the autonomy of artistic expression for women" (181). As a woman writer, Briet lives simultaneously in two worlds. On one hand, a domestic realm in which she is controlled by others and required to be dutiful, and on the other, a literary realm in which she is free to assume other identities—free, that is, until readers imagine they have recognized her domestic identity behind a textual mask.

For Jordan, the seeds of equality for women lie in the act of writing: "When [socially subordinate] persons claim the liberty of the pen . . . they are, in effect, claiming something like social equality, at least by virtue of the fact that they are being heard" (181) And yet Coulet's assertion that Boccaccio "creates" whereas Briet "remembers" leads us to wonder whether Briet has in fact achieved equality with her male counterparts in view of the fact that her writing continues to be judged by the degree of its correspondence to her life. Readers who limit their appreciation of her writing in this way may tend to discount the parts of *The Torments of Love* in which no such correspondence is readily apparent, or worse yet, criticize her for the very quality they praise in others: her departure from lived experience, her creativity. Briet's work is significant in the history of women's writing less for its representation of the author's personal experience than for its exploration of the literary resources of her time and its assertion of a woman's right to imagine and describe the experiences of others. Long recognized as the author of the first French sentimental and epistolary novels, Briet should perhaps also be credited with the invention of the first fictional autobiography in French.[20] By going significantly beyond her personal experience in *The Torments of Love*, Briet creates a space in which she can be a moral exemplar, a deceitful wife and lover, a melancholy, inept knight, and, importantly, a woman writer whose literary work is sought after by gods. The lucidity with which she claims the right to create and take pleasure in fiction should assure her place within the feminist tradition.

History of the Text

Sixteenth-century publishers must have seen in Marguerite Briet's literary work a potential "best-seller," for after Janot's first edition of the novel in 1538 there followed four others before 1545, three of which were slightly revised. (For example, the 1539 edition included the chapter divisions we have maintained in our translation.) In 1551, the title page of an edition published by Charles Langelier indicated that the text was "revised and corrected in entirety by the author" ("le tout reveu et corrigé de nouveau par elle"), though it cannot be determined whether Briet actually had a hand in the revision. What is certain, however, is that a little-known poet, Claude Colet, assumed the responsibility for changing "the obscure and Latinate words" into terms "more familiar and common" ("les motz obscurs et trop aprochans du Latin [en termes] plus familiers et . . . uscitez"; Demats, 102-3). At least this is what Colet wrote in a letter dated March 15, 1550, included in all editions after that date, in which he furthermore claims to have undertaken the task reluctantly at the request of certain "gracieuses Damoyselles" who were unable to understand Hélisenne's erudite style. In his letter, Colet ponders whether the author used such a style expressly in order *not* to be understood by those of "mediocre sçavoir."

Most critics have accepted at face value the contents of Colet's letter and, by extension, the necessity for such revisions; in fact, two of the three twentieth-century editions of her writings have reproduced his revised text without giving variants from the original edition.[21] But can we preclude the possibility that the revisions were undertaken as a kind of marketing ploy, an effort to make the works appear more "modern"? An analysis of Colet's revisions to Part One of *The Torments of Love* as they are listed in Paule Demats's edition suggests that few changes were necessary to make the text intelligible to a francophone reader, whether living in the sixteenth or the twentieth century. Of the six examples Demats gives to illustrate "errors of typography and coherence" that Colet "corrected," none comes close to obscuring the meaning of the text. (The middle French spelling of the first-person singular form of "émouvoir"—"n'emouve"—is changed to "n'emeue," "oppressée de si extreme destresse" to "presseé de si extreme destresse," "apparier" to "aparier," "il eut imposé fin" to "il eut mis fin." The name "Claudia" was changed to "Glaudia" in the first edition revised by Colet in 1551, but then, apparently when someone realized the mistake, it was changed back to the original and correct spelling in later editions; Demats, xlvii.) Thus it seems that Colet's changes to *The Torments of Love* may have been motivated more by a desire to modernize or standardize the text than to clarify its meaning. But despite Colet's efforts, and despite the novel's considerable success in the first half of the sixteenth century, the 1560 edition was the last, and Marguerite Briet's novel was soon forgotten.

The two modern editions of Part One both have their own peculiarities: Jérôme Vercruysse's is based on an edition revised by Claude Colet in 1550 but does not identify the changes in the text, whereas Paule Demats's more scholarly text, based on the original 1538 edition, italicizes words and phrases drawn from other works, notably from works by Boccaccio and Caviceo. So on the one hand, we have a version that conceals its revision or rewriting by a sixteenth century male editor, and on the other, an edition of the "original" version of the book that constantly highlights the female author's debt to male writers. Our translation is based on the 1538 edition as it appears in the unpublished dissertation of Harry Secors.

A Note on the Translation

Ideally, translators seek both to preserve the distinctive characteristics of their author's style and to produce a version suitable for contemporary readers of their own language. This is never an easy task (many, of course, have pronounced it impossible), and it is particularly difficult when one is attempting to translate a writer like Marguerite Briet. Features of her style that are not unusual in male writers of her period—for instance, the use of semisynonymous qualifiers or "doublets," Latinate syntax, diction, and spelling, as well as frequent neologisms—become vital when they are seen in relation to her effort to demonstrate her qualifications as a writer. These stylistic features thus become signs of her claim to participate in a realm normally reserved for male writers, and also of her determination to address her women readers in a manner that does not assume their inability to understand and take pleasure in elevated and even learned language.

We have not wished to emulate Marguerite Briet's contemporary, Claude Colet, who "translated" her text into a style he considered more appropriate—because easier and more familiar—for female readers. Thus we have been more than usually reluctant to eliminate in our translation the time-bound and alien characteristics of Marguerite Briet's language, though we have normally not retained those that seemed to us mere linguistic tics, such as the habit of beginning sentences with the conjunction "et." We have often chosen to translate erudite diction in the French by using similar words in English (e.g., "augment" rather than "increase," "transmigrate" rather than "move," "lachyrimations" rather than "tears"). The result is an English version that may occasionally seem wordy, pretentious, or extravagant, but which, we hope, conveys some of the flavor of the high humanist style as practiced by a woman writer of the early sixteenth century.

Synopses of Works by Marguerite Briet

Les Angoysses douloureuses qui procedent d'amours: Contenantz troys parties, composées par dame Hélisenne, laquelle exhorte toutes personnes à ne suyvre folle Amour (*The Painful Torments which come from Love: Comprising three parts, written by Madame Hélisenne, who discourages all people from following mad passion*), 1538.

Called the "first sentimental novel in France," this work presents a first-person account of a married woman's illicit passion, her lover's occasional lack of trustworthiness, and her husband's anguish, violence, and decision to imprison her in a tower (Part One); a first-person account of the lover's tale—told by the lover but, as the title to Part Two tells us, written nonetheless by "Hélisenne"—that contains numerous adventures of chivalry (Part Two); the lover's discovery and rescue of his lady, followed by the deaths of both lovers (Part Three); and an account, narrated in the first person by a companion, of the afterlife of the lovers and the destiny of the book Hélisenne wrote ("Full and Ample Narrative Made by the Magnanimous Quezinstra").

Les Epîstres familieres et invectives (*The Personal and Invective Letters*), 1539.

This collection of letters draws on the classical genre of the epistle but has no real precedent in French prose; it can be considered the first epistolary novel in French. The first eight personal letters, written by the character Hélisenne to various friends and acquaintances, contain themes common in Cicero's *Letters to His Friends* and establishes the moral fiber of the writer; the next two relate the writer's transformation when she falls in love; and the two that follow recount her rescue by her lover. The five invective letters include reactions by the letter writer's husband to what he perceives as her infidelity and to women's general lack of moral integrity.

Le Songe de madame Hélisenne, composé par ladicte Dame, la consideration duquel est apte à instiguer toutes personnes de s'aliener de vice et s'approcher de vertu (*The Dream of Madame Hélisenne, written by the aforementioned Lady, the consideration of which is intended to encourage all people to flee vice and embrace virtue*), 1540.

A dream allegory in which Hélisenne witnesses various allegorical figures (e.g., Shame and Sensuality, Reason and Chastity) who debate questions of free will, divine grace, and, especially, the dignity of women. Modeled after Jean de Meung's *Roman de la Rose*, *The Dream* is, however, more steeped in Church doctrine and more flattering toward women. Christine de Pisan's writings may also be a model, though the narrator evokes Cicero's *De Republica* as her inspiration.

Les quatre premiers livres des Eneydes du treselegant poete Virgile, traduictz de latin en prose Françoyse par ma dame hélisenne, à la traduction desquelz y a pluralité de propos qui par maniere de phrase y sont adjoustez: ce que beaucoup sert à l'elucidation et decoration desdictz

*livres, dirigez à tresillustre et tresauguste Prince Françoys, premier de ce
nom invictissime Roy de France (The First Four Books of the Aeneid by
the very elegant poet Virgil, translated from Latin into French prose by
Lady Hélisenne, to which translation are added through the phrasing
many remarks, which contribute greatly to the elucidation and ornamentation of these books, addressed to the most illustrious and very au-
gust Prince François I, unvanquished King of France),* 1541.

This unabridged prose translation of the first four books of the *Aeneid*
aims to "correct" and add to Virgil's poem in order to promote the belief,
widespread in the Middle Ages, that the French royal family descended
from the Trojans. Briet's marginal glosses follow the medieval practice, but
she dedicates the translation to François I, the patron of Renaissance arts.

Notes

1. See synopses at the end of this Introduction.
2. The word "sentimental" in Reynier's title refers to an emphasis on sentiments
rather than on events.
3. "No one doubts that the best document on the life of Marguerite Briet is the work of
Helisenne," writes Paule Demats, the editor of one of the modern editions of Part One (x).
This may be true, but mainly because we have practically no other source of information
about Marguerite Briet.
4. I will henceforth refer to the author as Briet to distinguish her from her pseudonym
and narrator, Hélisenne.
5. Reynier also proposes that Part One was published separately, though he does not
claim that it was intended as a self-defense (119).
6. A document from 1552 states that she separated "as to possession." Demats calls
Marguerite Briet's imprisonment "probable" (x).
7. Paule Demats has called Hélisenne's writing "a Pirandellian game of masks [in
which] nothing is certain . . . truth fades as soon as it appears and a mask that slips off reveals not the face, but only another mask." Hélisenne says as much herself in her *Epîtres*
when she advises a young woman on matters of love: "Since there is nothing in the world
more deceptive than feigning the opposite of what one wants, I beg you to pretend to deny
what you most desire so as to avoid arousing indignation in those who have control over
you" (VIII, 58-59).
8. Although there is some justification for considering the husband cantankerous, jealous, and even, on at least one occasion, sadistic—he fantasizes about killing the lover and
forcing his wife to kiss the corpse—I can find no grounds for claiming he resents his wife's
beauty. On the contrary, he enjoys walking with her in public to display her beauty. Notable
exceptions to the negative portrayal of the husband are offered by Reynier, who enumerates
the husband's many personality traits and then concludes that "such a husband does not
seem to be realistically portrayed [représenté d'après nature]" (118), and Coulet, in a fairly
detailed synopsis of Part One, describes the husband as pitying his wife, but fails to mention
the three blows he delivers to her (104). Irene Bergal offers perhaps the most thorough analysis of the husband, concluding that "Hélisenne's objective reporting of his words and actions renders plausible his excessive violence and even involuntarily justifies it through her
revelation of her own character" (112).

9. "It is as if the author, finding in her own experience the starting point for a novel, sought to fill out this material by attaching to the initial given a little chivalric tale and a tragic story of the type found in the sentimental literature of Spain or Italy at the time" (105).

10. In Part Two, the question of the audience is complicated by the fact that "mes dames benevoles" was substituted for "lecteurs" in editions after 1538. It is not known whether this change was made by Briet, by her second publisher, or by Claude Colet, who revised later editions of the novel (see "History of the Text," later in this Introduction). One can only wonder as to the reason for the suppression of the more neutral, gender-inclusive term "lecteur." As the last line of the cited passage indicates, the epistle addresses men in the hope that they will imitate the exploits they read about in books: "we read that Alexander the Great took pleasure in reading the *Iliad* . . . one may understand that this assiduity in reading inspired his deeds and inclination to chivalry which things written down could cause" (121-22).

11. It is important to note that Guenelic is not entirely passive in this specular exchange, though the emphasis is placed on his role as an object, and that Hélisenne does not relinquish her status as object of the gaze when she looks at him. The sentence preceding the passage cited reads: "He was also looking at me, which made me very happy."

12. A frame establishes a narrative instance: who is telling the story and to whom, and this narrator's relationship to the characters and to the events related. An embedded narrative is told by a narrator introduced by the primary narrator.

13. On this point, see Conley's analysis: "Hélisenne's innocent *Angoysses* are a naïve and thoroughly medieval piece of writing compared to that which Virginia Woolf explores in her essay, but yet the same cultural signs are apparent: the woman's constraint and abusive conditions seem to create a singularly feminist prose form as early as the waning of the Middle Ages" (330-31).

14. Her literary debts have been repeatedly pointed out since 1908 and as recently as 1971: "[*Torments*] clearly followed Boccaccio's *Fiammetta* very closely." Raitt quoted in Baker "*Fiametta* and the *Angoysses*," 303.

15. Boccaccio's *Fiammetta* was composed around 1343, first published in 1472, and translated into French in 1532; Caviceo's *Peregrino* was translated into French in 1527, and Jean Lemaire de Belges's *Les illustrations* was published between 1511 and 1513. *Fiammetta*, like Part One of *The Torments of Love*, is the story of a happily married woman who falls in love at first sight with a young man she sees from afar, and is then tormented by love, especially when separated from her beloved. But, as Baker points out, a comparison of the depiction of love in Hélisenne and Boccaccio's novels reveals a significant difference: "The sentimental situations of [the two novels] start from different premises. In *Flãmette*, it is implied that love may be fulfilling and satisfying . . . The relationship is finally a failure because of the fickle nature of the man involved. In the *Angoysses*, it is implied that sensual love is fraught with anguish, even when the man involved is basically worthy" (*Symposium* 304). Caviceo's work, like Parts Two and Three of *The Torments of Love*, is recounted in the first person by a male character who is searching the world for his lady who, like Hélisenne, is imprisoned. Two scenes from *Peregrino* closely resemble episodes in Part One of Marguerite Briet's novel: the husband's discovery of his wife's love letters and the betrayal of a servant. *Les Illustrations de Gaule et Singularitez de Troie* appears to have provided Marguerite Briet with a number of classical allusions; for instance, her description of the council of the gods in the Epilogue is inspired by the scene of the wedding of Peleus and Thetis in Jean Lemaire de Belges's text.

16. The statement is further complicated by the author's suggestion that her denial of passion is mendacious. " 'I have to deny it," she reasons, "for a proof can do nothing against a bold face."

17. In fact, already in Part One the female narrator assumes various voices in her dialogues and inner reflections. At one point, Hélisenne addresses herself in the second person: "What incites you to invent such lies?"

18. For example, in one passage of *The Torments of Love* (III:2), she takes references to Saint Augustine, Boethius, Plato, and Cato from Antoine de La Sale's *Jehan de Saintré*; see Demats, xix.

19. Marguerite Briet, like her predecessor Christine de Pizan, enumerates illustrious women from antiquity through the Middle Ages in order to point to the errors of men who deny women the right to pursue their interests. In this context, she could indeed be considered a "champion of women's rights." See Mustacchi and Archambault (18-25).

20. Reynier cites *The Torments of Love* as being the first French sentimental novel (101-2), the first autobiography, and the first woman's diary (118).

21. The only modern edition of the complete text of the novel, a photographic reprint of the 1560 edition, published by Slakine (Geneva, 1977), describes the revisions as having "eliminated the Latinate language that made the novel [*The Torments of Love*] unreadable" (vi). Vercruysse's edition of Part One of *Les Angoysses* (1968) reproduces Colet's changes but does not identity them in the text. Demats's edition of Part One lists the variants from all editions; in her introduction, she refers to Colet's work as having "assured [the works'] survival, [by rendering them] intelligible" (ix).

The Torments of Love

Containing three parts, composed by Lady Hélisenne:
Who exhorts everyone not to pursue mad Love.

Sold in Paris by Denis Janot in the rue neuve Notre Dame,
at the sign of St. John the Baptist,
near the church of Ste. Geneviève

Paris, 1538

Privilege

Denis Janot, bookseller and printer, is permitted to print and offer for sale this book containing three parts, titled *The Torments of Love*. And all other booksellers and printers are forbidden either to print or to have printed, sell or have sold the aforementioned books other than those that the aforesaid petitioner has had printed, until two years have passed and gone by, on pain of confiscation of the books they have printed and a fine to be determined; as is more fully set out in his request signed the eleventh day of September 1538.

Signed,
J. J. de Mesmes

[This privilege appeared on the verso of the title page, but only in the original 1538 edition. In the 1541 edition and subsequent editions, the following verses appeared in its place:

Hélisenne to Her Readers
Noble dames and fair maids
Full of virtues and sweetness,
Contemplating the seductions
Of the gaze that steals hearts,
The unseeing and unsure archer
Will strike you. Watch out!
Be always on your guard, for one
Who would snare is often snared!
I shall serve as your vanguard,
At my own expense, pain, and woe.

It is worth noting that the word rendered as "Readers" in the title is *lisantes*, which identifies these readers as women.]

The Torments of Love

Part One

Epistle to the Reader

Lady Hélisenne's epistle dedicating her work to all honorable ladies, offering them her humble salutations. She exhorts them thereby to love well and honorably by avoiding all kinds of vain and unchaste love.

The torments and tribulations of the wretched (as I think and imagine) are diminished when one is able to reveal them to some faithful friend. Because I am certain, for my part, that ladies are naturally inclined to be compassionate, it is to you, noble ladies, that I wish to communicate my extreme suffering. For I believe my misfortune will move you to shed a few tears of pity that will somewhat cool my burning pain. Alas! When I remember the afflictions with which my sad heart has been, and still is, continually troubled by my boundless desires and amorous urgings, it causes me a pain that exceeds all others, so that my trembling hand remains immobile. O dear ladies, when I consider that in seeing how I was caught, you will be able to avoid the dangerous snares of love, by resisting love from the outset, without persisting in amorous thoughts. . . . I beg you to try to avoid idleness, and to occupy yourselves with some honorable activity. Considering these things, I begin to revive and regain my strength, exhorting the mother and daughter of the creator who thunders on high to aid my wretched memory and to sustain my feeble hand, so that I might be able to write them for you in a suitable manner.

The beginning of Lady Hélisenne's amorous travail, which she endured for the love of Guenelic.

Chapter 1

In the season when the goddess Cybele[1] cast off her frosty and frigid garment and donned her verdant gown embroidered with various colors, I was born into a noble family; and my birth caused my closest relatives,

---

[1]Phrygian universal mother goddess, adopted by both the Greeks and Romans, whose attributes include fertility and rejuvenation.

who are my father and mother, to feel great joy and happiness, because they had lost hope of ever having any progeny. But now I have good reason to curse the hour when I was born! Alas, I was born under an evil sign! I believe that for me there was neither God in heaven nor Fortune[2] on earth. How lucky I should have been had my mother's milk been poison for me, for that would have caused the transmigration of my soul, without its having to be troubled by such great anxiety and distress! But since it pleased the Creator that I should be received into the world and procreated, the most I can hope for is to mitigate my great and extreme suffering; but this seems to me impossible to do.

To recount the first of my misfortunes: When I was only a year old, cruel Atropos[3] wronged me by depriving me of the person whose loss would have caused me the greatest pain, had I not been a very young infant: my father, whose death made my mother so sad, and which was so difficult for her to bear, that had she not loved me so ardently, her suffering soul would surely have left her body.

Thus I was left an only daughter, which was the reason my mother took such special pleasure in instructing me in good conduct and the proper way to live. When I had reached the age of eleven, several gentleman asked for my hand in marriage. But I was soon married to a young gentleman whom I did not know, because his home was very distant from mine. In spite of the fact that we had not met and knew nothing about one another, I found him very agreeable, and felt very grateful to Fortune, considering myself very lucky. And so I was my husband's only pleasure, and he loved me in return with a mutual and reciprocal affection. Living in such felicity, I lacked only one thing, my health, which had escaped me because I had been married at such a young age. But that could not prevent me from persisting in my ardent love for my husband. And when he was forced to be absent in the service of his prince, I was afflicted with such a great sadness that I consider it inexpressible and not comparable to any other, although I was sure his absence was good for my health.

Persevering in this love, my body grew, and when I reached thirteen years of age, I had an elegant figure, and was in every way so well proportioned that I exceeded all other women in beauty of the body; had my face been equally fair, I should have boldly dared to call myself one of the most beautiful women in France. When I found myself in a place where there were a great many people, many of them would gather around to look at me, as if to admire me, and they all said to each other: "That is the most beautiful body I have ever seen." Then, afterward, looking at my face,

---

[2] The goddess who personified good or bad luck.
[3] One of the three Fates, Atropos cut the thread of life spun and woven by her sisters Clotho and Lachesis.

they said: "She is beautiful, but her face cannot compare with her body." I was wooed by several men who were ardently in love with me, not men of low estate, but princes and great lords, and this caused people to talk about me far and wide. It happened that a king was accustomed to visit frequently a small town not more than two leagues from our residence. Having asked about me, he desired to see for himself, and so he came to our castle one day, thinking he would find me there. My husband, as if he had foreseen the future, had made me go away, knowing it would be impossible for me to resist such an important personage. But his visit caused such rumors to grow up in the region that for a time I was considered one of his mistresses. Soon afterward, however, people found out that the contrary was true, with the result that I won a brilliant reputation for laudable chastity; and in fact, no man I had ever seen, no matter how accomplished with gifts of grace and nature, had caused my heart to waver. I always remained firm in my resolve to conduct myself in the same way, despising and considering abominable women who had a reputation for being loose and disposed to commit such crimes.

The origin of Hélisenne's straying into shameful love.[4]

Chapter 2

So I went on living in the same way, noble ladies, and with good reason, because I never desired anything that was not promptly provided; and I believe that had husband known my secret thoughts, he would have fulfilled them without delay. Had changeable Fortune not envied my felicity, I should consider myself much obliged to her. But now I have good reason to complain about her, for she has dealt me cruel blows. What gave rise to the beginning of my misfortunes was a piece of land concerning which we were involved in litigation. For this reason we found it urgent and necessary to be in a city not far from the land in question. Because our adversary, who gave us much concern, was there and kept a close eye on matters, we feared he would gain the advantage, and decided to go there as well. I was not at all disturbed by this, not knowing the fate and misadventure about to befall me; but in accord with the nature of the feminine sex, which never gets enough of seeing and being seen, it seemed to me that the day of our departure would never come, and I continually urged my husband to make it as soon as possible. When the desired day had arrived, to win our court case we went to the said city, where the height of my future misfortunes awaited me. Now, would to God I had

---

[4]The division into chapters and the chapter titles (with the exception of the titles to the *Epistle* and to the first chapter) were added in editions after that of 1538.

had the Trojan Cassandra's powers, which allowed her, through the spirit of prophecy, to foresee the destruction of the illustrious and noble Trojan bloodline.[5] Alas! I should have saved myself the endless regrets which daily pullulate in my sad heart; but I believe it was divine predestination, because I know I shall serve as an example to others.

Thus once we had arrived at our lodgings, I immediately went to lean on the windowsill and look out, happily talking to my husband without worrying about the matter which had caused us to come there, and which was of great importance. That day was spent in all sorts of amusements and delightful pleasures. The next day, I rose rather early, as was my custom, and getting dressed, went to open the window. Looking across the street, I saw a young man also looking out his window, and whom I began to look at attentively. He seemed to me very handsome, and from what I could tell from his physiognomy, I thought him graceful and loveable; his face was cheerful, his hair curly and rather blond, and he had no beard, which was a clear proof of gentle youth. He was quite nobly dressed, but without superfluous ornaments. Because of the great heat, he wore only a black satin doublet. After having looked at him more than enough, I withdrew my gaze; but I could not keep from turning my eyes toward him again. He was also looking at me, which made me very happy; but I was inwardly astonished to find myself thus led to gaze at this young man; this had never happened to me with other men. I was accustomed to snaring and capturing men, and I only made sport with them; but this time I found myself wretchedly ensnared. I could not tear my eyes away from him, and I desired no pleasure other than this one.

Ladies, I exhort you and plead with you to judge the great power of love, considering I had never seen this person. You may find it very strange, for love usually results from continual contact.

Alas! I tried to resist, trying to drive love from my heart, for that evening, when I lay in bed with my husband, I began to think about the great friendship I had always had for him, and about my unblemished reputation, which up to that time was unmarked by anything that could tarnish my honor. Considering these things, reason corroborated me, counseling me to remain firm and not allow myself to be conquered, and said to me: "Why do you want to take the low road, filthy and fetid, and leave the beautiful path full of fragrant flowers? You are bound to your husband; you can take your pleasure in marriage. It is a fair road, and by following it you can save yourself. Oh, poor lady, do you want to choose lascivious love over the chaste and modest matrimonial love you have maintained under such close observation?"

---

[5] A Trojan princess upon whom Apollo bestowed the gift of prophecy; he later cursed her for rejecting his advances by making all those who heard her disbelieve her predictions.

When I considered all these things, how deeply I was moved and how my understanding was wounded by the ardent love that possessed me. Reason was once again dominant within me, for one good thought brought me another, and I began to consider and think over several stories, both ancient and modern, that mentioned the misfortunes that had come about from having infringed and corrupted chastity by exceeding the bounds of reason. I remembered the Greek Helen who caused the total destruction of Troy.[6] Then Medea was summoned to my memory; as remuneration and reward for having saved her lover Jason he expelled her from his country. For that reason she was forced to beg and to ask others to speak on her behalf and help her, and as a result the poor woman, in despair, killed her children with her own hands.[7] Next I remembered Eurial and the beautiful Lucretia who for a time lived in great happiness and joy; but afterward, Eurial had to leave home to follow the emperor, and this caused the premature death of his wife.[8] Several others entered my sad thoughts, such as Lancelot of the Lake and Queen Guenevere, who caused the ruination of the great King Arthur's fine reputation, and consequently that of the noble knights of the Round Table.[9] And in that same time, Tristan of Cornwall and Queen Iseult suffered great pains because their immoral love affair was discovered by King Mark.[10]

After considering all these things in my imagination, I had decided to refrain from love affairs, when sensual appetite attacked me with enormous force, trying to persuade me to follow it by accumulating in my wretched memory countless thoughts entirely different from the first ones, and these caused me to grow cold, and I found myself in an extremity so great it cannot be expressed by the voice, understood by the intellect, or represented by the imagination. The image, effigy or semblance of the young man was painted and limned in my mind. This lent so much weight, favor and aid to love that, intending to mitigate it, it made it grow and augment; and I said to myself: "It is foolish to be so timid; I must abandon the dismal fear of misfortunes that happened in the past and at-

---

[6]The daughter of Leda and Zeus, who was considered the most beautiful mortal woman who ever lived. Her abduction by the Trojan prince Paris sparked the Trojan War.

[7]When Jason and the Argonauts sought the Golden Fleece, Medea helped them flee her father's wrath. She married Jason, but he later abandoned her to marry the Princess of Corinth. In a rage, Medea killed her sons by Jason.

[8]A character in a novel by Aeneas Silvius, first translated from the Latin into French in 1493 with the title S'ensuyt l'histoire des deux vrays amans Eurial et la Belle Lucresse. Cf. G. Reynier, Le Roman Sentimental avant l'Astrée, chapter 3.

[9]In the tales of the Knights of the Round Table, King Arthur's wife, Guenevere, fell in love with Lancelot, causing great embarrassment for the king.

[10]Tristan was a vassal of King Mark of Cornwall, who sent him to escort Iseult, the beautiful princess of Ireland, to his kingdom. A magic potion caused Tristan and Isuelt to fall in love with each other. Mark later discovered their love and exiled Tristan from his court.

tend to the present time. I know several young ladies and girls who are said to have beaux who give them joy and happiness; I shall have to follow their example, for the power to resist has been taken from me. One thing comforts me, and that is that a person who sins along with many others is not worthy of such great blame. And as a final resolution, at least I want to have the delectable pleasure of seeing my beloved. I shall nourish love secretly in my heart without divulging it to anyone, so long as he remains faithful to me." And thus I began to drive reason away, whereby sensuality won the day.

Hélisenne, whom love has taken by surprise, is espied by her husband.

Chapter 3

I spent the whole night turning over these different thoughts. For that reason I was weak and pale the next morning when I tried to get up; I found myself indisposed because of the painful suffering I had endured on account of my vain and fruitless thoughts. Nevertheless, driven by a great and fervent desire, I dressed as quickly as I could in order to come to the window where I anticipated an exceptional pleasure; and as soon as I was there, I saw the man who was the true possessor and lord of my heart. Then I began to look at him immodestly, leaving behind all fear and shame, I, who up to that time had looked on men with simplicity and decency. He also kept his eyes fixed on me, which was the reason my husband, on seeing our faces, suspected us. To find out more he often said to me: "My love, so far as I can tell from your face, which is very different from the way it used to be, your heart is very oppressed and burdened with sadness and melancholy, and this surprises me, since you had such a great desire to be in this city. Is there something wrong that I can correct or change? Or if you want something that lies within my power, tell me without delay what it is, for I love you so much I would gladly do anything for you, even at the risk of my own life."

On the spot, I quickly invented a clever lie, saying to him, "No, I assure you that for the moment nothing is bothering me that you could help; for this sudden melancholy of mine proceeds only from my fears concerning the land in litigation, knowing that our adversary is very vigilant and that we are accustomed to living among worldly pleasures and delights; and for this reason it will be difficult for us to be as diligent as the case requires." Then my husband, acting as if he believed what I had said, answered me with a smiling face: "My love, I beg you, never fear we might be anticipated or taken off-guard, for I promise you I shall take such care that you shall never have cause for concern; don't worry about anything other than eating well and enjoying yourself." So saying, he pointed to my beloved and, as if he had not noticed that we were continually looking at each other, said: "Look at that young man over there, who is the most handsome I've seen in a long time; it will be a lucky woman who will have such a lover." As he was saying these words, my amorous heart was throbbing in my breast; changing color, I became pale and cold; shortly afterward, a vehement heat drove the pallor from my face, and I became warm and bright red. I was forced to withdraw because of the rush of sighs that agitated me, as I was exhibiting by clear signs, outward behavior, and spasmodic movements. When I tried to say something in the way of complaints and exclamations, the extremity of my distress interrupted my voice, I lost my appetite, and it was impossible for me to sleep.

It would be tedious as well as difficult to recount my thoughts, for I truly believe no woman in love ever suffered so cruelly. But I shall try to tell as much about them as I can. I persevered daily in my love affair, constantly casting my customary amorous glances. My husband saw all this, and he was clear-sighted enough to be sure I had been captured, but he showed me no sign of disapproval. On the contrary, he showed more fondness for me than usual, to which I paid little attention, for all the love I had earlier felt for him now belonged to my young beloved. I took such pleasure in looking at him that I thought no joy could be greater than mine, and I never ceased to think and imagine how I could speak with him. Sometimes I was so troubled that when my husband spoke to me I made him repeat himself several times, because unruly appetite had completely transported my mind by means of my idle thoughts. I saw my beloved sometimes play a flute, other times a lute. I took a singular pleasure in hearing him, and in short, I found all these things marvelously agreeable.

I enjoyed this smooth, sweet, and mellifluous delight only until the sixth day, because my husband let me know the suspicion he covertly and silently bore within his poor heart; for coming to lean on the windowsill alongside me, he happened to speak some words that seemed to me remarkably sharp. He turned toward me and smiling, said: "My love, that young man there is looking at you very hard; he keeps his eyes fixed on you. I know he is in love, for I know what love is. I would judge and believe, by his gestures and expressions, that he has been captured by your love."

The utterance of these accursed and insidious words pierced my heart through, and I was agitated, persecuted, and afflicted with new pains, so that I could not promptly answer. When I could speak, pretending to laugh I said: "I believe that such good fortune is not my due, for you think a woman who had such a lover would be blissfully happy. No, nonetheless I do not desire him. For even if he were as beautiful as Narcissus, who deemed no creature comparable to him in beauty, my heart could never waver or vacillate.[11] And surely also I believe his thoughts and ideas are not fixed on me, at least so far as I have been able to perceive."

After having excused my beloved, I retired, terribly upset. New and different thoughts passed through my imagination. I was incessantly spurred on by the beauty of the pleasing young man imagined and depicted in my memory. But when I had reflected for a time, I began to mitigate and temper my frenzy, inwardly saying: "I should not lose hope of enjoying my beloved, for my husband does not suspect me at all, but doubtless considers me firm and constant. If he has noticed the way my beloved usually looks at me, I shall find another suitable excuse. I must learn to suffer patiently, for there is no travail so great that it cannot be moderated by prudence, nor any pain so acute that patience cannot break it, and that, along with all that is prolonged, will not finally end." In this resolution I spent another four days. I no longer dared look out the window in my husband's presence, but in his absence, I looked out as I was accustomed to do, thinking that by this means my passion might be cooled. But it only increased my ardors and inflammations. One day, I saw my beloved going down the street. I conceived a desire to inquire into his rank and way of life, about which I was informed. He was of low estate, which made me very sad, but the great power of love, by which I was possessed and mastered, obscured what I had learned and took it away from me, so that although it caused me pain, my love did not diminish.

Hélisenne changes her lodgings, but not her heart.

Chapter 4

While I was thus living deprived of my liberty, my husband was melancholically angered to see my gestures and expressions. As a result, he wanted to move to a different place, which somewhat vexed me. But considering that my beloved would find the place and that love would urge and provoke him to investigate and look for it, I showed no sign of discontent. Thus we departed, and went to live in a place rather close to the temple where the divine oracles are delivered, and this immediately came to the notice of my beloved.

So the following day he was in the building closest to ours, and loitered

---

[11] An extremely handsome youth who considered all suitors unworthy of him. To punish his hubris, Nemesis, the goddess of retribution, caused him to fall in love with his own reflection in a pool. Unable to tear himself away from his own image, Narcissus was turned into a flower.

about the door, looking to see if he might glimpse me at my window. But as soon as I had seen him, I withdrew a bit so as to consult my mirror concerning my dress, appearance, and countenance. Then I began to look at him affectionately, and because of the intrinsic pleasure I felt in looking at him, I began to say to myself, as if I were speaking to him: "Certainly, my friend, you are very diligent. No negligence must be assigned or reproached you, and therefore you are worthy of being rewarded. At least you must be granted the privilege of being heard." While I was taking singular pleasure in my amorous thoughts, my husband came and leaned against me; he could not keep from speaking and unburdening his heart. Addressing me, he said with great fury: "I see your lover there whom you are looking at so hard. You may be certain that I know truly that you have been captured, and this displeases me. I see you giving him dissolute and immodest looks, and you are so perturbed that reason no longer rules over you. But I assure you that if you continue to look at him in this way, I shall show you that you have very seriously offended me."

When I had heard him out, it was not in my power to answer; but like a woman deeply afflicted by a languorous infirmity and very painful suffering, I had to sit down; otherwise I should have fallen. When I could speak, I began to say to him: "Alas, my love, who has led you to accuse me and so cruelly wound my heart by saying such things to me? You cause me such extreme pain that I was at first unable to answer you, for I should never have thought your mind occupied by such vain and idle thoughts. You have always seen me behave with such decency that those who know me, all of them, have had a good opinion of me, and I have not deserved any blame. But after thinking carefully and searching the farthest reaches and infinity of my thought, I can only imagine that you have been poisoned or contaminated by something said by a malevolent gossip, for they pullulate these days in large swarms and countless numbers. But if you consider how I have lived, you can easily return to reason, from which I see you are far distant."

When I had said this, he began to look at me, saying with great severity: "Ah! False woman, such excuses will never be accepted in my heart, for even though you have been chaste and modest, I see clearly that your heart has been subverted and inflamed with libidinous ardor; and you have contaminated chastity in order to follow lascivious love. And so I am right in cursing the day when I first saw you, for such dissoluteness will cause your honor and mine to be blackened and destroyed. If I find out about it, you may be certain that I shall take cruel vengeance."

So saying, he went away; and I remained so burdened with sadness and bitterness that it is impossible to know how to describe or recount it. But after being in this extremity for some time, I began to regain a bit of strength, and in a broken and halting voice I said: "Oh my dearly beloved,

15

the only hope of my sad heart, how can I now temper the great ardor that daily grows and multiplies in my heart, so that I burn and am consumed? I see no sign that I am beginning to cool, and even if I could desist, I should not want to do so, because of the pleasure I take in looking at you. Alas! Fortune, you constantly give me cause for despair, for if I am deprived of the sight of my beloved, I desire nothing other than that cruel Atropos should use her shears to prematurely cut my life-thread; that would seem kind to me, whereas she provokes others to feel trepidation and fear." No one could feel more tired and weak than I did as I said these words. While I was in this vain and superfluous travail, I saw my husband, who was returning from attending to some of his business; seeing me so pensive, he thought I was ashamed and abashed by the way he had insulted me in order to make me draw back from the excessive love I had for my beloved. But he was very far from the truth, for nothing short of death could have made me stop loving him.

Nonetheless, my husband had tempered his anger and said to me: "I beg you, tell me what makes you so sad. Is it that you have not had an opportunity to satisfy your lustful and unchaste desire? Or if it displeases you, be contrite that you have so long persisted in your continual looking, not wanting to give up your folly. Do you repent that you let your heart be taken by surprise and desired to begin a detestable and abominable life? If I thought you wanted to put an end to this love and drive it from your heart, and to bring yourself to return to a more decent way of life, I should not hold you in any less esteem, because I know that first impulses are not under our control."

As soon as he had finished speaking, I began to deny everything, for I had become bold and audacious, though up to that time I had been timorous, and I said to him: "How can you still hold such a wicked and damnable opinion? I see clearly that the devil is tempting you. You have been persuaded by some infernal, mad fury, which seeks to make you perpetrate and commit this enormous and execrable sin, which is causing the destruction of your body and soul. Certainly you are very wrong, for the integrity of my heart would never stain itself. And, contrary to what you say, you can see this by long experience." So saying, I angrily went into another chamber; and because it was bedtime, I decided not to return until he had gone to sleep; and that is what I did. Toward midnight, I went to bed, very melancholy because everything seemed to me displeasing, sad, and odious. But the next morning, I went to hear the divine prayers in a small church; and so when I turned to go home, I saw my beloved, who cast a glance on me so piercing that it penetrated all the way to my heart. This caused me such complete joy that I forgot all the torments and acute pains I had suffered on his account. I began to look at him without shame or pudency, and I paid no attention to one of his companions, who could

16

clearly perceive my immodest and artful glances. And the thought of going back was made more dismal because it seemed to me I had not enjoyed the sight of him; but since I feared my husband might inopportunely appear, I had to go away.

As you have heard, dear ladies, that is how I was treated by love. Sometimes extreme suffering constrained me to moan and lament; at other times I was given great joy and consolation by the pleasing way my beloved looked at me. I usually went to hear divine services at the main temple where everyone gathered; my beloved did the same, always accompanied by several other persons. I clearly saw his inconstancy and imprudence by the way he behaved toward me. And as I could not communicate or assume it by obvious signs, it was he who divulged our love and made it public. Moreover, I was assured of it by one of my ladies-in-waiting, who heard people talk about it. And he said this to one of his companions: "That lady is amazingly in love with me. Just look at the way she flirts with her eyes. I think that by continuing my pursuit, I shall easily be able to enjoy her."

When this remark was repeated to me, my heart's strength ebbed away, and my passionate vexation caused me to bend my head toward the earth, the way a violet inclines its purple color downward when it has been struck by the strong North Wind. I remained very pensive for a long time; then, raising my eyes, I saw my beloved, on whom I cast a glance that showed my complaint, and I said to myself: "Alas! Fortune, how bitter, adverse, ferocious, and cruel you are to me! I now know that there is only pretense and dissimulation on the part of the man I thought loved me with all his heart. Alas, he has no other goal than to deprive me of my honor in order to talk about me with derision. And yet despite the fact that I know him to be such, my heart belongs to him so fully that it is not in my power to take it back. But from now on, I shall no longer look at him, at least in public, for a good reputation is easily tarnished, and especially that of noble ladies when they are not modest, as their decency demands." With that resolution I left and went home to my room; and I stayed there alone all day. In the evening, when I was in bed alongside my husband, my mind began to fly about composing all kinds of new fantasies, which caused me great travail, so that I could not sleep.

Hélisenne longs for her beloved.

Chapter 5

While I was so tormented and anguished, I heard some musical instruments, which were playing in great harmony and melodious resonance. I suspected it might be my beloved. In order to find out the truth, I wanted to get up; although I had always been afraid of the nocturnal shadows, I became bold and assured. But as I tried to get out of my bed to go to the window, my husband said to me: "Where are you going? I truly believe it is your lover." And without saying another word, he went back to sleep. Oh! I was more upset and sad than someone held in a dark prison, because fear held me back so that I did not dare look out at the window, and this filled me with such irritation and anger that it was not in my power to control it. And so the night was passed.

However, my beloved returned several times. One time, my husband awoke, and turning toward me, began to speak to me in this way: "O wicked woman, you have always denied what I could clearly see by obvious signs, unless I were completely deprived of wits. I am certain, and I know without doubt, that it is your lover who is bringing these musicians to amuse you and to induce you to give in to his evil desire. But if he knew your heart as well as I do, he would not take such pains: for your unrestrained lasciviousness is powerful enough to make you provoke him; and if he were expert in love, he would have been able to discern (considering the way you look at him) the great ardor that constantly holds sway over you. Your sexual appetite has poisoned your heart, which was earlier pure and chaste. You are so deceived by his love that you have wholly changed your decent temperament, ways, acts, desires, and manners into the opposite sort. But be assured that I shall no longer endure it, for your disordered life causes me such pain and passion that I shall be forced to deal cruelly and ignominiously with your person." And when he had said this, he fell silent.

I rose like a madwoman, and without being able to say a single word in response, I began to tear my hair and to lacerate and bloody my face with my nails, and my piercing feminine cries penetrated the ears of those who heard them. When I could speak, like a woman who had completely lost her reason I said to him: "Certainly, I believe some familiar spirit has revealed to you my secret thoughts, a power I believed was reserved to divine prescience. Truly I do love him, passionately and with all my heart, and with such great constancy that nothing short of death can ever keep me from loving him. So come then with your sword: make my soul transmigrate out of this unhappy corporeal prison, I beg you; for I prefer to die by a violent death rather than by continual languor; it would be better to be strangled than to be always hanging. And so do not delay any longer. Pierce through my changeable heart, and draw back your stained and bloody sword. Do not have pity on me, any more than Pyrrhus did on Polyxena, who was sacrificed on Achilles' tomb; and if you don't do it, the madness and rage that possess me will make me leap on the sword myself."[12] As I said these words, my eyes were sparkling with a furious

---

[12]Pyrrhus was the son of Achilles; after the death of his father and the fall of Troy, he killed King Priam and his daughter, Polyxena.

heat, and I was striking my fist against my breast, to the point that I fell back so exhausted that I was almost dead. On coming back to my senses, I saw my husband and my attendants and other servants, who were frightened by such a syncope and fainting spell. When I could speak, I asked why they had gotten to their feet. My husband replied: "After you have lain down, I shall tell you." Without saying any more, he had one of my personal servants carry me to bed. And he began to say to me: "My God, I should never have thought (even though I shamed you and used harsh words) that love's ardor was so strong in you, so vehement and inextinguishable, for I see that you are dying from it, which makes me very sorry. Although you have committed a great error (as you have yourself confessed that you are engaged in a new love affair), I love you so much that it would be difficult and (I think) impossible for me to try to turn you away from your love. But I assure you I shall take cruel vengeance on your lover, who has caused so much sadness to accumulate and come together in my heart. But if you take it into your head to kiss him, before three days have passed I shall make you kiss his corpse."

On hearing these words my heart was as oppressed as the hearts of those who are condemned and given a death sentence, and I could not keep myself from answering: "I would much prefer that you take vengeance on me, as I have deserved, without injuring this young man, who has committed no offense. Why, if he is in love, does he deserve to die? That is proper and natural in young people." These words were spoken with many sighs that became tears, so that my grieving husband was forced to comfort me, swearing and affirming that since I was so bitterly opposed to it, he would not cause the young man pain or injury. But he begged me to give up my mad desire for my young friend, saying that I could easily do so if I put my mind to it, and that no matter how difficult it might be, it was still possible. Remonstrating with me in this way, he approached me to take Venus's pleasure. But I very quickly drew far away from him, and said to him: "My love, I beseech you to let me rest; for in such sadness and anguish as continually agitate my poor heart, I feel my members so debilitated I no longer hope to live in any condition other than languor and infirmity." So saying, I sat down on my bed, pretending to be seriously afflicted with sickness, which made my husband very sorry. He sought to calm my weeping, crying, pains and sighs; and when he thought he had somewhat consoled me he went to sleep and slept until dawn.

The husband's jealousy, with a description of an ugly woman.

Chapter 6

When the rising sun had brightened the sky, he awoke and took me in his arms to try to cheer me up and win back my love. But he was remarkably deluded, for my heart had already divorced itself from him and completely repudiated him; as a result, everything he did began to displease me, and had I not been forced to do so, I should not have slept with him. But in order to conceal and screen my iniquitous desire I had to make use of dissimulation, pretending to try to submit and return to the bounds of reason, on which my husband pinned his hopes. On that day, I refused to get out of bed, and had the windows closed, desiring only to be alone in a quiet place, as do people who are inconsolably contrite, because I was prohibited and forbidden to be where my beloved was. And still, my ungrateful fate allowed my husband—on that very day—to inquire of several of the neighbors about the music that was continuing to be played in front of our lodgings. They replied that it was customary only when there was a girl of marriageable age within. As soon as he heard this, he went to our landlord, who was a rustic with a crude, limited mind, to whom he said: "My host, haven't you heard these past days, more than once and at different times, the loud music played by flute-players in front of your house? I assure you that so far as I can see, it must be someone who is in love with your wife or with mine." The landlord replied: "Sir, I am at a loss to know what moves you to say such things, or why you do so, for I believe my wife to be as good and as chaste as any woman in town." So saying, he grew more heated, showing by clear signs that he was outrageously angered, which was a manifest demonstration of his small and rural mind, because his wife was ugly and odious, and I shall describe her deformity and ugliness for you. She was short of stature, hunchbacked and lame, and her face was also very wrinkled, with eyebrows as wide as two fingers, without there being any distance between them. She had little black eyes, deeply recessed in her head; she was snub-nosed, with an outrageously big mouth, with heavy lips, although she had only two teeth, disproportionately large; her neck was short, and her breasts lay on her belly; she was seventy-two years old. Therefore, all things considered, I think she would be rejected and sent away by all men, and with good reason. While my husband was amusing himself by listening to the landlord's talk, one of my attendants was present, and she immediately came to tell me all about it. Although I was very sad and deprived of every kind of pleasure, I could not keep from laughing when I thought about our host's folly; and as I was talking about this, my husband came in, and asked me how I was feeling. He said: "My love, I beg you to stop weeping and moaning, and bring your heart to console itself with joy. As for myself, I shall give you no reason or occasion for melancholy. Tomorrow is the day of a solemn observance, and therefore I wish and command that you put on your most triumphal garments in order to go to the temple with me; from now on you will be allowed to go out of the house only in my company, for I want to see how you behave in my presence, for I know your lover will be there." Such were the words my husband spoke to me, to which I made no reply, but held my tongue, although silently great joy and jubilation washed over me at the prospect of seeing my beloved; and because of my fervent desire, the night seemed very long to me.

But when Proserpina began to move through the house of the three-headed dog, and Phoebus, wearing on his head the diadem covered with dazzling bright rays to illuminate and shed light on the whole world, attached his chariot to the Zodiac, I quickly rose and began to dress.[13] I put on a white satin cloak and a gown of scarlet satin; I adorned my head with beautiful ribbons and fine precious stones. When I was ready, I began to walk about, admiring myself in my sumptuous garments, like the peacock with his beautiful feathers, imagining I should please others as I pleased myself. Meanwhile, my husband had been getting dressed; when he saw me, he was very pleased, and said it was time to go. And so we went out of the room in the company of my attendants I walked along slowly, maintaining a respectable gravity. Everyone looked at me, saying: "There you see the creature who exceeds and surpasses all others in the shapeliness of her body." After they had looked at me, they went to call the others, making them come out of their houses in order to see me. It was astonishing to see the crowd that gathered around me. When I had arrived at the temple, several of the young men formed a circle around me, showing me a semblance of love by the sweet and flirtatious looks shot from the corners of their eyes, in order to try to seduce and deceive me; but I paid no attention to them, for all my thoughts were focused on a single man. I looked in many different places, but I did not see the one in whom alone my eyes took pleasure. He did not come until the divine service had already begun. When he arrived, he did not look at me in the usual way, but only passed in front of me. I imagined he did that because my husband was present, in order to avoid making him suspicious, and so I was content. When the solemn rites were finished, we left to return to our lodgings, and passed the time in amusements and delightful plea-

---

[13]Proserpina is the queen of the underworld, whose gates are guarded by Cerberus, the three-headed dog. Phoebus is an epithet for Apollo, god of the sun.

sures, until we came back to hear vespers. My beloved did not fail to appear, and this time he did not show discretion, because in my husband's presence he gave obvious signs of his affection by his amorous looks and sweet allurements, constantly pointing me out to his companions, although he had not yet spoken to me. When I saw his inconstancy, I gave him a sweet, simple look to show and exhibit to him by signs that his behavior was causing my heart to suffer greatly; but for all that he did not cease his importunities, for he passed so near me that he stepped on my white satin cloak. I was particular about my clothes. This was a garment which gave me special pleasure. But despite that fact, I was not displeased; on the contrary, I should have voluntarily and wholeheartedly kissed the spot where his foot had touched my cloak. My husband saw the whole thing, which annoyed him so much he had to leave. Against my inclination, and to avoid any occasion for a quarrel, I followed him. As soon as we were in our rooms, he said to me: "Your lover amazes me; he was not able to hide his amorous folly even in my presence. He was very presumptuous to come step on your cloak. That seems to show that he is on very intimate and familiar terms with you. Thus to avoid causing me more suffering and vexation than my sad heart could bear, I prohibit and forbid you to be in any place where he is unless I am also there; and moreover, if I am present, even if it is at the moment when the body of Jesus Christ is elevated, as soon as you see him I want you to immediately leave. And if you do not observe this commandment of mine, I have the firm intention and design to separate myself from you. You have your own property, more lands and fiefdoms than I have, to which I shall not lay claim, for I should not want to profit from the wealth of a lascivious woman."

When he had spoken, I answered that I would obey his command, and that he should have no perplexity or doubt unless I gave him reason to do so, and he was satisfied, taking me at my word. Nothing more was said about it until the next day when I wanted to get up and dress myself in rich and sumptuous clothes, which my husband refused to permit. To please him I was glad to dress more simply. When I was ready, we went to the temple where I found my beloved, who persisted in his importunities, so that I was forced to move away three or four times; but he always followed me, talking about me with his friends. I guessed that he was talking about my husband, who was continually with me, for I heard one of his companions say to him that from what he could tell by looking at my face, which showed my anxiety, my husband suspected something. When my beloved heard these words, he began to laugh. Seeing that, and remembering my husband's command, I went away, thinking that I should sometime find a more appropriate and opportune place where we could both express our secret thoughts.

The two lovers seek to speak to each other.

Chapter 7

Thus I went on following the bad side of my spirit, and comments and derision—those of my beloved—were powerless to make me abandon my folly. But because on the preceding days I had observed my husband's command by dissimulating the ardent flame that burned and consumed me (which is not easy to do), I was allowed more freedom than I had had for a long time; for I went to the temple only in the company of one of my closest attendants, which made me very happy, for I thought my beloved would have an opportunity to speak. To invite him to do so, I remained inside the temple until no one else was there. And I continued to do so for several days. Nonetheless, he did not come up to speak to me, which amazed me, and I imagined that he was delaying out of cowardice. But I did not cease to persist in my plan. One day, I saw that he was more pensive than normal, and was walking alone, holding his cap in his hand, in order to please me by showing me his beautiful, finely combed hair. When he had walked around a while, he went into a chapel where the divine service was just beginning. And so I had a plausible reason to rise and follow him. I saw he was often looking about him, and I did the same, and I think our thoughts were not different, for in our hearts we both feared my husband would arrive. As soon as the divine service was over and done, he began to walk about, but before long he came to present himself before me, greeting me and looking at me with a sweet and amorous glance, and he said:

The lovers, in order to avoid being seen, resort to letters.

Chapter 8

"Milady, for a long time I have had a deep desire and yearning to speak to you, in order to tell you what you can easily imagine. But I do not want to speak very long, in order to avoid arousing the suspicions of people who could cause and give rise to a great scandal for you. Nevertheless, I beg you to simply tell me whether you would agree to receive a letter from me." When I had heard him speak, I told him that I should receive his letter freely, and that he should not hesitate to write me everything he felt, without holding anything back, and that I should do the same. As I spoke these words I grew pale, and I began to tremble all over; so many sighs rushed forth from my breast that one followed another. Thereby I declared clearly enough by my exterior behavior and by the inviting look in my eyes that my interior affection was the same as his. He made a show of being overjoyed, and humbly taking his leave, he thanked me. As soon as he had gone, I returned to my lodgings, where I stayed until we returned the next day to the temple. When we got there, I saw him, accompanied by one of his friends. But as soon as he saw me, he left his friend, and walking about, pretended to say his prayers, showing himself more modest and fearful than before, which he never did again. When he had an opportunity, he came to greet me, giving me his letter, which I took as subtly as I could, thinking no one had seen me, and told him he should have my reply the next day. Lowering his head, he remained silent for a while; then, breaking his silence, he began in this wise: "Lady, I am terribly afraid of your husband." Without giving him time to finish, I immediately interjected: "I beg you not to worry about that, for he does not suspect me in the least." At that, he began to look at me with amazement, imagining (as I have since been able to see) that the impetuousness of love had broken in me all the bonds of temperance and moderation, and made me exceed every sort of feminine audacity. Nevertheless, continuing what he was saying, he went on: "Milady, I am delighted to be assured he has no suspicions about us. We must moderate our desires with discretion in order to avoid giving him reason to suspect us. You shall give me your letter as furtively and secretly as possible, showing me by discreet and secret signs when you want me to approach and take them from you." Saying this, he took his leave. I followed him with my eyes, which were sparkling with amorous desires, for I was completely ablaze with erotic fire. Love grew so powerful in my heart that no one who has not experienced love could believe it.

Reading the lover's letter.

Chapter 9

As soon as I had received his letter, I returned in great haste to my lodgings, and going into my room, I opened them and read what they contained, which went like this:

"Milady, since the freedom to speak to you, in order to explain my amorous ideas, is not allowed me, Venus's son has persuaded me to write you the present letter; and to inform you of the extremity to which my excessive love has reduced me, I must tell you that when I first looked on your green and radiant eyes, there seemed to me to issue from them a splendor which pierced nearer my heart than Jupiter sharp arrow pierced Phaeton's.[14] At once, feeling myself taken by surprise by this sweet look,

---

[14]Jupiter struck and killed Phaeton with a thunderbolt when the latter was unable to control the horses of the sun's chariot.

I came to examine more particularly your extraordinary beauty. But in considering the excellence of your beautiful body, which is uncommonly well-proportioned, I was bereft of my power of judgment. Because of the recent memory of the bitter pain to which I was reduced, my understanding is so perturbed that it would not be possible for me to praise and extol you in a way worthy of the beauty of your form. Even if I were not shaken by any perturbation, knowing the feeble strength of my weak mind, I should not dare to undertake the task, because I believe that to describe your lovely appearance would be difficult for all eloquent tongues; for as I see it, the expression of such a singular thing must be reserved to the divine eloquence of Mercury.[15] Therefore I shall abstain from it, and I shall go on to reveal to you the secret of my heart, for I wish to observe the ancient custom of the celebrated Persians, which was never to present themselves before his sublime highness the king with their hands empty of gifts, not because they presumed their lord to be swayed by avarice of any kind, but out of respect and supreme reverence. Because, milady, I have nothing more esteemed than my person, as faithfully as I can I give it to you as a perpetual servant, begging you to accept it in the same spirit as I give it to you. Remember that gracious accepting is no less a virtue than liberal giving. Nothing more remains, then, than to give a faithful servant his reward. If my value is small with respect to your greatness, I beg you to reward me, not as my companion or equal, but as my lady and superior, so that through severity or negligence in succoring me you do not give me reason to die a cruel and violent death; rather, since you are sovereign over all creatures and full of gracious courtesy, be moved to pity and compassion, and do not allow me to so unhappily abandon nature. In the hope that you will be merciful, I shall put an end to my most faithful letter. Written by one who can boldly call himself a servant in love exceeding all others in loyalty and faithful service."

After having read this letter, I felt an incomprehensible and immeasurable joy and consolation, for in what he wrote he had declared himself mine in perpetuity. Then I began to cogitate and think over the response I should make to his letter. It seemed to me it would not be good to acquiesce so promptly to his request, because things easily obtained are little appreciated, while those acquired through great pains are esteemed dear and precious. For these reasons, I wrote him a letter suggesting that he had scant hope of reaching his goal, and it went like this:

---

[15]Chosen as the herald of the Olympian gods.

A letter the lady wrote to her beloved.

Chapter 10

"After having presented your letter to my eyes, and considered and meditated on its content, so far as I can see (unless your letter was composed in pretense or deliberate deception), I assume that because of the unbearable burden of love you are more anguished and afflicted than is suitable for a prudent man; for you must see you cannot persist in such a love, which does not consist in virtue because it would be impossible for me to satisfy your affectionate desire without tarnishing and destroying my reputation. This would be more bitter to me than a violent death, because I do not consider men and women to be alive whose reputation has been extinguished; they should consider themselves worse off than the dead. The contrary is true of those who have done virtuous deeds that cause their names endure sempiternally, despite cruel Atropos, even though their bones are reduced to ashes. The latter can consider themselves to be alive, and we ought to try to follow their example by living virtuously in the way that makes us immortal. To achieve this end, one must avoid allowing oneself to sink into lascivious pleasures in order not to be led to that ancient and usual unhappiness everyone laments, and from which follow many sad consequences. Had Leda's daughter led a chaste life, the Greeks would not have completely destroyed the famous city of Ilion.[16] And had the queen of Carthage persevered in her constancy, she would have followed with perpetual praise the shade of her lover Sychaeus.[17] Such stories ought to suffice to keep us from succumbing to similar crimes, and, because of a little appetite, being so ready to listen to the polished, elegant and suave words of young men like you, which are no more than deceptive snares to trap and deceive those who are too ready to believe what you say. This vice has caused the corruption of several famous ladies, since after men obtained the private and secret fruition of love from those whom they say they love so much, they are not content, but sometimes by indiscretion they brag about it, and glory in it. Whereby, all things considered, ladies who can save themselves from the fire of love are blessed indeed. In order to escape it, I beg you to put an end to this continual pursuit, for I fear that through your continual stimulations I might be persuaded to exceed the bounds of reason; for your sweet, attractive looks, along with the words exhibited by your let-

---

[16]Helen, Leda's daughter, was the cause of the war in Ilion or Troy.

[17]Dido's husband, Sychaeus, was murdered, after which Dido left her homeland and founded Carthage. There, she fell in love with Aeneas and committed suicide when he left her to continue his travels.

ter, could cause great effects and emotion in the hearts of young ladies, and some simple-minded ones might think they have in their persons many more gifts and perfections than God and nature put there. But not wishing to fall into the labyrinth of presumption, I take no pride in your praise and exaltations, for it may be that, through immoderate affection, your eye may wander. But you must believe that if Love had struck me with his golden arrow, no one but you would be the possessor of my benevolence. For that reason I beg you to agree to be content, and beseech him who thunders from on high to grant you happy peace."

Having put my seal on the letter, I eagerly sought out a subtle way of conveying it to him, and he received it with joy. And immediately after I had shown it to him, I withdrew to my room, where I preferred to remain alone, rather than in company, the better to pursue my fantasies in solitude. In this solitude[18] I took delight in reading my beloved's letter; afterward, I looked over the copy of my own, examining in detail all the terms of each of them. As I was busy with such a delightful occupation, my husband entered our lodgings unbeknownst to me, and with a great blow of his foot kicked open the door of my room, which disturbed me so much that I did not think to discreetly conceal the letter. He began to look at me with great displeasure and disdain mingled with anger, and spoke the following words:

The jealous husband's anger, and his wife's excuse.

Chapter 11

"O wicked woman, the time has now come when you can no longer deny your lasciviousness and your immoderate affection. Your deceiving words had the power to move, incite and incline me to set you free, and to give you some freedom because, believing your lies, I thought my daily remonstrances had moved and goaded you to return to your first way of life. But despite my exhortations and warnings, your inveterate and hardened heart has been utterly unable to change itself." Saying this, he took the letter, which I had left on my bed because fear had clouded my wits, and when he had read it, his fury was still further augmented. Deeply offended, he came and gave me such a blow on the face that I fell violently to the floor, from which I could not at first rise. When I began to recover my strength, I wept very bitterly, so much that tears streamed down my face in great abundance. The cause of my weeping was not the justifiable pain and remorse that I should have had regarding my detest-

---

[18]Secor's text has "solicitude" here; the context seems to suggest that this is a misprint for "solitude" and we have translated accordingly.

able conduct, but on the contrary my wounded pride; for since I had driven reason away, it ever after appeared to me distant and fleeting. Therefore, in my opinion, my husband was doing me a great wrong. He continued: "You should not be astonished if, contrary to my custom, I have struck you. But come here and look at this letter of yours, which you cannot deny, and tell me, without the clever lies you now know how to use, who is the person to whom you intend to send such writing."

Then I began to meditate and reflect, and I said to myself: "Alas! I can hardly excuse myself, for a letter in my own handwriting testifies very clearly to what I have been doing." Then I said to myself: "On the other hand, I have to deny it, for a proof can do nothing against a bold face." Then, with loud moans and exclamations, I said: "Alas! my love, what moves you to be so cruel because of the letter you found, which was composed only as an exercise and to avoid idleness? You should not insult and harm me in this way without having heard my reasons. What law in all the world is so unjust, barbarous, and severe that it permits punishment to be carried out before judgment is passed? Where is deliberate reason? Where is your prudent judgment, that you condemn me without having first heard me out?"

As I was speaking these words, and intending to go on, he interrupted me, saying: "Here is a letter that was sent to you. Where did it come from?" I replied that I did not recognize it. "No?" he cried, "to show my greater appreciation of your lies, I assure you I have recognized your letter in the hands of your lover, who, through inconstancy and indiscretion, gave it to two of his friends. And if you are so bold and sure of yourself as to want to maintain the contrary, I shall find some clever way to get it back from him. For his only desire and affection is to think up and imagine various ways and diverse acts damaging to you in order to deprive you of your honor by making them public. But from now on you shall no longer have the delectable pleasure of seeing him, because I forbid you to go out of your room or look out of the window. And if this sort of life seems too miserable to you, I will stand by my earlier offer to allow you to live separately."

Thus I was forced to endure and suffer all these travails, being deprived of the sight of my beloved, who was very surprised not to see me any more. But he nevertheless refused to end his amorous pursuit, continuing on many different occasions to come with singers, among whom I recognized his voice. Oh, how tortured I was because I dared not show myself! And then I was tempted several times to get up and throw myself down, leaping from my window to the ground. I was in such torment for about a fortnight that we were forced to leave in order to avoid a scandal, for the neighbors were beginning to talk about such goings-on being so prolonged. I was quite happy to move so that I might more easily be allowed to go out into the town, thinking I might sometimes meet my beloved. Nonetheless, after our transmigrations, I went three weeks without seeing him or hearing from him, which was very painful and almost unbearable for me. While I was languishing in this calamity, everything seemed to me sad and hateful, and I took no delight in the things of this world. And still Fortune was not yet satisfied with giving me cause for tormenting pains, and wanted to augment them. It tried to add to them a misfortune whose memory makes me sad. Although I am loath to recount it, still, weeping over and lamenting my unhappiness, I shall try to write it out. To tell you about the misadventure to which I nearly succumbed, one day among others I was in bed with my husband, and very pensive, so that the affections that troubled my heart were consuming my spirit, which made me so weak it seemed to me I could not rise. But in fact I was so impeded by my husband that I had to struggle to do so, although several times I had to lie down again, without being able to move my limbs. Alas! This was a clear presage of my future misfortune, but its meaning was hidden from me.

And so, without noticing or paying this any attention, I dressed with great difficulty and effort. Then we went to hear God's divine service in a pious monastery. As I was going inside, my husband said to me, "I beg of you, tell me, without trying to hide anything, if your lover happened to be in this temple, would it be in your power to moderate your will and appetite, so that you would not look at him as you usually do?" Then I turned my eyes on him, saying: "I pray to the creator that were I to do so, every elemental power should oppose me, and that tigers and wolves should tear apart and devour my body, or that the three sisters should prematurely cut my life-thread."

Then we entered the temple. I began to look around me. I saw a great multitude of people, men as well as women, and among them I saw my beloved. Then, although it was forbidden and prohibited that I should look at him, I could not dissimulate or temper my desire; for without hesitating to break and infringe on my promise, I looked at him very affectionately without recalling the pains and torments my husband made me suffer on his account. But just as a pregnant woman tormented by strong and excessive pains before the birth of her child finds upon seeing the fruit of her labor that her perfect joy and delight make her forget all the preceding pains, in the same way the intrinsic pleasure and sweetness I received from the delectable sight of my beloved made me forget all my previous travails and sufferings. My husband, seeing this, came to tell me to go into a place to which he led me. I did so, but nevertheless I did not cease to continue my foolish behavior, and without maintaining my dignity, as decency required, I was still watching to see if I could see my beloved pass by. My husband, seeing that it was impossible to restrain the vehemence of the love that possessed and dominated me, and not being able to endure such lapses into immodest looks, was compelled to leave. Thereupon I recalled his commandment, against which I had transgressed, and my promises which I had broken. And so I quickly rose and followed him.

When we had arrived at our lodgings, my husband began to blame and condemn me, saying: "O, wicked and unfortunate creature full of iniquity, desiring only to satisfy your lawless appetite! How dare you be in my presence? Aren't you afraid that in justified anger I might plunge my sword into your breast?" With these words, with such fury and impetuousness he gave me a great blow that made me fall and break two of my teeth, which caused me such extreme pain that I remained a long time without giving any sign of life. And when I had recovered from my faint, all pale and white, I began to look around me without saying a word; for because of my intense and unbearable internal pains, I was unable to speak. But shortly afterward a great multitude of sighs rose from my breast, and diverse and fantastic images came to me, so cruel and ignominious that the recent memory of them makes my hand so weak it trembles, and several times I stopped writing and broke my quill. But since this might cause me to be thought pusillanimous, I shall try to write them down.

Love's impatience despairing seeks death.

Chapter 12

In order for me to tell you about them, you must understand that all my thoughts came down to one, which was such that I wanted to seek my cure in death. An ardent desire to carry out my execrable intention burned in my troubled heart with such fury that raging madness called back to my weak and tormented body the strength that had been dispersed outside it. And seeing that I did not have an opportunity to satisfy my desire, like an injured and wounded animal I paced up and down in my room in the presence of my husband and a young maid, saying to myself: "O Tisiphone, o Megaera and Alecto, infernal furies who continually agitate humankind, help me use cruelty on myself.[19] Let such a gift be given me by you, as was given to Canache by Aeolus her father, a sword to pierce her body because of the crime she had perpetrated and commit-

---

[19]The Greek "erinyes" or furies were the avengers of wrong who relentlessly pursued the guilty and drove them mad.

ted.[20] Would that I could either leap to my death, as Isiphila did,[21] or put an end to my miserable life by means of some poisonous drink, like the one that caused the death of Socrates. Or let my great fury and rage be brought to an end by a death like that of the desperate Phyllis, who hanged herself from a tree, because her beloved Demophon was tardy in returning.[22] But since it is impossible for me to find a way of dying, because of my husband's presence, I wish I might share the fate of the beautiful nymph Hesperia; while walking in the grass with her bare, soft, and delicate feet, this chaste virgin was bitten by a venomous asp, whose fang's deadly poison caused her sudden death. Or let happen to me what happened to Dathan and Abiram, who were swallowed up by the earth."[23] Moved by such madness, I looked everywhere for a way to die. But I believe that some infernal fury I had invoked showed itself eager to serve me in accord with my ardent desire, because while I was searching everywhere a little knife presented and offered itself to my eyes. I picked it up as discreetly and furtively as I could, and hid it under my robe.

When it was in my possession,[24] I immediately began to tremble because of the dismal prospect of death; and trying to walk, I fell and felt within myself a great conflict between my suffering soul and my fearful life forces. But cruel Megaera persuaded me to follow my mortal purpose, making me remember that if I lived I could never more see my beloved, because my love affair was too public and known to all; but after my death, my soul could frequently visit him, and this made death seem happy and fortunate to me. Because of this future hope of seeing my beloved, Megaera[25] drove cold fear away from me, and I was inflamed by still more ardent desires for death. Although my face was painted in a pale color, I began to recover my strength; and without further delay, I got up

---

[20]Aeolus was the king of ancient Thessaly and the mythic founder of the Aeolian race, which settled all over Greece; he is also considered the king of the winds. Discovering that his daughter Canache was sleeping with his youngest son Macareus, he sent her a sword, with which she killed herself.

[21]Hélisenne probably refers to Ysiphile from Boccaccio's *De claris mulieribus* (chapter 17). Boccaccio does not, however, mention that she leaps to her death. Paule Demats proposes that Hélisenne has confused Ysiphile with Ilice, from the *Ibis*, who does throw herself from a precipice. Cf. Demats, 129.

[22]Demophon, the husband of Phyllis, became homesick for his native Athens and so left Thrace, promising to return soon. When he failed to appear, Phyllis hanged herself in grief and was transformed into an almond tree.

[23]In the Old Testament, the sons of Eliab, who joined Korah's rebellion against the leadership of Moses and Aaron; Yahweh caused the earth to swallow up all three of the rebels. See Numbers 16.

[24]"Et lors que je feuz saisie . . ." Literally: "When I was seized . . ." The context suggests this should be translated as if it read: "Et lors que je m'en feuz saisi . . ."

[25]This sentence gives no subject for the verb, a practice common in medieval French but archaic in Hélisenne's time. We have supplied the apparent subject.

with great agitation and urgency, wanting to go out of the room, which my husband refused to permit, since he imagined, considering my behavior, that the mad fury by which I was driven was urging me to leave in order to find my beloved. But when I saw I could not go out, I withdrew into a large alcove, and since I wanted to pierce my amorous heart with this dagger, I believe that by divine permission I was watched over and preserved, for the young maid who was in the room came in, and seeing such a horrible and fearsome thing, could not keep from crying out loudly, and approached me to take away the knife. I did everything I could to resist her.

Meanwhile, my husband came in, thinking that I had fainted again; but when he had seen and considered the mad rage that held me in its grasp, he was struck by anguishing pain because of the excessive love he had for me, of which he was unable to divest himself, and which had the power to restrain the anger which tortured his poor heart, and to convert it into compassion; and so he kindly came to console me, while chiding me in various ways. Among other things, he said: "My love, I see clearly that it is not in your power to put an end to your love, because you did not resist it from the beginning, but by long and continual thought you have nourished a lascivious love in your breast. By depriving yourself of your freedom, you have voluntarily enslaved yourself to your sensuality, whereby love has constantly augmented with such great power that you would sooner lose your life than your lover, without remembering or recalling that by such a death you concede to nature that you have lost your good reputation, in view of the fact and considering that you would have resorted to such cruelty against yourself; and I who have not deserved it, would be held in less esteem for the rest of my life. You should also consider that if your soul were separated from your wretched body, a dismal dwelling-place would be assigned it, on account of the enormous and execrable sin you would have committed by being your own murderer. But in order to keep you from succumbing to such calamities, I advise you to go away, as I have told you several times; this becomes still more urgent because it is impossible for me to endure any longer the aggravations I have tolerated in order not to cause a scandal for you. For the conservation of your honor I have to dissimulate, without daring to take vengeance on my enemy, even though he is a man of low estate, and I cannot tell you how painful and difficult this is for me. And for that reason, think about how you can put an end to my extreme distress, whether it be by our separating or by returning to a more honorable way of life."

The faithful servant's advice.

Chapter 13

While he was talking in this way, one of our servants who had been looking after our affairs came in. On his arrival he was informed by the young maid of the perilous danger to which I had almost succumbed, and seeing that it was something that should be kept in the deepest silence, he told her that he would sooner lose his life than tell anyone else about it. That said, he went to greet his master, who considered him a faithful servant, and for that reason my husband told him about my misfortune, though without mentioning my amorous folly. The servant pretended to be astonished by this, feigning that he knew nothing about it, and seeing his master in such pain and torment, he began to say to him: "Sir, so far as I can tell, your heart is terribly burdened, and not without reason; but nevertheless you must make use of your discretion to moderate and temper the passions of your poor heart, for a man's virtue is shown only in adversity, because a man who is full of great wisdom must restrain his will and desire, so that he is not elated by prosperity any more than he is cast down by misfortune and adversity. You must be consoled, considering that milady has always been virtuous; and, although her understanding is disturbed by agitations and afflictions unknown to us, still you should hope that reason will win out in her, for virtue cannot be driven out of a place where it has been for some time, nor without cause; and for that reason, my opinion would be that she should declare her extreme afflictions to some learned person who, through the efficacity of his words, could support and comfort her, and by this means she will be able to return to her original way of life."

My husband listened to these words and others the servant said, and although he was deeply troubled, he still took some consolation from them, and decided to follow his servant's advice. And so, turning to me, he gently admonished me, still thinking that through his exhortations my painful fury and extreme suffering might be diminished; but he did not understand that my illness was incurable. However, after I had listened to him, I pretended that I wished to reform, for no ire is so furious that it does not eventually cool in some measure. So I began to weep, and with great bitterness, to lament my outrageous folly. Nonetheless I did not repent having been captured by love, but I was irritated because I had not loved more temperately, without having let my husband discover it. Seeing the change in my expression, he thought his words had found their way into my heart and borne fruit there. So that I should be more inclined to annihilate my wicked desire, he took me to a pious monastery so that, through confession and without difficulty, I might agree to reveal my misfortune and unburden my heart to a respected monk who was very famous and renowned. This monk had been informed by the servant that my trouble was so great that it had led me to extremities. Being in this temple without feeling any devotion, I began to premeditate my confession to this monk, and I said to myself: "Oh, Lord, how tiresome and painful it is to feign and dissimulate! I say this because I have no will or desire to communicate the secret of my love through confession, for I am neither contrite nor repentant; I remain firm and steadfast in loving my beloved, for I should sooner expose myself to a thousand different kinds of death than desist from loving him. And so it seems to me folly to divulge it to this old man who has grown all cold, impotent and useless for nature's purposes. He will scold and blame me for what he earlier found pleasant, pressing and encouraging me to drive love away without having enjoyed it; and if I were to believe him, I should have only pain and torment, without receiving any pleasure of delight. Still, I have to answer him and tell him how I came to use such cruelty against myself, for I am certain he has been informed about my wretched desire. But when all is considered, I can tell him all about it; for since I shall tell him this in confession, he will never dare to reveal it. He cannot force me to follow his advice, and so I shall take pleasure in talking about the man I love more ardently than any lover was ever loved by his lady."

Pious admonishments will not make a love-struck woman desist from love.

Chapter 14

While my mind was occupied with such varied ideas and thoughts, I perceived the aforementioned monk, and as soon as I had seen him, I addressed him in a modest way; and after we had greeted each other and retired to a small, secluded and godly place, he graciously invited me to sit down, because he saw I was a little weak. Then he began to speak to me in this way: "Madame, I can presume and conjecture, looking at your very pale and colorless face, that you are suffering from passions so vehement you find it difficult to find even a small relief for your acute pain. But if you are willing to return to God, beseeching him very devoutly, you must believe firmly, with unshakable belief, that He will not abandon you, but rather aid and comfort you. You must try to feel contrition for the offenses you have perpetrated and committed, for sometimes through our vile and exorbitant sins we arouse Divine wrath and indignation, which leads us into great confusion, and we cannot return to a state of grace until we have first done appropriate penance. I was astonished to learn that today you nearly fell into such a calamity as to lose your body and soul by trying to take your own life. What misfortune or adversity can have happened to you that is so great as to give you cause and reason for despair? Have you no regard or consideration for the fact that we die and leave this world and our soul is divested of this miserable corporeal clothing, and if by cupidity or wickedness it has become fetid and stained, it is assigned a doleful dwelling place in perpetuity and forever? I believe that if you are aware of such things, you can easily reform yourself. And so that I may aid you in this, I beg you to tell me the source from which such mad fantasies come to you."

After making my salutations, I tried to speak, but before I uttered the first word I began to tremble, and such an extreme chill entered my bones that because of the pain I was suffering, regrets cut off my voice; and for a long time I looked more like a simulacrum or statue than a living creature. Reduced to this extremity, I was unable to find peace or tranquillity in my heart; but sighing until I began to weep I bowed my head, showing by my external gestures that I was terribly upset and pained. Seeing this, the monk, with very efficacious words, sought to calm me and showed great compassion for my grievous suffering. But his good words were of little use or value to me, because my thoughts were occupied by the venomous love that was tormenting me to death.

Nevertheless, after a time, I recovered some vigor, which gave me strength and the ability to speak. And then, in a voice broken and halting (because of the burden weighing on my heart), I began to speak in this way: "Alas! Sir, if all those who have eloquent tongues were to gather together, it would still be difficult to relate the unbearable passions which continually agitate and persecute my soul, without ever having any hope that my misfortunes end before they cause my death. Therefore do not be astonished to see my face pale and colorless. Rather, so that you may not be ignorant of the cause of my lachrimations, tears and moaning about my misfortune, I wish to make it clear to you, even though I cannot relate it without pain, for remembering it is a great torment to me. Alas! the thoughts and infinite regrets that so unbearably torment and torture me are not for the justified pain I ought to feel on account of my wicked sins, but proceed from the countless desires and amorous impulses which oppress me, and which I am incapable of resisting. For I love so ardently that I should prefer to be deprived of my life rather than of the sight of my beloved. Considering my unbearable woes, that should easily lead you to take pity on a woman whom, because of her excessive love, you see in a languorous infirmity far worse than a violent death.

"You urge and exhort me to return to God, offering him devout prayers and intercessions. Alas! How is it possible to ask him to make me desist from my love? For you may be certain that I could not force my heart to do so. Although, as I have already told you, I suffer unimaginable pain and suffering, I nevertheless take a kind of pleasure just in looking at him. A single glimpse of my beloved can give me color if I am pale; if I am sad, it can cheer me; if I am weak, it can give me strength; if I am ill, it can restore my health; and if I were about to die, it would have the power to resuscitate me. For these reasons I could not desire to abandon my love for him.

But even if I wanted to desist from my love, I am not so presumptuous, and I do not esteem my pusillanimous virtue so much as to believe I could do it, seeing and considering that our predecessors most learned in this domain were not able to resist such ardor, but rather, in spite of the sublimity of their minds, let themselves be humbled and captured. David committed homicide in order to enjoy Bathsheba.[26] Wise Solomon was an idolater in love. Aristotle, the prince of nature, worshiped Love in the person of his beloved Remia.[27] The son of Alcemene, who was a conqueror of men and monsters, was not able to avoid being vanquished by love, so that to please his lady Iole, he put powder on his face and moreover, acted as a nanny and a chambermaid.[28] To tell you about other cases would only use up our time. So to avoid superfluous talk, I leave them aside, begging you to consider that since love has had such great power over our predecessors, it cannot fail to have power over their successors.

"Therefore would it not be madness for me to imagine myself superior to love, which men have not been able to resist? And for that reason, all fear left behind, I have to fulfill the desire of my youth or I shall die from misery. You have made me several remonstrances that I know to be true; I am sure that when my soul has transmigrated from my body it shall be judged, according to my merits or demerits, by the just judge. But I believe there can be no place so painful to it as my wretched body, for the greatest infernal pain is the intellectual comprehension of divine justice; that is an immeasurable torture for [the damned].[29] And I, poor wretch, am tormented in body and in soul by love's flame, which burns and consumes

---

[26]David was a king of the Jews who became enamored of Bathsheba, the wife of one of his warriors whom he sent into battle with the intention of having him killed so he could take the widow as one of his wives.

[27]The image of Aristotle being bridled and ridden like a horse by a woman was common in the Middle Ages. Demats, who emends the spelling of the woman's name from Remya (as it appears in all sixteenth-century editions) to Hermya, notes that Hélisenne draws this passage almost word for word from Caviceo's *Peregrino*. The exact identity of the female alluded to here is not known; tradition has it that she is Alexander's mistress. Cf. Demats, 129-30.

[28]Heracles, the son of Alcemene and Zeus, wore dresses while in the service of Queen Omphale, at whose court all gender roles were reversed.

[29]The French here reads: "cela leur est ung inestimable supplice." The only possible explicit antecedent for the pronoun "leur" is "places," which makes no sense in this context. We have supplied what we take to be the implicit referent of this pronoun.

me with the countless regrets that agitate me, without having hope of any cooling. Hence one may deem [the damned's] pains not comparable to mine. And yet I do not fear death, but continually seek it out eagerly. In that respect I shall not be inconstant, for since my love has come to the attention of my husband, I am certain that he will force me to go away, in order to deprive me of the sight of my beloved, thinking that this will cause me to forget him. Alas, then! How should I go on living? For although my body departs, my amorous heart shall take up residence with my beloved, until my body and soul are separated, which will soon occur, for what preserved me and kept me alive was only the singular pleasure and sweetness I felt in seeing the one who is the lord of my life."

A woman's heart fixed on love is impossible to reform.

Chapter 15

When I had finished speaking, weeping bitterly and heaving a great abundance of sighs, the devout monk remained silent for a long time; after a while, he began to look at me, and with gentleness and clemency he spoke to me in this way: "Madame, so far as I am able to judge, I believe you have wholly revealed the secret in your heart without holding anything back, and this gives me hope that your pain can be tempered by restraining the violence of the passion that dominates you. For the great distress you are suffering can grow and multiply if it is kept silent and hidden, which is an incredible torment to lovers. I have very carefully thought over and considered the unfathomable pain of your afflicted heart, which provokes great compassion in me; for on the basis of what you have expressed to me, I believe no lover was ever in such an extremity as you are. But all the same, although you are tempted to commit such a cruel and ignominious offense against yourself as to try to kill yourself with your own hand, and although you do not consider the pains of hell comparable to yours, nevertheless you must try as hard as you can to resist, and see and verify whether there is any virtue[30] in you. For the present, however, I truly believe it is not in your power to show it, because of the agitated state of your soul, and also because of the heated frenzy which has not yet cooled. Reason is not welcome in your heart; but

---

[30]This is a particularly interesting case of the polyvalence of the word "vertu." For here it is a matter not only of adherence to moral codes requiring resistance to desire but also of the strength, power, or courage to resist.

when the violence of your passion begins to diminish,[31] you will recognize your madness and furious fantasies, and find them horrible. You say you are not so presumptuous as to think you could vanquish love, seeing and considering that men have not been able to resist it. On that account you should not lose hope, although your sex is more fragile and less constant, for men freely submit to love, and do not think themselves reprehensible, for they do not consider love a vice. On the contrary, they boast and are proud of themselves when through their deceptions, ruses, and adulations they succeed in beguiling your sex, which is overly credulous and too eager to listen to them; this should serve you as an example showing that you should not so easily believe their blandishments; and you must forego familiar intercourse with them, for continual conversation causes love to grow. And for that reason, it is necessary that you avoid the presence of the man who causes you such pain and torment; for although you say you take a singular delight in looking on him, you are not considering the bitterness mixed with this sweetness, which is worse for you than a poisonous venom. Therefore, since the pain is so violent and since it exceeds the pleasure, you may call yourself blessedly happy if you are able to moderate the ardor of love and return within more modest limits. This you can easily do, by means of absenting yourself far from his sight, which is the thing you most fear. It seems to you impossible to live without him, not realizing that he alone torments you, to the point that he is opening the path toward death. I am well aware that when you have moved away, at first you will suffer very grave pain because of the recent memory of past pleasures; but through prudence, with honorable practice you will mitigate and temper your excessive pain, and in the course of time the madness will pass and consume itself; in this way you will be able to recover your liberty, of which I see you deprived at present. To induce and aid you in driving love away and destroying it, if you will not take pity on your person, you should be concerned about your honor, which could easily be tarnished, and consider that through careful observance a thing is to be preserved and maintained that can never be recovered when once it is lost. I want to remind you and urge you to follow other ladies who preferred to risk death rather than corrupt their chastity. Among others, you should remember Penelope's continence; because of her sincere love for her husband Ulysses, she always refused to acquiesce to the importunate requests that were pressed on her. And then you must consider the marvelous constancy of the nymph Oenone; for despite the fact that her spouse had treated her very badly in repudiating her to attach himself to the Greek Helen (which later caused him to lose his life), the

---

[31]Here we have chosen to follow the 1538 text rather than the 1541 text, which substitutes "dominer" for "diminuer."

noble nymph retained her original love in her pure and chaste heart; and so, seeing him dead, she was afflicted with such extreme distress that embracing the body of her late husband, she heaved her last, mortal sigh, and her loving heart broke within her breast.[32] Then we must not forget the pudency of the Roman Lucretia, who refused to live after the treacherous rape committed on her by force and violence. I find your desire very contrary and different to that of this noble lady, who cared more for her honor than for her life; whereas you, more willful than wise, want to follow your sensuality, and you would sooner deprive yourself of life than fail to enjoy your voluptuous pleasure and satisfy your unruly appetite, without regard to your offense against God and your husband, the fear of which ought to be sufficient to make your inveterate and hardened heart draw back. Don't you imagine the circumstances, fearing the evil that might ensue in the future? I had never seen your husband before today, but I esteem his noble character so much I am sure his heart could not endure or put up with such importunities. Since your love has become known to him, he will be able to take cruel vengeance on your beloved and on you; and if such a misfortune occurred, your reputation would be forever tarnished and soiled with perpetual infamy. Therefore, to avoid such a peril and danger, you must consider that those are blessed who in all their acts consider the result."

When he had put an end to his remarks, I remained very pensive and did not know how to answer him. I had a great desire to go away, since I found what he said sad and odious, because he was persuading me to expel love from my heart. But it was only time wasted to chide and warn me about that, for I was so obstinate that no matter what annoyances, pains, and torments I had suffered on account of my beloved, love had never diminished; and I was determined always to persevere. For that reason it seemed to me that the monk was doing me a great wrong in scolding me, considering that he had declared that it was not in my power to desist from love, and so I began to say to myself: "Oh, cursed old man, I thought even before I spoke to you, that such words would be terribly bitter to me, and would only irritate and depress me. And so I wish you were submerged in Scylla or Charybdis,[33] and that my beloved[34] were in your place wearing your habit! In that way, without arousing suspicion, we could talk about our love, which would give us more pleasure and solace than

---

[32]Hélisenne does not mention that Oenone dies of both grief and remorse. Her husband, Paris, returned to her wounded from the war and asked her to heal him, which she at first refused to do. Although she relented in time, it was too late and Paris died.

[33]Scylla was a multiple-headed monster who had a taste for sailors and lived across from Charybdis, a giant whirlpool that would do away with the sailors that Scylla missed.

[34]Secor's text reads "mon mary," but this makes no sense here; we have assumed the text is in error, and have substituted "beloved" for "husband."

39

anything I can think of or imagine. But this felicity cannot be mine, because fortune, which is my cruel enemy, favors me in no way, but continually provides me with new occasions for despair. And for a final resolution, I desire only death, in which is reserved the last of my pains, which would otherwise be intolerable to me."

I was led into a cruel and mad fantasy, and the continual change in my face's color gave the monk clear evidence of it. Seeing that I was in such pain and beside myself, and that it was not in my power to respond with a single word, he went on to say some words of comfort to me, which produced no effect, for the more he admonished me, the less I wanted to give up my follies. Realizing that his words were wasted and carried away by the wind, as decently as he could he dismissed me, promising to say devout prayers and intercede for me so that through His special grace, it might please God to cure my lamentable illness. As soon as I had left this secluded room, it seemed to me that I was relieved by being away from a person who so greatly annoyed and irritated me. Then I saw my husband walking about; after he had noticed me, he came up to me, and with his humane kindness, asked how I was; to which I responded that I felt completely consoled and that I was in a very good mood, which made him very happy. But alas! That was the very opposite of the truth, for I was compelled to keep my internal pains concealed and secret so that he might think I intended to abandon the love I had so long nourished in my breast by persisting in vain and useless thoughts.

Thus I had to dissimulate my agonizing pain under a false joyful face, which tortured and tormented me all the more. But when we had returned home, I withdrew into my chamber, and finding myself alone, I began to grieve and complain; and in a lamentable voice, I expressed grave and piteous complaints yearning for my beloved, whom I could not see, and whose absence displeased me more than anything else could. I continued in this difficult and painful way of life, which caused an illness that will accompany me to my death, and which led me into such an extremity that I usually had to remain alone in my room, not being able to walk, my limbs being debilitated by their trembling. My husband, seeing this, wanted to try different kinds of medicines, which I cared nothing for, knowing that there was only one medicine that could cure me, and I thought it was impossible to recover because my husband kept such a close eye on me that he wanted us to be constantly together. In this way, I went a long time without seeing my beloved. I constantly thought and imagined new ways of getting my husband to go away. Sometimes I told him that it was very urgent that he be in certain places on his lands and domains, giving him to understand that through his negligence in visiting them, they might become less valuable and this could greatly prejudice our situation. But no matter how I tried to persuade him, I could never make him agree to do as I wished; hence I remained confounded until I begged him very urgently to allow me sometimes to go to the court where our case was being heard, in order to avoid melancholy, and also to help him put our affairs in order. Because of my requests and continual urging, this was granted me. Nevertheless, he kept me in his company, which was very annoying to me. But if one cannot do what one wants, one has to do what one can. I never showed my feelings at all, and passed that day with less pain than the others.

A woman's way of seeing her beloved.

Chapter 16

The next day, as soon as I saw the sun, I got up and put on rich and glorious clothes, hoping to see the man whom I should have braved any peril to please. While I was taking delight and singular pleasure in my amorous thoughts, joy entered my heart with such vehemence that I utterly lost my composure. Seeing this, my husband was astonished, not knowing the cause from which this sudden change proceeded, and not inquiring about it. As soon as I was dressed, he asked me if I wanted to go to the place where justice was done and disagreements settled.[35] Without delay I replied that I did, and that henceforth I was determined to involve myself in caring for our affairs—were it his pleasure to employ me in this matter—which would be much more helpful to me than to remain constantly idle. Smiling, he replied: "Certainly, my love, you are right, and I assure you I am quite willing to do as you say." Saying such things, or things like them, we left our lodgings.

When we arrived at the lawcourt, I began to look around me, and in looking, I saw a great multitude of men and a few women, several of whom came to form a circle about me and began to praise and extol me, making diverse comments. Some of them said they had been in many countries and had seen a number of ladies and maidens, but they affirmed that I was the most perfect in bodily beauty they had ever seen. I pretended to be looking elsewhere, but I was listening to them; and I should have taken special pleasure in such trivial vanities, had it not been that my spirit was completely transported by the intolerable vehemence of love, which dominated me with such great force that it dissipated and annihilated all my powers. For a long time I continued to try to glimpse my beloved, but seeing that he was not there, my desire was frustrated and I

---

[35]Hélisenne frequently uses such expressions, perhaps for lack of a suitable term designating a court that heard civil cases. To avoid needlessly multiplying such cumbersome periphrases, henceforth we will generally translate them by the term "lawcourt."

wanted to leave because of the pain I could no longer endure, which was hidden in my wretched heart, and whose cause I dared not name. When I was in my chamber, I began to complain and lament as I usually did. During my calamitous passions, I went many times to the said lawcourt before I was able to see my beloved, which gave me such continual distress and was so very bitter to me that I should have been incapable of enduring it had I not been aided by a slight hope from which I took some comfort. But among other things I was greatly displeased by my husband's suspicions about me. That caused him to vex, wound, and annoy me, and this made me so impatient that I continually returned to my mad fantasies. While I was virtually without hope, and assumed that it was impossible that I should be able to possess my beloved, I decided to remain alone in my chamber to continue my weeping as secretly as possible; but my husband refused to allow it, thinking my corporeal illness was the cause of my sadness and melancholy. Alas! He did not know that my suffering proceeded from the passions of the soul, and that excessive love was its cause, for he thought I had abandoned the mad love that possessed me and lorded over me. Therefore, one day he wanted to take me to the lawcourt, saying that continuing to remain so anxious might increase and augment my illness, and that to cure me and restore me to health it would be more suitable and profitable that I should occupy myself in pursuing our affairs. When I heard what he said, I dared not disagree, and was compelled to obey him; and so we immediately went to the judicial lawcourt.

Having withdrawn into a place where I thought I could rest (which was difficult for me, for an unhappy person finds repose difficult), I began to look about; searching everywhere, I saw a large group of young people, among whom I saw my beloved. He cast a look on me that penetrated all the way to my heart, and had such power that at that moment I myself was bereft of and completely lost my composure. But my husband, who had moved away from me a bit to deal with his affairs, immediately came back, and because of the great multitude of people, he had not seen my beloved; and so with a sweet greeting and a happy face, he came to tell me it was time for us to leave. Then my fear caused me to begin to tremble and grow pale. But he thought that it was my usual malady, and came to comfort me by holding out the hope of an early cure, saying I had to force my heart to be quiet, because wanting to be healed is an important step toward healing. From these words I knew, through his kind words, that he had not noticed my beloved, and I regained a bit of strength. In order not to be ungrateful, I began to thank Love, saying to myself: "O lord Love, if sometimes I have been mistaken in complaining about you because I was granted no favor in your service, I now repent, for I feel myself incapable of expressing the thanks due and fitting for participating in such a pleasure. What felicity or beatitude could equal mine? O happy look that has so much power that when I am in extremity it can revive and fortify me; whereby I deem my travail to be little or nothing in comparison with the reward. Alas! I remove my body, but my heart remains in such thoughts." We arrived at our lodgings, and this time I did not want to follow my usual custom of weeping and lamenting; on the contrary, I had the secret determination to live in greater pleasure and joyousness in order to dilate and open up my constricted and oppressed heart so that I might regain the beauty I had lost on account of my grievous and anguishing pains, and not be ugly and displeasing to my beloved.

Fortune, however, remained my enemy, and did not give me the opportunity to do so, because my husband, who was clear-sighted, incessantly watched my gestures and expressions; so that by continually looking where I cast my artful eyes, he espied my beloved, and then he began to say, pointing him out to me and pretending he had not seen me looking at him: "My love, there's that wicked man who causes the pullulation of continual dissensions between us; even now, so far as I can see, he refuses to desist or put an end to his outrageous folly. But nevertheless I do not want to prohibit or forbid you to come take solace in listening to the proceedings at the lawcourt, at least if you undertake on your honor not to absent yourself from the places where I leave you when I am constrained to pursue my affairs. And I also desire and command that you shall not look at him in your accustomed way; and if you do so, you will make me so angry that the violence of my wrath may make me exceed the bounds of reason."

After he had said this, I did nothing but heave pained and profound sighs, which showed beyond a doubt the martyrdom I suffered. Therefore several people, seeing me in such sudden calamity, had compassion for my suffering. Being in such misery and passionate chagrin, I desired only to be alone in order to recommence shedding the tears I had temporarily abandoned, but timidity and fear held me back, making me observe my husband's command, and I dared not leave the place where I was. My beloved was still walking about, and he passed near me; but to avoid his looks and in order not to arouse the ire and indignation of my husband, I was compelled to remain leaning on a bench, without daring to turn my face toward him, which so tormented me that neither peace nor repose returned to my wretched heart. Alas! I felt myself deprived of all my pleasures and consolation, without hope of ever realizing my affectionate desire; and the farther I felt from that goal, the more I suffered from ardor and burning. I remained a long time in such a grievous languor, still continuing to abide in the lawcourt where my beloved did not fail to be and to continue his amorous pursuit; and several times, when he did not see my husband, he was about to come and speak to me, but changed his mind, fearing he might be caught. One day, after he had looked in several and diverse places without being able to see my husband, thinking he was assured of his absence, he approached me, and after making amorous salutations, we remained some time without it being in our power to speak, because of the exceeding joy we felt. Then afterward, like a man who fears punishment and asks for mercy (as one could judge from the way he grew pale), he began to speak and said:

The lovers' devices for making approaches.

Chapter 17

"Milady, were it not so difficult to express the pains and travail that I endure, I should think that such felicity would be granted me as to see my service deemed pleasing, hoping this much from your sweetness and kindness, that they[36] should not wish to be ungrateful, but rather promptly recompense and reward me with a commensurate guerdon, without leaving me continually in such great languor and infirmity. Alas, milady! If it is not in my power to tell you about the agitations and afflictions that occupy my soul and the great cares that incessantly accumulate in my unfortunate attempts to acquire your benevolence, my face pale in color, and my continual sighs, must undoubtedly make you certain of it. Alas! The pain I must endure without being able or wishing to resist it is violent and insuperable; it is a wound no medicine can close; it is a fire inextinguishable by any power of water; it is an ardor no ice can cool. If you are so cruel (and I think you are not) that you refuse to provide the deserved succor,[37] then the misery and distress, the languor and martyrdom to which I am reduced, shall lead me to a premature death; and if that should happen, you would be accused of the vice of cruelty for not having preserved from death the man who would brave any peril in order to please you. Alas! What torments me most and causes me to despair of ever reaching my goal, is the continual presence of your husband, who threatens every day not only to strike or harm me, but to make me give up life altogether through a violent death. And yet, consider with what power love rules over me! There is no threat that deters me; there is no peril that I fear, nor importunity that will drive me away. By these evident and manifest signs you must consider me your perpetual servitor."

While I was listening to his words, I was suddenly so aroused by excessive love and ardent desire that my amorous heart was beating faster than

---

[36]The French text has a singular pronoun here, but it clearly refers to both *doulceur* and *bénignité*.

[37]Secor's text reads: "que ne voulez entendre, O meritez secours! la misere . . ."; in this case we have adopted Demats's reading: "que ne voulez entendre aux meritez secours, la misere . . ."

the airy wings of the swallow when it flies. Moreover, the fear that my husband might arrive tormented and vexed me so much that all my limbs began to tremble, as they were wont to do. Still, finding myself in the presence of the one I loved most, after a short time I began to think how I should answer him. But considering his external behavior, I understood that he was very bewitched and captivated by love for me, which was the reason that for the moment I concealed from him the secret of my heart, not to banish him or drive him away, but to inflame him with even greater ardor.

Then I said: "After having carefully thought over and considered your actions and behavior, I have been able to conjecture that your thoughts are occupied with very weighty and serious cogitations, for love is a passion in the soul which usually reduces us to perplexity and sadness because we cannot enjoy what we love. When such a fate befalls lovers, they remain submerged in the depth of extreme distress and misery when they prefer lascivious love to true love, which consists in virtue. You should consider that if your persuasion were to press and urge me so that I granted your wish, that could not be done or accomplished without damaging my good standing; and thus, because it is not the sign of a prudent man to seek his pleasure by destroying the reputation of others, I beg you to abandon this immoderate affection, showing yourself to be a virtuous man, so that reason dominates and is superior to sensual appetite. I shall not blame you or consider you vicious if you are not able promptly to separate love from your heart. But through prudence and honorable efforts, you must moderate and apply your flourishing youth to more honorable ways of life than trying to seduce and deceive ladies or maidens. And especially you must not continue to pursue those who have always kept company with chastity, among whom I count myself. Had you been well informed about my life, you would have found that no one has ever had a poor opinion of me, even though several times I have been tempted and begged by princes and great lords; but in spite of this, their sublime highnesses did not have so much power as to make me acquiesce to their importunate requests. But had I been born under such an evil star that I was constrained to make myself the slave and subject of love, there is no man in the world who would sooner obtain my benevolence than you, with your sweetness; I assure you that you should be preferred to all others. Therefore I beg you to agree to be content, putting an end to the amorous pursuit by avoiding the presence of the object of your love, for continual commerce causes you the ardors and inflammations that could make you fall into despair . . . at least if you are as afflicted as your behavior and words suggest."

Continuation of the amorous colloquy.

Chapter 18

While I was telling him these things and others like them, he sometimes interrupted me and said that he was terribly afraid of my husband. To which I replied by saying: "I beg you to cease being afraid; I assure you there is no foundation for your fear, for he neither doubts nor suspects me. If I thought his mind was occupied with such ideas, I am the one who would have to give up hope of living, because I am certain—and I know it by long experience—that he loves me more than any man ever loved a woman. Therefore you must believe that I would have indeed reason to be fearful, for one who is capable of loving ardently is also capable of hating cruelly. I am astonished that such a fear disquiets you. You are the opposite of all other lovers, who through artful cleverness find a way to become intimate with the husbands of their beloveds, knowing that by doing so they can often have an opportunity to safely speak and converse with their ladies privately in public."

When I had finished, he immediately replied in this wise: "Madame, I am certain, and see it clearly, that your husband is afflicted with a great and passionate anger because of his suspicion regarding my intentions." As he was saying these words, he noticed my husband and pointed him out to me, which worried me so much I did not know how to behave. And then, just like the sea's waves agitated by a wind, I began again to quake and tremble all over; and for a long time I was silent until the fear of losing my beloved came back to my memory, which made me forget everything else and restored to my tortured and weakened body the strength that had been dispersed outside it. Looking at him, I realized that he was afflicted by a similar passion, and to reassure him, I told him that he shouldn't worry about anything, and that we were in neither danger nor peril because there was nothing strange about speaking and conversing, affirming that I was sure he would not ask what we had been talking about because he thought me chaste and modest, not only in acts, but also in words and conversation.

But no matter how much I said and affirmed, I could not persuade him to believe it. In his tender young courage there was not enough strength to allow him to say a word, but rather heaving a great many sighs, he departed; and I remained extremely irritated, fearing that through his pusillanimity my beloved might end his suit. This thought was so distressing to me that I did not recall the pain I might suffer because my husband had seen me; he had left, not being able to endure the violent rage that seized him. Seeing this, one of my attendants brought it to my attention.

Thereby I understood that he was troubled by a great concern, the memory of which caused my pain to grow, so that in extreme fear I left for our lodgings, thinking I should suffer like the daughter of King Priam, when her body was sacrificed on the sepulcher of Achilles.

Not without great labor and difficulty, I arrived at the place where I expected to suffer no less pain than Aegyptus's forty-nine children suffered at the hands of their wives and cousins.[38] And when I tried to go into my room, I met my husband, who began to threaten me cruelly; seeing this, the two attendants I had with me tried to take me away into another chamber. But he very promptly followed me; taking the first cudgel he could lay his hands on, a torch, he dealt me such a great blow that it knocked me violently to the floor. And still he could not satisfy or restrain his anger, but gave me two or three more blows so vicious that in several places the white, tender, and delicate flesh of my body became black, without, however, breaking the skin. While he was beating and battering me, my attendants and household servants tried to calm him. Meanwhile, his rage began to diminish, and so he went away, leaving me weeping and in terrible pain. Out of impatience I began to say: "O woman more wretched and unhappy than any other woman living, that is what you may well call yourself! For you have no hope ever to be delivered from your present wretchedness and calamity except by means of cruel Atropos, who is the only refuge of the desolate; she alone can put an end to your tears and sighs, to your pains and torments and furious desires." Uttering such words, I cried out several times, and heaved loud and piteous exclamations from my breast, still continuing my wretched regrets. Each of my attendants did her best to comfort me and alleviate my grievous and unbearable pains, which were to be my lot until I died.

While I was in such torment and travail, I heard the voice of my husband, who through long experience with sadness was more temperate in suffering pain than he formerly was; and so he tried to moderate his anger, considering that he would have to endure and suffer until my detestable way of life had been divulged and become more widely known, at which time he could repudiate me without being reproved or blamed by my relatives. And for that reason, without any outward sign, he remained silent, so I had no evidence that might allow me to understand what he had in mind. That day passed with me continuing my painful laments. When came the night, which is always worse than day for all sorts of suffering, since the nocturnal shadows are more in conformity with misery than is

---

[38]Aegyptus, the king of Egypt, and Danaus, the king of Lybia, were brothers with fifty children each. The children were all betrothed to one another, but Danaus feared his brother planned to murder his daughters after the marriage, so he ordered them to murder their husbands. On the marriage day, his daughters hid daggers in their cloaks and every one of them, save one, murdered her spouse.

light, I was in my bed accompanied only by my closest maid. I was not feigning when I cried out and wept bitterly, and I spent the whole night in such anxious and painful travail.

The glittering son of Hyperion,[39] holding the golden reins that were once foolishly desired by the presumptuous Phaeton, was already giving back to everything its proper colors, which had been blackened by the princess of the shadows, when my husband sent to ask whether I wished to go with him to the lawcourt where justice is done, which much amazed me, for since he had seen me talking to my beloved, I no longer hoped I should be permitted to go there again. Alas! I did not know for what reason he did this, which I have since discovered, to my dishonor and disadvantage. Nonetheless, somewhat comforted, I rose and dressed very hurriedly, although I could not do so without great difficulty, since I felt sharp pain because of the wounds I had suffered the preceding day. But the memory of my beloved was so deeply rooted in me, and so strongly anchored and alive in my heart, that it gave me the strength to endure all sorts of pains and travails. And so I did not fail to go to the aforementioned place as I was accustomed to do. That very day, in the evening, knowing my husband would be very busy with his affairs, I craftily found a way to encourage my beloved to speak to me. After he had offered and received amorous greetings, he mused and remained silent for a while; then he said:

The lover's complaints.

Chapter 19

"Since I spoke to you yesterday, Madame, I have continually consumed my time in great agitation, fearing that your husband might have mistreated or harmed you, without your being able escape his impetuous ferocity, which I understand to be very great, because he saw me speaking to you. Alas! If I thought you had suffered on my account any rashness or distress, it would cause me a pain worse than death; therefore, I exhort and beg you to tell me what happened, so that in the future I may moderate my desire and affection, dissimulating the excessive love I bear you. And besides everything else, I am astonished and cannot conjecture for what reason I was one day threatened by someone who said he was a household servant of yours, and who, speaking covertly, said some unintelligible words to me; and hence I can only assume, and greatly fear, that

---

[39]Hyperion and his son Helios are often referred to collectively; they share the role of sun god with Apollo.

you have revealed our love to him; but because we were in the street, I did not try to ask him about it, fearing I might offend you."

When I had heard him out, and listened carefully to what he said, I said to him: "O Guenelic, be assured that I am very sorry to see you in such a distressing and painful state. To judge by your words, it seems I am some lascivious woman. Haven't you given any thought to what I predicted to you? If you wish me to do so, I am willing to repeat them: I told you that my husband has always seen me behave with such decency and modesty that he does not doubt me at all; and indeed I can be proud of the fact that up to this point my life has been conducted in such a way that I have not been worthy of any blame. I beg you to desist from your fear, which is without foundation. As for what you have told me about my servant, who seemed to threaten you, I cannot imagine why that happened. You must not fear that I have so lost my senses as to divulge to him what should be sealed up in the deepest silence." After I had said this, we remained for a time without speaking, for we were both heaving continual sighs while we cast on each other sweet and amorous glances, so that it seemed to us that nature itself was struck dumb. Then Guenelic began to speak again and said:

"Milady, I beg you not to be angry, and not to impute to ill-will what I have told you in friendship, for the fear of the conflagration that could arise from this should your husband have any suspicions has compelled me to utter such words. And if you believe I have in any way offended you, I am a man who is prepared to suffer the worst punishment to repair or make amends for my crime; for on your will depends my whole present and future beatitude and felicity, or my perpetual calamity. If I am accepted into your good graces, my life shall be sweet and tranquil; if you decide otherwise, I shall promptly put an end to my life. But I am somewhat corroborated and comforted by my certainty that I am in the power of the lady who can, even if without clemency and sweet gentleness, judge me; and because it is human to have compassion, I beg you to soften your heart, and deign to punish or reward for enduring so much travail a servitor who is wholly and profoundly yours. Since we now have a convenient and propitious moment to do so, let it not displease you to inform me of your ultimate and final decision." After these sweet and gentle words, I began thus:

"My friend, I understand your words and deep eloquence, which is so efficacious that it could pervert the intentions of the chaste Penelope and seduce the invincible heart of the beautiful Lucretia; but it may be that your sweet and attractive words are false and simulated, for you young men commonly make use of such tricks and adulations to circumvent naive feminine credulity, which is sometimes not very constant and too liberal, and you seek no other end than to destroy the honor of those whom you say you love so much. But if I thought your love firm and stable, and that your will was not at all mutable or transitory, so as not to be ungrateful toward such a great love, if the opportunity were offered me, you would be my first choice, and I should recompense and reward you for your services. But as I have asked you on several occasions, how can your desire be satisfied without tarnishing and destroying in me that which must, even more than life itself, be preserved with the greatest care? Consider that everything that is lost can be recovered, except corrupted chastity; whereby, if I take pity on you, I shall be cruel toward myself in setting little store by my honor, and I might succumb to the dangers of pestiferous gossip, from which, by taking great pains, one can protect oneself by behaving properly."

He did not delay in responding to these words, but with elegant and sweet elocution said to me: "My sole lady, can it be that you are so cruel as to lead me to die because of your excessive hardness? Your words, which give me scarcely any reason to hope, cause me no less pain than Deianeira's cloak caused Hercules.[40] Alas, my love! Were I to be granted the felicity of being able to satisfy my desire and affection, would you think so little of me as to believe that I might, through a perverse and iniquitous desire, divulge the secret of our love? I should sooner expose myself to a thousand deaths! On the contrary, I should try to be as confidential and careful in matters of honor as in matters of love. If you think I am saying these words in dissimulation and pretense, you shall be far indeed from the truth; for it is not my custom to use embellished or adulatory expressions, since I never sought intimacy with any living creature other than you. And so you must not defer satisfying my request, driving all severity from your noble heart; and I beg you to liberate me from such great anxiety and pain and not let me go on languishing."

When he had finished saying these sweet and mellifluous words, I was full of such joy that I said nothing in return; but heaving a great multitude of sweet sighs, I signified to him the inner pleasure I had received from what he said. Suddenly, however, the fear of my husband came back to my memory, and this caused me extreme distress. Because I dreaded being found speaking to my beloved, I bade him a sweet and loving farewell, saying: "Live in hope, for you may be certain I shall remember you." Continuing his humble, sweet, and beseeching words, he left me, and was not yet far away when my husband approached. When he reached me we immediately returned to our lodgings.

After our amorous conversation, I continued to frequent the place dedicated to rendering to each justice and accord; but it was a long time before

---

[40]The robe was saturated with the blood of Nessus, who had told Deianeira the blood would act as an aphrodisiac. Instead, the robe stuck to her husband's flesh and fatally burned him.

I had an opportunity to bring us together in conversation. I do not know whether my beloved was putting off our meeting out of fear, or was doing so out of craftiness, so that love might grow yet stronger in me; because sometimes through continual intercourse one becomes bored and weary, for a thing less familiar and well-known engenders more admiration. I constantly thought and imagined reasons that might occasion so much restraint and silence, and I often recalled the words we had said to each other, and took a singular pleasure in them. Sometimes, turning over different thoughts of this kind, I said to myself: It's the fear of my husband that keeps him from speaking to me; for, so far as I can understand or imagine, he does not believe what I said; he does not realize the excessive love I have for him, since I am trying to persuade him to believe the contrary of what he sees clearly demonstrated. But what keeps me from declaring my love to him is my fear of losing[41] him.

I spent and consumed several days thinking about and meditating on diverse and novel phantasies, to the point that persisting in this I fell into an insidious fever that debilitated me and dissipated my body so violently I could not have long endured it; and so against my will I gave up my pleasant and comforting visits to the place where lawsuits are conducted. My husband continued to go there as usual, and sometimes he told me he had seen my beloved, in order to see how I would react. One time he said to me: "I saw that wicked man filled with iniquity, the sower of all evils, filled with lust and infamy. I mean that villain your lover, who kept following me. I don't know whether he thinks I don't recognize his manifest follies, since I don't show any sign of recognizing them, for fear of creating a scandal for you; therefore he can go wherever he likes in safety, for in order to preserve your honor, I should not want to harm him in any way. But I'd like to catch him in my woods. Then I'd take cruel revenge on him by making him suffer great and innumerable torments. Then, after my appetite was sated with torturing him, I'd make you a present of his body, all broken and lacerated; and at the same time I'd shut you up in a tower where by force and constraint I'd make you lie with him. Then afterward I'd make him wear out his detestable and wretched life through the cruelest and most ignominious death I could think of for him." While

---

[41]The French reads: "la crainte que j'ay de le perdre." The verb *perdre* means both "to lose" and "to doom" or "to betray," and it is not easy to say which is the correct translation in this case. Hélisenne has just suggested that Guenelic might be trying to increase her love by playing hard to get, and here she may be indicating her fear that if she declares her love for Guenelic he will lose interest in her. But she has also just mentioned Guenelic's fear of her husband, and her own, and she may be expressing her fear that if she declares her love for Guenelic, he might do something rash that will cause her husband to harm or even kill him. The verb *perdre* here thus reflects—and perhaps maintains—a crucial ambiguity in Hélisenne's character.

he took pleasure in saying this sort of thing, I listened to him, terribly angry, and, in a low voice, I began to speak, addressing myself to God:

"O eternal, exalted and sublime God, if it ever pleases you to hear wretched sinners, lend your ear to my prayer and supplication, and do not consider my sins and iniquities. Instead, through your infinite goodness, gentleness, and clemency, accept and grant my request, which is that you may preserve and guard my beloved from my husband's cruel ferocity. O poor hopeless woman that I am! I realize and know that I have gravely offended you by the infinite desires I have had to satisfy my disordered appetite, and still I cannot repent, because I am entirely deprived and dispossessed of my liberty. O sovereign God! I am certain you know the secret of my heart, for the divine prescience knows and recognizes everything without any exception, and you see that I am continually tempted to try to kill and put an end to myself without regard to the perdition of my wretched soul. For that reason I exhort and beg you to grant me death, which is the final end of all, in order to avoid being compelled through excessive pain to perpetrate such an enormous and abominable thing, which I should not be able to resist, were my husband to commit homicide on the person of the man I love so firmly that I should suffer death a thousand times and endure a thousand kinds of tortures and painful torments, before I should be able to cease loving him. And so to avoid the greater evil, may it please your goodness and benignity to keep my beloved alive. If I am not worthy of such grace, and if my voice cannot touch your greatness, eternal God, I beg the glorified saints to agree to be intercessors for me, so that by this means my humble request might be granted."

After having made this prayer and supplication, I felt somewhat relieved. Nevertheless, I remained a long time without being able to recover. But the singular desire I had to speak to my beloved compelled me to get up and go to the lawcourt as soon as I was cured. When I arrived there, I found my beloved, whose behavior seemed much changed, for on first seeing me and several times afterward, he did not take the trouble to greet me in the accustomed way, but rather, passing often near me, talked with deceptive dissimulation about lawsuits, and it seemed his mind was occupied with great worries. I was terrified, and did not know what caused him to hold his peace in this way. I suspected some new love affair, and said to myself: "my long absence may have estranged my beloved from me; for he is inclined to love—and indeed, worthy of being loved—and he may have found a woman to his taste who is also inclined to love. And so I shall be deprived in a brief hour of the pains I have suffered so long. Or it may be that he is angry with me because of something I don't know about. And if that is so, it will not be possible for me to remedy it, because a physician who does not know what is wrong cannot cure it."

These fluctuating ideas were very painful and virtually unendurable for me, because such vain opinions kept me suspicious, and my fear caused me to have a fever so cold that I fainted. But after my countless considerations, I resolved to endure my calamities more patiently, busying myself with thinking and imagining in what ways I might determine the cause of such a strange transformation. I was plagued and pierced by diverse thoughts, cares, and worries for several days, seeing my beloved persevere in such haughty pride; and had he not been accompanied (as he always was), I should not have been so slow to speak to him in order to find out the cause. But nonetheless, sometimes I was so pressed by a furious attack of love, which inflamed me, that I was not able any longer to endure the extreme internal pain that was in me. And so, without shame or embarrassment, seeing my beloved walking about, I followed him and, without deciding in advance what I should say to him, I was so bold as to pull on the hem of his robe. Thus he looked at me as if greatly astonished and stopped, and I immediately lowered my eyes and thought a bit. Then afterward, not having been able to find a more respectable way to begin, I asked him if he had seen my husband, telling him that I was looking for him to show him some letters I had received. Then he replied that he had not, and left without saying another word. But a few days later, with great audacity and proud arrogance, he came to speak to me, and said:

The beloved reproaches the lady
for having languished too long.

Chapter 20

"Madame, I now know, and see clearly, that your thoughts are in remarkable disharmony with what you say, at least if I remember correctly the last words you said to me, which were these: 'Live in hope, and I shall remember you.' But you must not imagine that I am so blind and unseeing that I am unaware of the way you, and your husband as well, mock and deride me every day, and which you cannot deny, for someone who heard what you said reported it to me. This angered me very much, considering that I never received anything from you but vexation, sadness, and a very woeful life. But if you are determined to be rid of me, you ought to make use of more suitable and decent means, and unconceal and declare what is in your heart, for hiding what is manifest is an act of affectation rather than of the prudence of which I thought you truly and clearly mistress. I imagined your strength and virtue to be so great that all vicious things were detestable to you, and believed that you would have not only avoided them, but would have discreetly reproached them in others who were stained by them, in order to help extirpate and abolish them. But if you consider it well, it is not virtuous to indulge in such mockeries. I should be very discontented with them, were it not that one thing comforts me, and that is that I am not the only man abused by the fickle feminine sex, and the one refuge of the wretched is to see others oppressed by similar sufferings."

After he had said this, although his words were spoken with great fury, I felt my heart filling with a certain happiness so great it would be difficult to express. I hoped to make him believe the contrary of what the false witness had told and reported to him, which he ought not to have believed, for he could see, by clear signs, that I loved him beyond human belief; and if sometimes, pretending to laugh and take comfort, I had spoken about him, it was to please my husband, cleverly dissimulating my love so I might be given more freedom than before. While I was thinking and imagining what excuse I might give my beloved that he would find acceptable, he pressed and urged me to reply, and out of impatience he said: "I am sorry that you are so slow and tardy to speak; thereby you give your detractors reason to think and to say even more evil things than they already have."

I immediately replied: "I am greatly astonished, and not without reason, by the distressing things you have said, and I cannot conjecture or imagine what moves you to attribute to me such a fault as derision and mockery, which I never thought of. If some false reporter has persuaded you to believe it, the fault must be ascribed to your inconstancy; for it may be that some sharp-eyed person has noticed your continual pursuit of me, and to cut short or alter our love has been the messenger of a crafty lie. So you must not impress such habits on your mind, for credulity and consent to lies[42] are manifest signs of a blind person. It displeases me very much that you hold my honor in such small esteem. I see readily that you hasten to say in public what ought to be kept in silence until we are in a suitable place. One should be wise, discreet, and circumspect in matters that always concern our lives and honors; and for that reason I beg and pray you to be more considerate, or if you are not, it will be a clear demonstration of your great villainy and wickedness. If I see that, I shall succumb to such a great heartache that it will cause me to end my life."

As I was saying these words, I withdrew to the places that seemed to me the most secret and silent. Seeing this, my beloved tried to speak more loudly, and said to me: "Madame, your speech is eloquent and well-suited to the occasion, and so efficacious that I am persuaded to believe it. But in order that we might not consume our time in pointless talk, I beg

---

[42]Secor's text reads "le consentir ou mensonges"; we have followed variants in other editions that give "le consentir au mensonge."

you to say whether or not I shall reach my goal. I say this to you briefly, but the fear I have must serve me as a reasonable excuse." When I heard his proposition, I drew back a little from the people who were passing by in great multitudes, and in a low voice I told him that the following day he should come to the temple (which I named), where we might have an opportunity to converse at more leisure. At these words he promptly responded: "Madame, as for conversation, I've had enough, and require no more of you; for if you consider the amount of time spent, at length, service deserves to be rewarded. If you are so ungrateful for such great love, you will pervert the order of your gentle nature, which seems to have been born to love. Remember Cydipa who was severely punished by Diana for being ungrateful to her lover."[43]

As he was goading me to respond, I was moved by various impulses. Love and fear tormented me, and I said to myself: "Experience shows that this young man here has converted love into disdain because it seems to him I am too slow and tardy in satisfying his ardent desire, and, through impatience and indiscretion, he wants a prompt response from me; and so I may conjecture that he is determined and resolved to lead me into perpetual infamy; for if I give in now to his request, someone will surely hear about it who will cause my total ruination and diminution." Preoccupied by these considerations, I told him that since I feared my husband would arrive, it was urgent and necessary that I return to our lodgings, but if I found a suitable time and place I should inform him of my desires. So saying, with great sadness and bitterness I bade him farewell. And showing his discontent and grumbling, he took his leave. But when I had withdrawn, and began to reflect on my beloved's iniquity, it caused me an extreme and tormenting pain, and for the rest of that day I did not cease weeping and lamenting. But when night had come, I was forced to cease my pains, tears, and moans in order not to let my husband see that I was persisting in my amorous folly.

After my beloved had said such harsh words to me, he continually provided me fresh reasons for vexation in every way and manner he could imagine: everywhere I was present, he was also, accompanied by several of his friends, and he swore and affirmed I was his lover. When I saw such outrageous cruelty, which was still only the first of his slanders, I sought ways of addressing him to remonstrate and express to him the anxieties and pains I suffered through his importunities. Thinking I should realize my intention, I proceeded to the usual temple where I hoped to find him, since it was a day on which a solemn rite was to be celebrated, and there

---

[43]Cydipa, an Athenian maiden, neglected the attentions of her suitor, Acontius, who had prayed to Diana for help in winning her hand. Each time Cydipa was engaged to marry, she fell gravely ill. Finally the cause was discovered and she was married to Acontius.

was a great multitude of people there, both men and women, doing various things; some were saying devout prayers and orisons, others were walking about, taking pleasure in looking at the most beautiful ladies. But after I had looked in several and diverse places, trying to find my beloved, I withdrew into a secluded and quiet place where I could continue in great solitude to pursue my fanciful thoughts; but shortly afterward, glancing around me, I saw him with two of his companions, looking at me in his usual way and trying more than ever, by means of various signs and expressions, to induce me to acknowledge him as well, so that through my gestures, which seemed full of feminine lasciviousness, I might more openly indicate my excessive love for him. And once more, in order to have greater experience and certitude of our love, he was the inventor of a clever ruse, so that his companions might have no doubt that what he said was true. After he grew bored and tired of walking about, he approached and passed near me, and said rather loudly that he wanted to return home; afterward, he said in a low voice to his companions: "Let's go hide behind a pillar, and I am certain she will go away without delay; for she has stayed here such a long time only in order to speak with me." I heard these words, which was the reason I stayed. Thereupon he began to stroll about, but I immediately left, terribly distressed, seeing that I was prevented from realizing my intention, which was to speak to him in order to reproach him a bit.

But when I had returned to my room, an incredible suffering caused my green and radiant eyes to distill a great abundance of tears; and an amorous desire assailed by despair deprived me of my true sentiment. When I considered the inconstancy of my beloved, it was an unimaginable torture, but although I recognized that he was a scoundrel and a bad man, it was not in my power to diminish my love, for it was so strongly imprinted on my heart that continually, day and night, his image was represented to my wretched memory. Whence it happened that the following night, when I had lain down next to my husband, very weary and tired out, and my eyes were very tempted by sleep, I remained awake in order to meditate and think. Finally I grew so drowsy that I was overcome and fell asleep. Certainly sleep was more pleasant to me than waking, because it seemed to me I was in a beautiful garden, pleasant and delightful, and without any fear I held his hand and begged him to be prudent and discreet, reproaching him for the great suffering he caused me through his importunities. It seemed to me that he replied that the blame must be set down to love, which through impatience forced him to exceed the bounds of reason, but that henceforth he would give me no further reason for annoyance. Hearing his sweet and mellifluous words, it seemed to me that I interrupted his voice with frequent kisses and embraces. But alas! what pain I felt when, in order to attend to some business of great importance, my husband awakened me, and left me very melancholy.

Rosy Aurora was rising from the golden bed of ancient Tithonus, her husband, when I began to say: "O, vexed wife of old Tithonus, who moves you to be so prompt to incite beautiful Apollo to illuminate the earth? Certainly, you are bored and weary of resting in your husband's arms, being the one who most desires Cephalus's kisses, to the disadvantage of Pocris.[44] O, vexatious woman! What harm was done you by the singular pleasure I received from merciful sleep, which made me believe to be true that which waking shows me to be the contrary? Why didn't you permit that delicious night to last as long as the one Jupiter was granted when he was in the delicate arms of fair Alcemene, mother of the hero Hercules, when for three days and three nights the nocturnal darkness was not driven away? Certainly I believe that you were then lying in the arms of that Cephalus from whom you did not want to separate yourself." Saying these things, I saw it grow ever lighter, and so I was compelled to get up. But I strongly desired that the night might return so that in sleep I might again receive the pleasure of which waking had deprived me. But I was never again able to enjoy such a delight; on the contrary, on several occasions I seemed to see my beloved in a horrible and terrifying form, so pale and white that I was horrified by the sight of him, to the point that several times I cried aloud, so that my husband woke up and asked me whence came such fears and terrors. And I, being reassured, realizing that it was only a dream and empty things, quickly found, through diligent feminine reflection, some clever lie. Then when he had gone back to sleep, I would begin to think and imagine, extraordinarily perplexed and full of doubts on account of such dreams, that it was a certain presage and demonstration that in the future I should fall into even greater misfortunes than those in which I now found myself. I suffered even more anxiety because I knew that my humor was melancholy and cold, and that in such persons virtue dominates so much that they understand as much while sleeping as others do while waking. In such travail I rose; then I asked all the augurers, seers, divines, and conjecturers to interpret my dreams so that I might be certain of their meaning.

I spent several days doing this until fortune permitted me the opportunity to speak to my beloved without any constraint, because on that day my husband was busy with a young relative of his who had just arrived; because it would have been neither proper nor honorable for him to leave his relative alone, I was allowed to go to the lawcourt accompanied only by my closest maid. But as soon as I got there, I saw my beloved accompanied by a young man, and he did not delay coming to speak to me. But after we had conversed pleasantly for a while, as subtly and ingeniously as I could I hinted that I had something secret to communicate to him.

---

[44]Cephalus, the husband of Pocris, was kidnapped by Aurora, who tried to seduce him.

Then, pretending I had something to do, I went off alone, leaving my beloved behind. His mind went on wandering from one thought to another, and was stimulated by a fervent desire to know what new thing had happened. And so he followed me, and by continual efforts sought to persuade me to tell him what it was, which I denied him for the moment, promising to reveal it to him that evening. Then his desire to know grew, for privation is the cause of appetite. Therefore, through urgent entreaties he continued to beg me not to conceal it from him while we had the opportunity to talk, telling me that my husband might be there in the evening, thereby causing his desire to be frustrated. Seeing that he persevered in his urging, I gave in and agreed to satisfy his desire, and I told him that to avoid exposing myself to dishonor, we should go to a small temple not far away from the lawcourt. I had no sooner said these words than he rose from his seat beside me. With great haste we transported ourselves to the designated place. When we had arrived there, I began to say these words: "My Lord! I should never have guessed when I first saw you and gazed at your physiognomy, which shows you to be inclined to good will, that you could be so cruel and pitiless as I now know you to be, at least if what I have been told is true. Alas! my very bones tremble because of it. My mouth is closed. My tongue is mute to tell of such cruelty. Still, to satisfy your aspiring desire, I shall recount it to you in a few words. It is that you do not cease to denigrate and speak ill of me, which amazes me very much, seeing and considering that I have never offended you in any way. This gives me certain proof that the love you appear to have for me is only a false and simulated pretense. O too ignorant feminine nature! O unfortunate pity! How we are deceived and circumvented by adulatory words, by sighs and continual cares, and by false oaths! But despite the fact that I am aware of all these things, my bitter fate has so bound me that it is not in my power or capacity to unbind myself in any way."

The rejection of the false report.

Chapter 21

As soon as I had said this, he immediately replied in this way: "Madame, life cannot be lived without feeling the vituperative bite of pestiferous tongues. But to liberate you from all suspicions: if it be true that I have said anything to your dishonor or prejudice, I pray that the wrath of the creator of heaven and general arbitrator confound me, or that the infernal furies never leave my side, or that the three sisters cut my vital thread before my time, or that the furious goddesses who avenge all human misdeeds enter my soul, and torment me perpetually through their violent agitations. But, madame, if I am not guilty of the crime of which I am accused, why do you wrongly mistreat me? And if your secret purpose is to drive me away from your love and to reward me with the ingratitude natural to women, you ought to say so in a more honorable way. You ought not to be so prompt in believing my detractors, seeing and considering that you yourself reprove those who are too ready to believe false reports. If you consider carefully the false betrayer's acts and behavior, you will find that he has invented all this to destroy our love in order to win your good will and to deprive me of my hoped-for reward, for that mordant envy, that fox-like subtlety, along with a malevolent nature always disposed to denigrate, generate countless frauds in order to deceive those who believe such lies. Therefore it is very important that one not believe more than is fitting for a prudent and sound mind. I take some comfort in the fact that your goodness has deigned to tell me the fault imputed to me; not knowing about it, through no fault of my own I might have fallen into your ill graces, because I was not able to clear myself or demonstrate my innocence."

He had no sooner put an end to this speech than I said to him: "O Guenelic, excessive passions usually win out over virtue. I was so angry and upset, hearing affirmed the things I have clearly told you, that it was impossible for me to restrain my ire. For that reason I beg you not to ascribe the words I have said to any ill will, but may all the fault and inveterate malice be attributed to the person from whom they proceed! I mean, to the reporter of falsehoods!"

As soon as I had finished speaking, he said to me: "Madame, if you are so benevolent as to consider me worthy of learning the name of the person who made this false report, I would be sempiternally obligated to your grace, and it would be a perpetual contentment to me as a clear sign of your good will toward me. It would also offer me the opportunity to avoid the company of that person, for conversing with vicious people is no less scandalous than detrimental." Having said these words, he thought a moment; then, he named a person whom he suspected of having made this report. And in fact his suspicion was not false, but wellgrounded, for on this occasion and on several others this person persevered in relating even more amply these accusations, concerning which, for the present, I shall say no more until the suitable time comes for telling and reciting it.

Nonetheless, considering that if I were to tell him, he would not keep it secret, I decided not to tell him, for in such matters in which there is so much peril and danger of dishonor, keeping silent is much more decent and suitable than speaking. And so I did not want to deny what he said, but said that it should be enough for him that I undoubtedly believed what he told me. And from then on I decided to be more constant, so that anger might not take the place of reasonable consideration. Conversing in this way, we left the aforesaid solitary place and went along together until we were compelled to separate, out of concern for our honor and to avoid giving evil tongues cause to wag. Then, with appropriate good wishes, we said our final farewell, for I never again spoke to him.

When I had returned to my lodging, I withdrew to my room, where I found myself greatly relieved, because I had unburdened my heart; and my spirit felt inestimable consolation and secret joys, which I was unable to enjoy for long, because an insidious fever put me into such an extremity that I had no hope of surviving. But although its working grievously tortured me, I endured with less patience being deprived of seeing my beloved than the pain I suffered; and so I cursed and detested my bitter fate which continually heaped on me countless anxieties and heartaches.

My husband, seeing me in this misfortune, was diligent in sending for doctors and physicians who, when they had arrived, prepared several medicines intended to help me; they did hardly anything for me, because I was as tortured by passions of the soul as by corporeal illness. Seeing this, my husband was thrown into a great sadness, for although I had greatly erred, his original love was so deeply anchored and alive in his heart that it was not in his power to avoid its influence. Thus, to incline the divine goodness to aid my salvation, there was no place dedicated to the name of God that my husband did not visit and where he did not offer sacrifices. One time, when he returned, he told me he had met a gentleman with whom he was rather intimate, and who was accompanied by my beloved. He told me the gentleman had left [my beloved] to come greet him; but a little later my beloved had not hesitated to approach him, and began to converse with them. When he had told me this story, I was greatly amazed, since my beloved was customarily so fearful. I thought and imagined what his intention might be, and this was a fresh cause for worry. My grave concern and the sleepless nights filled with sharp pains led me to such extremities that sighs and tears were my food and nourishment. After I had gone on for several days in this wearisome and wretched way, I thought it would be better for me to try to recover my health, for being deprived of it in this way I could not see my beloved, which was the gravest of all my misfortunes. This consideration caused me to recover my spiritual forces; whereby in a few days my face, which had changed to a pale, faded violet color, regained its vivid color, and I resumed my earlier state of health. But my ungrateful fortune let the man who had told me of Guenelic's misdeeds come to see me, and he was graciously received by my husband and myself. Afterward, several things came up that led him to speak of Guenelic, and seeing that my husband was present, in a low voice he said to me: "Madame, I am very astonished by this wicked detractor, who, it seems to me, will never get enough of calumny. I think there is no woman under the sun so common and vile

that she is worthy of such great vituperation and execration, for he publicly boasts and prides himself on having violated your chaste honor;
hence I consider him an ignorant and senseless man because he seeks to
stain and denigrate the good reputation of such a lady." When he had said
this, because of the bitter pain that oppressed me, my face changed from
one color to another and my painful heart stood still, like Oenone on the
mountain watching the Greek lady go with her beloved Paris into the
Trojan ship. All the same, I prepared myself to make some response when
my husband, who had clearly perceived the way my face had changed
color, asked if I felt ill. I replied: "Indeed, my love, I am very afraid of re-
lapsing into my usual illness." And I immediately arose from my place to
withdraw all alone into my chamber. My pale face, my bleary eyes, and
my impetuous way of walking made me look like a servant of Bacchus
wandering about.[45]

Hélisenne's piteous exclamation against her beloved.

Chapter 22

When I was finally led into my chamber, I began to weep and to cry
out furiously: "O iniquitous and wicked young man! O enemy of all
pity! O wretched false face, speech fraudulently and deceitfully composed, vessel of treachery, Proserpina's sacrifice, Cerberus's holocaust,
source of iniquity incessantly flowing forth! See how your pestiferous
tongue, a diabolical organ, dissipating all goods, consuming the world,
without cause now seeks to denigrate and annihilate my good reputation!
It is indeed time for you to close your lying mouth and to restrain your
impudent and vicious tongue. O, how I ought to curse the day I ever saw
you, the hour, the point and moment that I ever took pleasure in you!
Surely, I believe firmly that some infernal fury must have persuaded me
to deprive me of all felicity, for of all the men in the world, I know I have
elected the cruelest, whom I thought the most loyal and faithful. O, unhappy woman! How much better off you would have been had you observed a chaste life rather than following your stumbling appetites, whose
end is always unhappy! How perilous are these sad and unconsidered
pleasures! Blessed are those who through prudence learn to overcome
them. Alas! The beginning seemed to me so sweet, but the end is sour and
bitter. O holy goddess, who has far too ardently inflamed me! O cruel

---

[45]The followers of Bacchus, the god of wine and revelry, were either nymphs or mortal
women possessed of his spirit; they were usually mad, wild beings who danced, clashed
cymbals, and tore apart people, chiefly men, whom they encountered.

child, who wounded my heart![46] If I ever received an injury from your arrows, in the name of this pain I beseech you to take pity on wretched me. Undo these bonds, extinguish this ardor, and give me back my original liberty!"

With such words, I threw myself down and turned about with disordered and impetuous movements, as if I were tortured and moved by anger or some similar passion, to the point that I was exhausting my spirit and dissipating my body through such unbearable travails; and I remained in such pain and calamity for several days. Among other things, I repented having so outrageously rebuked my beloved, and thus I began to say to myself: "O mad woman! You are troubling yourself without cause! Don't you know that heaven and earth are full of tellers of false tales and detractors? What prudent person would want to judge before looking into the matter?[47] One may well doubt, but not decide without having other indications or clear presumptions. It may be that he never intended to utter such calumnies. And if it happened that he could clear himself of these charges, you would have gravely erred, for serious punishment is due one who wrongly complains." After I had said such words, several other ideas returned to my mind which made me utter words completely dissimilar to the others, and I spoke thus: "Ah! so I must assume you said these things because you one day came so audaciously to speak to me, and this makes me believe you did not love me, but only took pleasure in thinking to deceive in order to boast about it and take pride in it, as they say you do, and this astonishes me very much. What incites you to invent such lies? (Although I could make them true.) Don't you think that if your calumnies come to my husband's attention you are putting my wretched life in peril? If my existence is painful to you, I beg you to put an end to it yourself, for death would seem sweet and happy to me if your hands were stained and soiled with my heart's blood. But if it is the case that the crime of which you are accused is falsely attributed to you, I beg you to come justify yourself in order to free me from such great anxieties, which have led me to such an extremity, in order to preserve the life of this creature, of whom you are more the lord and master than I. If it seems to you that your long service has long since earned you the right to be rewarded, and that through impatience you want to escape from love, consider that it is no small reward, for having suffered a little, to be a lover permitted countless sweet gazes. Some people believe that Love is nothing other than a contemplation of the thing loved, in which more

---

[46]Venus (Aphrodite) and Cupid (Eros).

[47]"Quelle personne prudente vouldroit juger premier que proceder?" The sense seems to require that "proceder" be translated on the model of a legal proceeding that comes before sentence is passed.

pleasure is to be had in thought than in the corporal act; but I do not wish
to decide that question. I do believe that where the act is lacking, the
sight can substitute for it. With hope, the lover should continue to pursue. Even if the strength to continue the pursuit should fail, the will to do
so should never be extinguished, considering that all illustrious and elevated things are difficult. If the lady is slow in rewarding, the love will be
more perfect. For the more difficult to ripen a fruit is, the better it preserves itself, because it has better compassed its humor. Everything easily
created is much more subject to corruption. A well-considered affection
is much more to be esteemed than one that is extemporaneous and rapidly demonstrated. For that reason, then, knowing that your beloved is
favorably inclined toward you, do not be one of those pusillanimous men
whom the power of love makes imperfect, destitute, and desolate, for if
impassioned with amorous flame you show yourself timid and fearful,
one can never hope that you will someday be magnanimous." When I had
thus spoken for a long time as if he were hearing my words, I felt somewhat relieved, and nothing remained other than that I should be able to
speak to him to assert my opinion about that concerning which I was in
doubt.

O my noble ladies, considering the extremity to which I am reduced, I
do not wish to be like those in misery, whose sovereign refuge is the sight
of others oppressed by similar passions; on the contrary I take pleasure in
setting my misfortune down in writing so that it might become a clear
example for all ladies and young women, considering that I was once a
noble and renowned lady and am now become a servant and a subject. For
although the man who possesses my heart is not my equal in either nobility or property and wealth, to me he is sublime, and I am low and
small. Alas! how happy is the person who by another's example avoids
this sensual love which customarily renders its servants unhappy and unfortunate! Love is nothing but the forgetting of reason, and is not suitable
for a prudent person because it disturbs the judgment and breaks elevated
and generous spirits; it weakens all power; it makes people sad, choleric,
prodigal, bold, proud, harmful, forgetful of God, of the world, and of themselves, and ultimately it keeps them in misery, distress, languor, martyrdom, and inhuman affliction. Usually it leads them to a cruel death
through pernicious despair. Alas! I speak of this not as an ignorant
woman, but as one who has experienced it all. Thus only death remains!
But although I know such pains and anguish, I cannot desist. My mind,
my reason, and free will have been taken by surprise, subjected and enslaved, because from the outset, scarcely resisting, I let myself go. It is
easy to conquer those who do not resist.

Fortune left me in such calamity and continual pain, which grew nei-
her better nor worse for a time, until I was betrayed by one of my ser-

63

vants, because there is no one, no matter how clear-sighted he may be, who can prevent domestic treachery. Usually there is no integrity in the hearts of servants; to that perfidious and wicked race no secret can or should be entrusted. I took no precautions with this servant, and in her presence did not hesitate to express my anger and sighs, and to formulate my painful complaints, because she had been present at all my misfortunes and adversities. But this perverse and iniquitous person conspired against me with such treachery that all my acts and behavior, and even the words which she had carefully noted and retained, were conveyed by her to my husband. Perhaps driven by avarice, hoping to profit from it and in order to give the clearest proof of what I was doing, she told him that what she said could be verified through my own writings.

On hearing such painful words, my husband was no less distressed than was the son of Laomedon[48] when he realized what was in the wooden horse's belly, which caused the extermination of his life and his land. For the moment anger and disdain moved my husband so strongly that he could not restrain himself from promptly trying to find out if I was guilty of the crime of which I was accused. To determine this with greater certainty, knowing that at that moment I was in alone my room and had neither doubt nor suspicion, he came in great ire mixed with impetuosity and struck with all his strength such a blow on my door that he broke it. Then I was very frightened, and trembling and fear seized my heart not otherwise than does Zephyr[49] when it blows upon the waves, or when it shakes the dry and sylvan herbage. I saw my husband in the grip of anger, his eyes sparkling with hot rage. Misfortune and unhappy influence of the stars allowed his sudden intrusion to so greatly perturb me that I didn't think of hiding my writings, in which were set forth and amply declared all the good and bad fortune that had befallen me since Cupid had won domination and mastery over me. And that was the cause of my total ruination, for after he had read them and clearly understood everything, with his face full of indignation he turned toward me and said: "O wicked and detestable woman! By this I am well informed, by writing in your own hand, of your unrestrained lasciviousness. O wretched woman! I see you submerged and drowned in this pernicious sensual pleasure. Your lust is so ingrained that you desire only its libidinous execution, which would cause both you and me to live in perpetual infamy. But to avoid your doing something so scandalous, I have decided to deprive you of life; and in doing so I shall consider that I am acting rightly, for it will be a true sacrifice to God and to the world to purge the earth of a creature so abominable, and wholly shot through with iniquity." So saying, and

---

[48]Priam.

[49]The west wind or god of the west wind, brother of Boreas, god of the north wind.

holding his sword in his hand, he was coming toward me with the firm intention of carrying out his will when he was forcefully restrained by one of his domestic servants, who had come in without his noticing, because he was so deeply troubled.

My servants quickly carried me into my room, against my will, for I desired only to die; and so I said: "O wicked servants, women of servile estate, what has made you so audacious as to lay violent hands on your mistress? For a long time with particular affection I have desired only death, which you have denied me. Alas! I should have been delivered from this inhuman pain and unbearable tribulation that incessantly torments me." In saying these words I cried out and wept, striking myself with my fists as if I were fighting in a violent combat. Then in this fury I went on:

"O wretched lady, unhappy and unfortunate, what could bring you aid in such a great misfortune? What magic art of Zoroaster and Berosus? What Orphic mystery? What Aristotelian device? What Pythagorean secret?[50] What Platonic majesty could console me in such desolation?[51] O unfortunate star under which I was born! I believe all the gods conspired against me on the day of my birth, for within me are all the pains particularly and separately suffered by the wretched. O my body, so delicate and slender, how can you suffer so many inhuman ills? Acteon was lacerated by his intimates. Thiaceus was devoured by dogs.[52] Portia put an end to her life by swallowing glowing coals. Pernissa leapt and threw herself down from the top of the highest tower in Crete.[53] The Sagontes or Abidians, fearing Hannibal of Carthage and Philip, king of Macedonia, burned and incinerated their goods and homes as well as themselves. But all those together did not suffer as much as you [my body], for their death came suddenly, while, wretched as I am, I am tortured by continual cruelty. O, how happy I should have been had my mother's milk been poison to me, or if my cradle had been my sepulcher! O, Lachesis and the sister

---

[0]This list of classical allusions is an example of the kind of phrases Marguerite Briet takes from other sources, in this case from Caviceo's *Perigrino*, III:26. See Demats, 119, 133.

[1]We adopt here, as does Paule Demats in her edition of the text, the variant reading "desolation" rather than "discretion," which seems to make no sense in this context.

[2]The references to Acteon and Thiaceus are in error in Caviceo's *Peregrino*, from which Marguerite Briet drew. The allusion to being devoured by "intimates" concerns not Acteon but Pentheus, who was mistaken for a wild beast by his mother, who then tore him to pieces. Thiaceus could be a misprint for Thrasus, who, in Ovid's *Ibis*, is devoured by dogs like Acteon. See Demats, 133-34.

[3]The name "Pernissa" is in error in Boccaccio's *Fiammetta* in which "Pernice" is written for "Perdice," the hero "Perdix" (also known as Talos), whom the jealous Daedalus threw down from the Acropolis. Perdix was changed into a partridge or "perdix." See Demats, 134.

goddesses of fate, why do you so prolong the thread of my miserable life? O, Charon, why doesn't your boat come to take me away from this bank and transport me to your side [of the Styx], which to me would be a sweeter dwelling place? For I do not believe that even in the fearsome place where Minos and Rhadamanthus reside there is any pain so sharp as mine, for I am ignorant of my life and very certain of my suffering."

When I had spoken and loudly cried out, I was so tired that I could speak no more, and I remained as if half-dead. My servants were gathered around me, for they had not dared leave me alone, fearing that I might have killed myself with my own hands. For the rest of that day and night I spoke no further. But when the conductor of the celestial chariot, his horses in the ocean, began to rise, word was sent to me to go speak with my husband, who had mitigated his great fury by deciding to send me away. When I was in his presence, he said to me: "Since I see and realize that you are inveterate in your iniquities, it is urgent that I remedy this by sending you away, for it would be impossible to defend oneself against these vulpine feminine wiles. I see that you are presently disposed to love; and I am certain that you are sought after by several men. Therefore, considering the difficulty of keeping something desired by several others, you must obey my will, for it may happen that some day, through your lascivious acts and behavior, I shall be forced to take vengeance on you without its being in my power to control my fury. For that reason, take steps to prepare yourself. I am going to give the order for your departure." So saying, he went away and left me.

Hearing these words I was filled with a fury greater than any before, for if the suffering of the preceding day had been very serious, this was even more excessive, and in a furious rage I said: "O wretched Hélisenne, more wretched than any living woman, seeing the culmination of your misfortunes! Rightly may you curse the detestable hour when you were born. The incarnation was prodigious, the birth very unfortunate, the life horrible, and the end will be execrable. O proud lions! O cruel tigers! O ravening wolves! O ferocious beasts and all cruel animals, lacerate and devour this poor body! O heavens! O earth! O bodies on high! O shadowy spirits! O restless souls, conspire in my death and put an end to my wretched life! O Alecto, Tisiphone and Megaera, daughters of the Acheron, the horrible river, present yourselves to me with all your serpent-hair, after the vile Charon has carried me over the river called Styx, and transported me to my perpetual abode in the depth of the abysses called Chaos, which is eternal confusion, for I consider myself unworthy because of my repeated crimes and exorbitant sins. Let Mercury, receiver and guide of souls, the gods' messenger, conduct me to the Elysian fields where the fortunate reside, where only ambrosial fruits grow, and all the liquors are nectar."

Thus I was so distressed that I was exhausted, seeing that it was impossible for me to realize my cruel desire for death because I was always under close guard. And so, looking at my beautiful white and slender hands, in a furious rage I said: "O iniquitous hands that have embellished me, and have served me in accord with my diligent desire to please the man I love so ardently, for whom I am reduced to this extremity by being deprived of his sight, you have partly caused this misfortune to which you would put an end by piercing this changeable heart that has allowed itself to be surprised and conquered by love. But the power of doing so has been taken from you because all iron instruments have been taken from you. For that reason I must wait until I have ropes or cords, deadly herbs or knives; and then you shall perform your work of pity; and you shall use my body cruelly; and by the blood which shall flow in great abundance you shall remain stained and soiled. Nevertheless, it was not long ago that I believed you were not created to do such vile things; but fortune, the cruel enemy of felicity and the subtle inventor of all sorts of misery through its unstable nature, has led me to such despair. O fortune more inhuman than the hydra, more violent than the vulture, more bitter than the asp, more uncertain than the waters! Now I know your deceits and frauds, since you are not so adverse and harsh to anyone else. For my ills and sufferings are interconnected in such a way and manner that the first were the harbingers of the later ones, announcing and declaring other ills and infinite torments which have incessantly tortured and exhausted me. Because of the extreme and very cruel suffering I have endured and endure continually without having any respite, I am as weak and feeble as it is possible to be." Saying and uttering these words, my voice failed me completely, and my heart as well, and I fell into a faint because of the tormenting pain and suffering I felt; and I remained a long time in this syncope. Then, after I had regained my strength, the light I had lost returned to my eyes, and I saw my maids weeping and crying around me, who, by sprinkling me with waters suited to this purpose, had cared for me in this wretched misfortune.

Hélisenne's departure from the place where she loved.

Chapter 23

Shortly afterward my husband returned to our lodgings, having arranged matters so that I could leave the following day, as I was immediately informed. Seeing that he persisted in his resolution, in great anxiety and pain I continued my weeping accompanied by woeful sighs; and ecause of my suffering, I could neither speak nor use my voice, but only ignify by my eyes the extreme pain my wretched heart felt. In such dis-

· tress and bitterness I spent the day and the night. Phoebus's porter was announcing his arrival when I was alerted and roused by my maids so that I might prepare myself for the painful departure; I did not want to listen to them, but considering that my husband would force me to get ready to leave, with many regrets and with laborious effort I began to do so, and I was no less doleful than those who are condemned to the ultimate punishment. Nonetheless, in order to delay no longer, accompanied by despair, I came to present myself before my husband, whom I found ready, and we set out immediately. When I was in the countryside, I began to look back on the place from which I had departed; and then, dissolving in tears and sighing, I said in a low voice:

Hélisenne's regrets for having been transported to a place unpleasant to her.

Chapter 24

"O noble city! If I am sorry to go away from you, that is no great marvel, for in you I leave behind my heart, my soul, my life, my spirit, and my whole power," and in so saying, I lifted my eyes to the lofty skies above and said: "O star-studded heavens! O sovereign governor of the Olympian manors, if your irrevocable decision has been, for the social company of humankind, to produce me in this hemisphere, why didn't you preserve me from the power of proud Cupid, whose power is cruelly felt and not seen? O happy those who are kept far from the flame of love! But unhappy those who, without refreshment or rest, always toil, burn, and consume themselves, who, like me, are wretched and miserable, and nourished on incessant sobs and lamentations. I am so agitated and persecuted by that burning that not only my veins but also my joints, nerves and bones are cruelly tormented, so that my suffering soul, weary of being in this wretched body, desires only to be separated from it, knowing that it could not suffer more grievous pain than it felt at such a departure. Neither Portia for Brutus, nor Cornelia for Pompey, nor Laodomeia for Prothesilaus, nor the magnanimous Carthaginian queen for Aeneas, taken all together, ever felt such a loss as I feel, poor unfortunate woman that I am." Continuing my painful lament, I went away from the place where my desire was, and did not know where my husband wanted to take me. But through his diligence, we arrived there in a few days. When we got to the place intended to be my perpetual abode, I saw that it was a place I had formerly found pleasant and delightful because it was a little castle situated in a very lovely place. All around, and surrounding this castle there are towers, one of which is rather large and spacious. This castle is called the Cabasus castle, and bears the principal name of the region and land of Cabase. Those who have visited this land may well have heard of this castle. As soon as I arrived, I was put into the great tower, and shut up there, accompanied only by two maids, one of whom was very old, and had been chosen by my husband because she had served me from the time when I was first married, and I had found her very faithful in her service; and for that reason, she was persuaded to keep me company, having been promised sufficient remuneration.

Hélisenne was imprisoned in a tower, and had with her only two maids.

Chapter 25

After I was shut up in this tower, which seemed to me a sad and gloomy abode, even though I had earlier found it pleasant and delightful, I continued my lamentations and exclamations interspersed with many sobs. Sometimes, without considering the presence of my maids, I wanted to cry out in anguished rage and extreme distress. My laments and sighs assaulted me in such a way that my sweet voice could not find issue from my aching breast. But when I could speak, I recited the story of my love, from beginning to end, and all the words we had exchanged. Seeing this, the elderly maid, who was very constant and moderate, had manifest proof, by clear signs, of the anxiety and pain that oppressed me; she was moved to compassion and, thinking to mitigate the passion that she understood to be so powerful, she said these words to me:

The elderly woman's counsels, comforting Hélisenne.

Chapter 26

"Madame, from what I can understand from your behavior and words, which I have carefully noted and considered, you are extremely tortured and distressed because Love has wounded your heart, which is tender and delicate. I am certain that it is very difficult to resist the madness inspired by the son of Venus, if one does not do so at the outset; for anyone who has for a long time nourished lascivious love in her heart, can with the greatest difficulty expel or refuse the delightful games to which one willingly submits. But as I have understood by your words, Love has not yet attacked your honor. You must understand that there are five points or five degrees peculiar to love, namely: looking, kissing, speaking, touching, and the last is the most desired one, toward which all the others tend. As a final resolution, it is the one which, through concern for decency, is called the granting of favor. I see very well that it was not your fault if you did not arrive at this last stage; rather, the continual presence of your husband prevented you from doing so. Thus you have had only the looking and the speaking, even though it was in extraordinary fear and trepidation. Hence you are very agitated by inexpressible regrets because you have no hope of ever realizing your fervent and ardent desires. Hence you spend your time weeping and moaning; you blame the stars under which you were born, you despise fortune and seek death, which one can suffer only once, and, imagining that it is the end of all suffering, you desire it with great affection. Because madness dominates reason, you do not consider that such a violent death is the beginning of a horrible and unbearable pain that endures forever, while your amorous passions can terminate and come to an end. For that reason, if you only considered the perpetual along with the temporal, you would arrive at a different judgment, and you would strive to extirpate from your heart the venomous love that has so long dwelt there, which has blinded your eyes, so that you have strayed from the true light of reason, to which it is indeed time to return, in order to free yourself from the painful anxieties that have accumulated in your sad heart. You might answer that it is very easy to say this, and very difficult to act on it, and that love has so deeply penetrated your heart, and is so alive there, that you could not separate them no matter what the torment that awaited you. But at least if it is impossible for you to desist, allow more moderation and do not continue such weeping and crying, for although nature has granted us tears out of pity, this has not been done in order that we might thereby consume ourselves. Therefore abandon these bootless tears which serve no other purpose than to erase the color from your fair face, and do not fill the heavens and the earth with vain clamors. Do not beat your white breast with enormous blows, but reserve your life for a better use and live in hope, thinking that just as one cannot be certain that any worldly thing will happen, neither should one despair or lose hope of something good happening, for in this mortal world, we encounter diverse fortunes, both good and adverse. Therefore take comfort in good advice, hoping that some day Dame Fortune will be favorable toward you. If you must obey love, whose power seems to you invincible, you will more easily satisfy your affectionate desire through patient endurance than through such injudicious and ill-considered importunities. For that reason, it is urgent that you moderate its ferocity, considering that it is better to bow than to break, and to bend through obedience than to be uprooted through obstinacy. If you show yourself to be virtuous, it may be believed and granted that your husband will take pity on you; whereby, you shall not long be detained in this tower. If you are freed from such a calamity, it will not be impossible to accomplish what you desire, for in love there are many secret acts and ingenious tricks, which lead love affairs to their desired end. Even if you are not delivered, still you should not become so sad that you want to deprive yourself of life, but rather, by the most subtle means that can be imagined and thought up, you will have to let your beloved know about your unhappy misfortune. When he sees that, for persevering in loving him, you are enduring a painful, tormented, and anguished way of life, if he has retained any spark of the amorous flame, he will not let any peril prevent him from delivering you, but rather, at the price of countless torments and dangers, even with the heavens opposing him, he will pursue his lofty enterprise, being certain of arriving at the fruition of the desired pleasure to which he aspires. Perhaps this seems to you difficult because you know this tower to be strong and inaccessible; but believe me, no matter how exhausting the task may be, it can be accomplished by a man who is determined. That this is so, the histories demonstrate very clearly. Haven't you read about Jupiter, who through a clever ruse found a way to enjoy his beloved, the fair Danae, though she was imprisoned in a marvelously strong tower? You must also remember Leander, who did not fear to expose his body to the dangerous perils of the sea in order to reach the celestial pleasure of gathering the amorous fruit of the game of love. And so, knowing that love, by means of its great power, has extirpated all boyish timidity and fear from the hearts of the men just named, you should be persuaded to believe that your beloved will not be pusillanimous any more than the others our predecessors; for I do not deem the human race in principle so divided that what is granted to one person cannot be applied to another. Therefore I see no reason why you should succumb to such despair as you show yourself to be in through your behavior and words."

Hélisenne's decision after hearing the elderly woman's remonstrances.

Chapter 27

After I had carefully listened to such remonstrances, in which I took some comfort, my thoughts were more agitated than any ship with sail or rudder abandoned among tempestuous and terrifying winds. Thinking and meditating on the way and manner in which I might inform my beloved of my sad misfortune, but after several and diverse ideas, I found no means more suitable than to recall to memory the pitiful lament that I had earlier written with my own hand, which my husband had burned in the impetuosity of his anger. It seemed to me that if it could be delivered into the hands of my beloved, that could cause my sufferings to come to an end and give rise to a joyful life. Having made this decision, I immediately began the present work, thinking it would be a very happy labor for me. If I am granted the felicity of having it fall into my beloved's hands, I beg him not to deprive me of my hoped for and expected delight, and I beseech him to consider that of all things under the sun, there is a copious amount, indeed a great abundance, except for loyal lovers. Since it would be impossible for him, no matter how long he lives, to find a man or woman who would love him as faithfully as I, it seems to me that it would be very cruel if, having learned of my misfortune, he did not feel pity and commiseration, knowing my soul to be in continual travail, my mind preoccupied, my body overcome, my limbs weak, and no one except him can help me. Alas! Although I am more tormented [than ever], I often remember, among all the other words he said to me, these which he briefly uttered: "Madame, in my view and according to what I can judge from your face's change of color, you have lost your health; but if you were willing to believe me, your health should be restored in a short time, for I know no physician who has medicines more apt to cure you than I." He said these words to me with a sweet smile, which I shall remember all my life, for although they were said by way of entertaining me, nevertheless they were true; for he is the one who, in the midst of the great sea of the Ocean, would be my solid ground; among perils, my indubitable security; in fire, delicious refreshment; in poverty, extreme wealth; and in serious illness, health; for if I had him, it would be an eternal contentment to me, because I cannot desire anything beyond him. And were that beatitude granted me, then in consoled delight I should recount to him all my suffering and travails; and what has been sad and painful for me to endure, would be a pleasure for me to recite to him. Alas! If I had Daedalus's ingenious art and Medea's enchantments, I should be swiftly borne on gossamer wings to the place where I thought I should find him. But when I consider that it is impossible that I should ever see him, or he me, if he does not strive with magnanimous courage to release me from this captivity, as an ultimate recourse I exhort and beseech the lord Cupid, that with all his strength he move [my beloved's] heart in order that the number of his worshipers not diminish. In this hope of my prayer being heard, I shall put an end to my dolorous complaint, begging you, my ladies, that you consider what is or might be my misfortune, being a prisoner in the flower of my youth."

The end of the book.

Chapter 28

Most dear and honored ladies, may your hearts be moved to some astonishment in considering whence proceeds the boldness to take it upon myself to title the present work mentioning unchaste love affairs, which according to the opinion of some timid ladies might be judged more worthy of being kept in profound silence rather than published and vulgarized. But if you understand with what strength Love has constrained and labored me, I shall be blamed by none of you. With that in mind, as I said before, and having several times laid down my quill, the affectionate desire I have in your regard, my noble ladies, has caused me to strive to tell you everything without holding anything back; for through the knowledge of my mad folly, I can counsel you and offer you advice which will be useful and profitable to preserve you from such a conflagration. I am very certain that this little work of mine will be found the product of a crude and cloudy mind when compared with those you may have read which are composed by orators and historians, who, through the sublimity of their understanding, compose books whose subject matter is no less amusing than difficult and arduous. But in that respect I must make use of the excuse that our feminine condition is not so knowledgeable as men's naturally is. Moreover, I am not nor do I wish to be so presumptuous as to believe I have gone beyond or even equalled some ladies in literary knowledge, for I believe some are endowed with such lofty minds that they would compose in a language much more elegant, which would make the work more acceptable to readers of good will. But if my work is not in a more ornamented and modest language, it is because of my feeble knowledge and not my intention and aspiring desire, as one who seeks and wants in every way to make you know my affection. And so, my ladies, I beg and beseech the creator who thunders on high that he grant you all the continence of Penelope, the wisdom of Thetis, the modesty of Argia, the constancy of Dido, the chastity of Lucretia, and the sobriety and frugal happiness of Claudia, so that, by means of these gifts of grace, you may remain free and unfettered, without succumbing to similar misfortunes.

FINIS.
De Crenne.

The Torments of Love

Part Two

The Second Part of
The Torments of Love

Composed by Lady Hélisenne,
Speaking in the person of her beloved Guenelic:
In which are included the battles fought by
Quezinstra and Guenelic, while wandering over the earth
in search of the aforesaid lady.[1]

De Crenne.

Epistle to all noble and virtuous ladies.

Having shown you, benevolent readers,[2] the vehement passions that sensual love can cause in the tender and delicate hearts of women in love, I have conceived the desire to narrate and recite to you the calamities and extreme miseries young men may suffer as a result of indiscreet love. While I was occupied with this meditation, I recalled to memory another occasion that stimulates me even more strongly to prepare my trembling and feeble hand to take up once again the quill I relinquished. You must believe I am moved by an aspiring desire to divulge and make clear some warlike and praiseworthy enterprises which, through reading this little book of mine, shall be shown to have been accomplished with virtue and magnanimity of heart, which I hope will be of great utility; we read that Alexander the Great took pleasure in reading the *Iliad* of the prince of poets, Homer, to the point that several times, through the fatigue of continual study, insidious sleep overcame him. One may understand that this assiduity in reading inspired his deeds and the inclination to chivalry which things written down could cause.

Hence I have no doubt that the present work will not only stir modern gentlemen to martial activity, but will in the future stimulate our posterity to be true imitators of this art. When I consider this, it makes me find the difficulties of my little labor rather slight. But I fear some of you may be astonished that my Guenelic, whom I said in my Torments[3] to be a man of low estate, should have thus practiced the military art; and hence

---

[1]This "argument" is very similar to the one at the beginning of Chapter 1 in this part; it should be noted, however, that here the emphasis is on the valorous feats of arms performed by Guenelic and his friend Quezinstra, and in the second case it is on the sufferings of Guenelic.

[2]In editions after 1538 this was changed to "mes dames."

[3]The text does not capitalize this word, although it seems clearly to refer not to Hélisenne's experience but rather to her written account of that experience. We have not italicized it, however, in order not to suggest that it necessarily refers to an earlier book whose title is *The Torments of Love* (that is, *Les Angoysses douloureuses qui procedent d'amours*).

I wish to explain very clearly my reason for saying so, which is simply that he was not my equal, since I had in my possession several castles, lands, and properties, and thus had such an abundance and affluence of goods if wealth can be so named, and not because I want to extol myself in order to diminish the honor of a man who, since that time, has through his deeds rendered himself rather praiseworthy. And so I wanted to remind you of what I said earlier, and why I said it, seeking to persuade[4] you thereby that I do not mean to say that he was not of noble birth, but only that he was a not a wealthy gentleman. But his virtues exalted him, and this is indeed the opposite of those who are sublime and elevated by gifts and properties received from Fortune, and who through pusillanimity debase themselves, which makes them worthy of extreme vituperation, and they are very unfortunate to continue to live after having been discredited in this way. For it would be more advantageous to die with honor than to live with shame; therefore, he is a fortunate man who leaves this world with praise and reputation, and such a death should be deemed glorious. I say this for Guenelic and Quezinstra; I hope their perseverance in their virtues shall be such that their splendid fame shall be ineradicable by death. This would give me considerable pleasure, were it only because the anxieties lurking in my loving heart desire the company of some consolations.

And so, when I cannot do anything else, I have begun to think over and delve into the sublimity and infinity of my thought, recalling all my former sufferings. Being engaged in such mental occupations, I have remembered that on several occasions I wrote in my Torments about Guenelic's importunities and the accusations against him, wherefore, I believe, some readers may find it strange that after I had depreciated him in this way, he should have been able afterward to endure so many travails in order to find his lady. You might say to me that a devoted lover is not accustomed to maligning or listening to others malign his lady, for the true nature of those who love is to serve, love and obey. For that reason, you might think Guenelic's love not very great. Nevertheless, if you have recently read my writings, and consider them carefully, you will see that I was never certain the reports I heard were true. Hence I believe, and you should also assume, that bearers of false tales imputed such crimes to him. It is very true that through his indiscretion, accompanied by impatience, he was the cause of a great calamity, as he has since recognized, repenting his lack of consideration, as you shall see through his torments. You must not marvel if you see in the account of his travails unspeakable pains he has suffered in seeking to reach the fruition of love; for such is

---

[4]Secor's text here reads "persuadent"; this seems to make no sense syntactically, and we have rendered it as if it were a misprint for the present participle, "persuadant."

the male human condition that during the time when they have not yet enjoyed the thing they love, they will risk any peril for the sake of satisfying their desires, as you young men know. And on that subject I shall end my Epistle, exhorting the divine clemency to free my spirit of all perturbation in order to complete the present work.

The Second Part of
The Torments of Love

Composed by Lady Hélisenne,
Speaking in the person of her beloved Guenelic:
In which are related the torments
of the aforesaid Guenelic.

Chapter 1

Although it is credible and admissible that by disclosing and declaring the torments and pains one has suffered, they may be mitigated and tempered, nonetheless I hope only that by relating my distressing vexations I might be granted some diminution of my travail; and hence I have not initiated the present work in that intention, but only in order to exhort all young men to avoid the unbearable burden of love (at least if they do not want to be ruled and governed under the empire and lordship of Cupid) by observing the customs of true lovers, which are: to be magnanimous, modest, discreet, solicitous, persevering, and patient in all things; and not proud, difficult, or obstinate, but rather sweet-tempered, flexible, and obedient, as the case may demand, so as not to succumb to the kind of extremity into which one might fall through lack of such perfections.

Alas! Poor miserable wretch that I am, who realized too late my imprudence and inconstancy! I have no just cause for complaint against Love, although the excessive pain that incessantly tortures and torments me comes from him, not through my lady's fault, but through my folly and indiscretion. This consideration causes me so much distress and sadness that my languorous life is to me more bitter than a cruel and violent death, because of the afflictions that constantly churn my soul. But all the same, although the story of my intolerable sufferings cannot be narrated without augmenting my pain, still I want to try to put it down in writing, considering that what I want to tell is worthy of perpetual memory. For that reason I beseech and implore the great creator who thunders on high to grant me the ability to write and make public the present work.

At the time when the son of Hyperion, following his course through the Zodiac, having dwelt so long in the southern skies that he had reached the fishes' tail and begun to turn the reins of his noble steeds back toward our climate and hemisphere and to prepare the delicate and temperate season; and gentle Philomela, still recalling the base calumny and insult made against her by the false traitor Tereus,[5] was recommencing her sighing and harmonious complaint; and the perverse and furious Mavors,[6] mounted on his swift chariot, was stimulating all noble hearts to martial exercise, I, being in the flower of my youth, twenty-one years old, was entertaining various thoughts, vacillating back and forth because I was unable to discern which would be more useful to me: to take up the military art or to continue the literary work which I had commenced in order to succeed in elevating myself to Minerva's abode.[7] At that time my young mind had not yet been touched by the ardent flame of love. I did not understand what the life of wretched lovers was like. I did not know what blazing fires are usually felt by those who make Venus and Cupid their gods on this earth, whose heat has since attacked me with such great violence that I believe no marshes, rivers, torrents, or anything capable of cooling could cool its inextinguishable fire. Alas! I was still free and unfettered, and I attended only to my lucrative and honorable concerns, when love (I know not for what reason) wounded my heart with an arrow such as the one that formerly pierced Phoebus. This happened to me through a lady's single glance, which snared and bound me, and shall hold me captive until I am reduced to dust. I tried from the outset to resist, which it was not in my power and capacity to do. Seeing this, I gave up all hope of being able to desist and began to consider the quality of this lady, in whom I knew to be combined the beauty of the Greek Helen, the gravity of Martia, the modesty of Argeia, the merry elegance of Julia, the pity of Antigone, the fervent tolerance of Hipsicrates, the sweet urbanity of Cicilia, and the lofty excellence of Livia. After I had considered all these things, love grew and augmented, and took possession of me with such violence that my spirit could not sustain it, for it seemed love's fire had been ignited by my powers.

Being thus vanquished, bound, and captive, I began to meditate and re-

---

[5]Philomela was raped by her brother-in-law, Tereus, who then cut out her tongue to prevent his wife from learning of his act.

[6]Mars, the Roman god of war.

[7]Minerva (in Greek mythology, Athena) is the virgin goddess of wisdom and knowledge.

call the loves of others who had not been able to resist conflagrations of this kind; and into my mind came the Trojan shepherd who to his great disadvantage saw Cythera.[8] Then appeared before my memory the mighty Achilles, who was invulnerable because his mother, the goddess Thetis, had immersed him in one of the infernal rivers called the Styx, but for all that he could not avoid being wounded by Cupid's golden arrow. Afterward the memory of others came to me, such as Hannibal, Certorius, Demetrius and Philip of Macedon. After that, I considered with what force love had overcome Aristotle, Plato, and Virgil, who, despite their knowledge, were subjugated by the invincible power of love.

Having thought over each of these things, I formed the firm intention and irrevocable decision to make myself obedient; and then I dismissed all other cares and solicitudes in order to turn my understanding toward these puerile exercises that youthful age customarily observes, namely: boasting, singing, and dancing. In such acts I consumed my life, reputation, time, and abilities, and I took delight in such vanities; and love lent me credibility and favor, so that after some letters had been exchanged, and also after having spoken a few times, nothing remained but the opportune time and convenient place in order to satisfy our affectionate and fervent desires. But because she was married, this was difficult, and this was the reason I began to grow weary and impatient.

Two friends reveal to one another the secrets of their love affairs.

Chapter 2

Phoebus had already twice illuminated the Zodiac since I had allowed myself to be overcome by Venus's son; and for that reason, wearied by so many vain solicitudes, through impatience I began to blame my lady, accusing her of the vice of ingratitude. Nonetheless, I continued my pursuit, and through my inconstancy I let her husband clearly see what goal I sought to achieve. Seeing this, he did not delay in sending her away, as is amply shown in the first book of her Torments. She had already been gone for a long time before I found out she had left; therefore, I was very astonished that I no longer saw her.

I often discussed this with my faithful companion, whose name was Quezinstra. He was descended from a noble and very ancient family; from his childhood onward he had been instructed in the military arts, and in this respect showed himself not unworthy of his ancestors. But fortune, which usually raises up the bad and casts down the good, had been a cruel

---

[8]An allusion to Paris; Cythera is an epithet for Venus.

enemy to him, for he had been thrown out of his parents' home. The reason for this was his supreme beauty, which inspired such desire in his stepmother that she was impelled to exhort and beseech him to satisfy her lustful and incestuous craving.

He refused to agree to this, for honor and reverence for his father made him ashamed of her continual objections and attempts to persuade him. But when the young lady saw herself repeatedly refused, she began to transform her love into mortal hatred; hence she conspired to have him definitively exiled, making piteous complaints to her husband, saying her son had wanted to violate her noble chastity. For that reason he was banished and thrown out of the house, as Hippolytus and Bellerophon were for similar reasons. But I want to tell you whence proceeded the faithful friendship maintained between us. On the very day love took me by surprise, we met and became acquainted as I was walking in a little wood near our city, and we told each other about the reasons for our woe. Because it seemed to me that he exceeded all other men whom I had ever seen in discretion and prudence, I put what little I had to offer at his disposal, for which he heartily thanked me. In such conversation we entered the city, which Quezinstra found pleasant and delightful; and so he decided to take up residence there, and did so. Since we conversed daily, it was my custom to report everything, both favorable and adverse, that happened to me in my love service. Being young in age and old in wisdom, he always counselled me to desist from such excessively puerile worries and cares, exhorting me to devote myself to activities that were manly and praiseworthy. One day, as he was remonstrating with me, my bitter fortune allowed me to find out what I continually sought to learn—the reason why I had been deprived of the sight of my cherished lady Hélisenne—for I was informed of her absence by one of my servants.

In the season when the trees drop their verdant beauties, Vulturnus, the cold wind, coming from the north, was the harbinger of the winter cold, and his companion Boreas froze the liquidity of the flowing rivers and transformed them into immobile crystal; it was at that time the sad news was made known to me: the painful departure of the lady who was my sovereign empress. Alas! When such bitter words were said to me, they entered my understanding with such great terror that I nearly fell dead; and had it not been that my perfect and faithful companion was there with me, I should have succumbed to some irretrievable affliction. But seeing me grow pale, he understood the extreme distress I was suffering, and showed himself diligent in succoring me. Still I did not hesitate to complain and lament in his presence, and I began to speak in this way:

"O blind and unstable fortune! Insidious traitor to all good understanding! Fabricator of all woes and illusions! I clearly see by your clever ruses how ingeniously you have deprived me of seeing the lady without whom it is impossible for me to go on living. Alas! I do not know if the gods are angry with me and to avenge themselves have allowed you to use me so cruelly; in any event, I cannot say what might be the reason. O sovereign Jupiter! I am not he who with the giants besieged your sacred realm. O Saturn! It was not I who disinherited you of your father's kingdom. O Titan! I am not the one who deprived you of your hereditary right. O beautiful Venus! It was not I who made the clever nets that ensnared you and Mars. O illustrious illuminator of the whole world, Apollo! I am not the one who struck your son Phaeton with a thunderbolt. O Mercury! I never betrayed any of your counsels. O Phoebus! I never disturbed you in your long love affairs. O Juno and Minerva! I am not the man who pronounced the judgment on the golden apple and depreciated your divine beauties. O custodians of the underworld! I did not lend my aid to the great Hercules or to his loyal companions in order to despoil your reign. Alas! Why am I so cruelly tortured? For what reason do you conspire against me? Alas! My heart consumes me with such fury that I desire only the end of my wretched life. O Lachesis, Clotho and Atropos, who dissolve every human life! Come to me, I desire you so greatly. O shades lacking the honor of burial! O damned spirits! Why will you not enter my body to destroy me? O sovereign god Jupiter! I beseech you to use your mighty hand to strike me with your swift thunderbolts, or, if possible, to put an end to me by still more horrible torments. I beg all the gods, celestial, sylvan, and alpine, to bring my painful and wretched life to an end without delay."

Saying such things, I was overcome by tears as hot as Mount Etna's flame, and I was so pricked by anger and pain that it was impossible for me to utter any further words. When Quezinstra saw the extremity to which I was reduced, he kindly tried to comfort me, and said: "Dear friend, your tormenting pain makes me succumb to extreme distress; and it would pain me even more if from the outset I had not tried to dissimulate my distress, intending to dissuade you from giving yourself over to such sad ways, which, once established in a man, cannot be extirpated or abolished without great difficulty. For this sensual appetite is an incurable infirmity from which arise forgetfulness of God and oneself, loss of time, diminishment of honor, discordant contentions, emulations, envies, denigrations, exiles, homicides, and destruction of the body and soul; and in the end, nothing good comes of it, as you can already see. Nevertheless you are unable to desist, because for a long time you have followed your pointless desire more than reason; thus you are completely disposed to persist [in pursuing your desire]. But you should still consider that solicitude in which there is no ground for hope is mad and not sane. You see that through your inconstancy, and by not having proceeded by suitable means, you have brought about your lady's departure, and you don't even know where she is residing. Since the object of your desire is lacking, how will it be possible to achieve what you so ardently desire? Certainly I have no hope for a cure in your case, unless by means of good judgment you strive to mitigate your madness, and are not among those men who are so melancholy and disdainful that when things do not happen in accord with their desires, they immediately want to die, which is a clear demonstration that they are sunk deep in their lasciviousness, and for that reason are impatient and importunate, usually because they have lost contact with reason. The fault which should be attributed to themselves, they ascribe to fortune, which in their ignorance they deem a god. How detestable are those who so presumptuously attribute divinity to that unrestrained sensual desire which should be condemned by all prudent minds!

Hence you must strive to gain control of yourself, and turn your eyes away from your murky thoughts, from the iniquitous love which has so much occupied you, and receive my friendly testimony, following the course contrary to the one your heart urges. Man is subjected by three things: by nature, by education, or by discipline; sometimes viciously, sometimes virtuously. Therefore demonstrate that by none of these means are you enslaved by vices, and do not permit an unfortunate event to annihilate the gifts of grace with which you have been endowed by God and nature."

After I had heard his remonstrances, whose elegance and agreeable delivery exceeded that which long ago flowed from the mellifluous mouth of the eloquent Nestor, I replied in this wise: "Quezinstra, in this way, by rather persuasive arguments, you seek to confound and dissipate love's power, which is so great that the whole company of Parnassus would not suffice to describe it. You might have read the histories, both ancient and modern, which mention a number of people, both men and women, bound together, who have sought to unbind themselves, which they were not able to do, but rather died through this passion like Dido and Phyllis, who for love ended violently their lives, as I shall soon end mine. For by natural inclination, I am constrained to love someone gentle, noble, and beautiful, as my lady is. Before I would give up my pursuit, I would expose myself to a peril greater than the one Theseus of Athens faced in conquering the monster Minotaur, or than the one encountered by Jason in the conquest of the golden fleece. For I am a man abandoned by fortune who ardently desires death, which would deliver me from my pains and unbearable travails. Alas! It would have been an act of pity had my genetrix mother dealt with me the way Procne or Medea[9] dealt with their children, for continuing to languish in such a passion is too insufferably bitter to me." While I was uttering these words, I was striking my breast and

---

[9]Both killed their children.

84

tearing my hair more than Agamemnon did when in mad pain he tore and destroyed his beautiful mane. My companion immediately sought to say comforting words to me, and among other things he said to me: "Guenelic, I beg you in the name of the friendship you have always had for me to bear and endure your misfortune with due equanimity, without wishing to resemble the emperors Marc Antony and Nero, or Niobe and Artemisia, who through their lascivious acts abbreviated their lives without learning the virtue of true patience. I am certain you are grievously tortured by the vehemence of love, for the more love finds himself in a clever and delicate subject, the more he grievously torments, vexes, and troubles him. Since it is clear to me that you have vowed to be lord Cupid's perpetual slave, it is very urgent that, following Assuerus's example, you free yourself from one bond and bind yourself with another, as the aforesaid Assuerus removed himself from Vashti's love by means of the beautiful and gracious Esther.[10] There is no other remedy for your bitter pain, and otherwise it will be intolerable for you. But as Aristotle puts it, as by the diversion of a river which spreads itself into several streams, one diminishes because of the other, and the later ones reduce and dry up the first, so in the same way when several desires are added to each other, the later ones cause the earlier ones to be forgotten. You know that in this city there are a great many fair ladies disposed to love and be loved. Therefore dispose yourself to conform with the desire of some fair lady, who will readily submit to your pleasure, as much because of your beauty as because of your blooming youth. By this means, you will recover your liberty from the other lady."

As Quezinstra sought to persuade me to divert myself from the love of my dear lady, in great haste I tried to confound what he said by an efficacious example, and said to him: "Quezinstra, I am sure, and this is certain, that when a tree is transplanted it usually withers, because the soil in which each was planted is more natural to it than another which is alien and unknown to it. I gave my heart to this lady so fervently that I cannot withdraw it from her, because it would be not be noble, legitimate, or admissible to alter my love, seeing and considering that this lady of mine possesses so many gifts of grace and nature there is no one who can compare with her. And so I beg Jupiter, ruler of the gods, to let his wrath confound me, or to let the brother and sister, the son and daughter of Lathona[11] deprive me of their splendors, or to let the fetid and stinking

---

[10]Asseurus was a Persian emperor whose head wife, Vashti, refused to present herself to the princes at her husband's command. She was banished and a new queen, Esther, took her place. Esther had to hide her Jewish identity from Asseurus.

[11]Probably a reference to Apollo and Diana; Lathona is presumably another name for the nymph Leto. At the beginning of II:3, Lathona's daughter is referred to as Phoebe, an epithet for Diana.

Harpies infect my place of residence with their excremental infections, or to let my body be torn apart, as Hippolytus's was, if I am ever so fickle as to change my affection and divide up my heart among diverse objects. For this reason I beseech you to insist no longer on opposing my desire, begging you to remember our true love, so that your counsel and aid might not fail me at the present time. I have understood that love is an essence whose fruition is achieved through travail, labor, endurance, and unbearable suffering. Hence I am determined to confront every peril. I want to search every inhabitable land, surpassing Ulysses' peregrinations, to find my lady, considering that diligent and solicitous people are worthy of everything. Hercules, Theseus, Peirithous, Aeneas, and Orpheus descended into the underworld to satisfy their aspiring desires; I am no less desirous than they were. And so I fear nothing, for good intentions make a man bold, and thus there is nothing that love cannot accomplish." When I had ended my remarks, Quezinstra began to speak in this way:

"Guenelic, I am well aware that against a heart totally disposed to love, no castigation, request, or counsel can have any force; and since it is very clear to me that my exhortations are in vain, I shall never again return to them; and I am prepared to lend you whatever aid I can, for I have such friendship for you that you may make use of me as you will, for I am more yours than mine. Nevertheless, searching so many lands as you have proposed will be a very arduous and difficult task. Moreover, if you reflect on it, you shall see that it cannot be done at present, because the time is not opportune; for we will have to wait until the winter cold is past, so that Aeolus's ferocity might be mitigated; for sometimes through imprudence one is led to harm oneself. The prince of poets praised Aeneas for knowing fear; flight is no less a virtue than steadfastness when the occasion counsels it. And so you must patiently await the opportune time; and meanwhile, to give you some consolation and cheer, we shall often speak of the sweet memory of Hélisenne."

On hearing these words, my mind was occupied by diverse thoughts and ideas; but I was somewhat comforted by the promise Quezinstra had made me. Weeping, I straightaway said to him: "O, my dear friend! The comforting words you have spoken to me have tempered my tormenting pain; for since I know through long experience the purity of your affection and the integrity of your noble heart, I am certain I shall not find your deeds in disaccord with your acts; and so both dead and alive I shall remain your debtor. Your discreet advice, accompanied by truth, makes it easy for me to patiently await the opportune moment."

Encounter with brigands on the road, and their defeat.

Chapter 3

We spent that day in such talk, and ever since I have suffered with more moderation. But on countless occasions I prayed to Apollo, saying: "O Apollo! If you still have any memory of the noble laurel, I beseech you to complete your course as hastily as you can."[12] Then afterward, when Lathona's splendid daughter began to show her horns, I said: "O Phoebe! If any memory of your beloved Endymion still abides within you, have compassion for me, and show yourself diligent and rapid in your course in order to abbreviate the time."[13] I passed several days in such activities, until the season began to turn in accord with my ardent desire. Not wishing to delay any longer, Quezinstra and I immediately resolved to leave. We acted on this resolve, and on the pretext of wanting to make a pilgrimage and visit some holy places, I said farewell to my family and friends, and we set out on our way toward a noble city whose name was Sirap.[14] But before we arrived there we met with a perilous adventure I wish to tell you about. This happened as we were passing through a great forest. Our bitter fortune caused us to encounter a company of people who lived a detestable life, for they had no other occupation than robbing those who passed through this forest. Seeing such people, I was moved to some fear, for the faces of these unhappy brigands suggested they were no less cruel than Busiris or Diomedes;[15] but my companion, who had great faith in his strength, began with magnanimous courage to exhort me, telling me that we were called upon to defend ourselves in a manly fashion. Meanwhile, these accursed people approached us, and one of them, who exceeded all the others in height and in the strength of his limbs, said to us with great audacity and arrogance that we must without delay hand over to him all the money we had along with our horses and clothes. Quezinstra replied that we were not willing to do this, and asked them to let us go, without trying to harm us or lay violent hands on us. As soon as they heard his response, they began to attack us. Then Quezinstra, taking

---

[12]A reference to Apollo's beloved Daphne who was transformed into a laurel tree by her father in order not to be raped by Apollo. Presumably Guenelic is asking the sun to hurry back toward the south, to make the spring come.

[13]The goddess of the moon was often depicted with a crescent moon affixed to her forehead, and this gave her the appearance of having horns. Phoebe was an epithet for Diana, though the moon goddess who loved Endymion was not Diana, who disdained men, but rather Luna (Selene).

[14]Paris (spelled backward).

[15]In Greek myth, Busiris was a king of Egypt who, in order to end a drought, sacrificed all strangers who came to his kingdom; Diomedes was the king of the Bistones, whose man-eating horses were slain by Hercules.

his sword in his hand, began valiantly to defend himself, and at the outset he struck a great blow to the head of one of the men, who was grievously wounded and fell violently face down on the ground. Then Quezinstra strove with all his might, and with his right hand gave such a marvelous blow to another man that he was pierced through and through. Immediately, following his example, I defended myself, and fortune was favorable to me, so that with my hand I wounded two of them so badly that it was no longer in their power to harm us. Seeing this, the others began to be afraid. Nonetheless, the man who had first started the struggle urged them on and exhorted them not to abandon the fight. Then they drew together and assembled, and found a way to kill our horses, which greatly angered us, and especially my companion, whose body and heart were in no way weary; he continued and persevered with magnanimity, nobility, and courageous strength. Thus he went to confront the man who was the most powerful and who vexed us most, giving him such a great and enormous blow that he split his head all the way down to his teeth. Then with another blow he lopped off the arm and sword of another, which fell to the ground. Seeing this, the others fled, fearing they would be cut down like their fellows. Nevertheless, in order to purge the earth of such abominable and detestable people, we pursued them diligently. Seeing they could not evade mortal peril, they turned around, fighting back as best they could, so that Quezinstra—who had up to that point scarcely been injured—was wounded in the left shoulder, and I, being near him, was seriously wounded in the arm. But for all that, we did not cease to try to subdue them. However, bright Phoebus then began to drive his chariot downward toward the western regions in order to plunge his flaming steeds into Thetis's waves. And so we were forced to abandon our enterprise, for because of the nocturnal shadows we were unable to discover where they went. Then we sat down under a tree, as wearied and vexed by having to remain there for the night as by the tormenting pain we suffered from our wounds. Alas! I was in such an extremity that my tortured life no longer had any sort of salvation other than the piteous memory and recollection of my lady, whose absence was so excruciating to me that I could not refrain from complaining and lamenting. But Quezinstra imagined that the cause of my anxieties was the pain and hardship we had that day endured. So with gentleness, urbanity, and clemency he said to me: "Guenelic, I wonder greatly for what reason you are consuming your life in tears and moans, considering that the sovereign God has accorded us such favor that we have overcome and defeated those who firmly intended to put us cruelly to death; whereby we can hope to prosper on our journey. Need I remind you that no glorious triumph can be won or retained without suffering? Are you ignorant of Pompey's great misfortunes? Of Julius Caesar's difficult youth? The long and arduous travels of the eloquent Ulysses? The perils and shipwrecks of Aeneas and Ajax Cyleus?[16] You must understand that all elevated and generous spirits usually are opposed by fortune, and for that very reason their names remain to us in sempiternal praise. Take comfort, then, considering that when you have found Hélisenne, the memory of your extreme suffering will be sweet. The Greek ladies had no greater pleasure than hearing narrated the pains and hardships suffered and endured by their husbands, for what is painful to endure is a delight to remember when one is happy. And so you must not be so weak and allow yourself to be upset by every adverse event; but rather regain strength from your heart, and in the end love will make you victorious."

As Quezinstra was kindly consoling me, I said to him: "Alas, my dear friend, the cause of my tears is not the weary tribulations I have borne today; I am tortured only by the fact that in the painful travail I have endured for the sake of love, I see no reward that presages future comfort. For that reason love and fear have besieged my aching heart, and continually agitate and torment me. In addition, I am no less pained by the misfortune you endure for my sake than by that which my ungrateful fortune daily sets before me."

As I was saying these words, the air began to grow dark. Aeolus, the master of the winds, wished to unleash his fury at that moment; and suddenly the air grew so murky that one might have thought all the planets and stars both fixed and errant had been unfastened from both hemispheres. Then came thunderbolts hurled by the fury of the first of Saturn's sons, along with a superabundance of water; the air grew dark and took on a countenance so terrifying that we could hope for nothing better than cruel Chaos. Finding ourselves in such perplexity, we resorted to beseeching the one who is mother and daughter to the thunderer on high, and who gave birth to the salvation-bearing child in a corrupt world, that she might preserve us from being submerged as humankind earlier was, without anyone escaping this peril except Deucalion and his wife Pyrrha.[17] When our humble prayers and supplications were finished, the

---

[16]Pompey was a great Roman general whose successes earned him popularity but also the jealousy of other powerful men who finally killed him. Julius Caesar was assassinated by a group of men that included his friend Brutus. Ulysses, who figures prominently in Homer's *Iliad* and *Odyssey*, is bound by his oath to join the Greek expedition to recover Helen, and then endures hardship on his return home. Aeneas is one of the Trojan leaders in the Trojan War and the subject of Virgil's *Aeneid*. Ajax fought with Ulysses in the Trojan War and, when defeated, went mad with shame and later committed suicide.

[17]In *Torments*, direct references to Christianity such as this one to the Virgin Mary are often oblique and combined with allusions to classical mythology. Rather than mentioning Noah, the author refers to the myth of a flood caused by Jupiter, of which Deucalion and Pyrrha were the only survivors.

clouds began to break. Then Bise and Zephyr[18] dried up the earth, which gave us reason to take some comfort, and we thanked the one who quenched the Samaritan woman's thirst with saving water.[19]

When fair Aurora had risen from the bed of her husband Tithonus, and made her appearance in her scarlet robe to shed her light on the earth, we set out to investigate and search this woods to find out if any habitable place might be found there. Looking in several and diverse places, we spied a small hut where a pious hermit lived. Examining and looking at this little abode's location, which suggested great saintliness, we approached it; and as we were about to knock on the door, the holy brother came out. When we had reverentially greeted him, he invited us into his home. After having relieved our fatigue a bit, we began to narrate our misfortunes, on which he took pity and compassion. He promised to cure us and heal our wounds, telling us that he had long studied the art of surgery, in which he was rather experienced, so we should rest assured and not be afraid. Thus were we comforted by this good and religious person, who shone with purity and sincerity.

Quezinstra said to me: "O Guenelic! We are obliged to thank, venerate, and adore the sublime God through whose providence the heavens, the earth, and human life is ruled and governed, who has made us worthy of all kinds of mercy, such as finding this holy person for our consoling refuge." As we were conversing in this way, the hermit left us, then soon after returned and offered us herbs and roots for our bodily nourishment, of which we took as many as was suitable for our needs. By this means our debilitating hunger was satisfied. Then he began to look at our wounds, and when he had examined them, he assured us we should soon be healed. Next he began to apply a soft and fragrant ointment whose perfume equalled that of ambrosia and nectar. He did this several times, so that within a week we had regained our health. But we were extraordinarily weak because during this time we had eaten only herbs and roots, and drunk only water from the clear spring.

However, despite our debilitation, I did not want to put off our departure, for Hélisenne's image persisted with such vehemence in my memory that my thoughts were occupied by no other idea. To satisfy my desire, Quezinstra agreed to set out on our journey, and so, addressing his words to the good hermit, he said: "It is clearly not in our power to render you all the thanks due such great merit, or all our hearts' gratitude, for having taken us in and kindly treated us. But that Lord whom you serve with such care shall be your remunerator by rewarding you for the charitable way you have dealt with us." These words said, we left the good her-

---

[18]The North and West winds, respectively.
[19]Jesus; see John 4.7.

mit, who accompanied us until we had left the woods, promising to remember us in his prayers and orisons so that the Eternal God might grant us felicity and prosperity on our journey.

The adventures of the two companions during their peregrinations.

Chapter 4

After we left the hermitage, we traveled a week before reaching the city of Sirap. When we arrived there, because we were extraordinarily tired and weary, it seemed suitable to remain three days to refresh ourselves a bit. On the fourth day, as soon as Phoebus showed himself in his lofty abode, we got ready and went to enjoy ourselves by the water.[20] While we were conversing, we took singular delight in looking on the very beautiful face of Juno, who was completely serene, for Iris, her handmaiden, had purified the air. Then we saw how the beautiful nymph Flora, accompanied by her friend Zephyr, had undertaken to spread out her lovely carpets decorated with beautiful flowers and aromatic plants that gave off such a perfume that the whole region was imbued with it. Afterward we began to consider how calm and tranquil the water was, allowing us to navigate Neptune's salty waves. And so we decided to set out under the protection of Venus, who came from the sea. Because she is the princess of love, I hoped she might be favorable to us, and thus I deemed no sea monster, no Leviathan so bold, nor any pirate corsair so enterprising, as to dare to try and harm us. Neither had I any fear of Proserpina's virgins, who through their supplications entreated the gods to give them wings, and were changed into sirens so that they might achieve their goal, which was to find their mistress, who had been carried off by Pluto; but they are still busy investigating and searching, and have since been the cause of several ships' sinking, for they are full of deceptions and sing so well that, by means of the great harmony and melodious resonance of their sweet voices, they put people to sleep, and then cause them to perish. Nevertheless all these dangers did not worry me at all. Having found a vessel which was departing for Cyprus, we negotiated the cost of passage with the mariners, and then got on board and left. The wind was extraordinarily propitious at the beginning, but in its changeableness it soon turned against us. Thus against our will Aeolus carried us to the port of a fair and spacious city, whose name was Goranflos. When we arrived

---

[20]The French term is "rivaige," or "riverbank," and since the scene takes place in Paris, one would assume the water in question is a river. We have, however, maintained the ambiguity suggested by allusions a few lines later to Neptune, salt water, and the sea.

there, glancing around I discerned the lord of this region, who was walking along the beach to divert himself. But as soon as he had set his eyes on Quezinstra and me, he came up to the water's edge, and out of his human kindness began in a cordial way to inquire and ask us where we came from, and what was the occasion of our voyage. With reverence and humility, Quezinstra promptly replied, naming our homeland. In addition, he told him that the motive of our voyage was merely to satisfy youthful curiosity, which sought only to see and visit diverse lands.

When the magnanimous lord heard these words, I believe some divine power inspired him to invite us to be admitted and received in his palace in order to refresh ourselves and rest, which pleased us very much. I said to him: "Illustrious prince, it is not in our power to render you the thanks and gratitude that befit your great merit, to which, as I see it, neither Ulysses' wit nor Nestor's wisdom would be equal, but the urbanity and clemency which it pleases your highness to show toward us redounds no less to your praise than to our pleasure." These words said, we were without delay conducted into the city, which was constructed and built in a very singular way, for one could see there magnificent edifices erected and rising to great heights, which were pleasant and delightful to look at. Contemplating this beautiful city, we arrived at the palace, which was of various kinds of marble, and made with such subtle skill that it would difficult to describe it. Several ancient stories were depicted on it so cleverly they equalled the art of the sculptor Pygmalion, who was overcome by love for the image he had himself fabricated. While we were feasting our eyes on these artful pictures, along came a young man, who was the duke's son. On first glancing our way, when he had espied us, he came to meet us, and asked who we were. Quezinstra replied with discretion and modesty in the same way as he had to the lord.

We spent this day in such conversations, and ever since, the son of the prince (whose name was Zelandin) continued to come to talk with us, and conceived such a singular friendship for us that we remained in his city longer than we had intended. During this time we occupied ourselves with various activities, and usually, when the numbering hours had awakened Tithonus's beloved, the duke's son rose and dressed, and then sent for us to accompany him into the fields. Sometimes with dogs, sometimes with falcons, we took the trouble to explore the lands abounding in game and prey. Then when we were tired and weary, we returned to the castle. After we had taken our refection, to divert ourselves Zelandin led us into a spacious room where the ladies delighted in dancing, which they did with such great agility and modesty that it was an extraordinary thing to see. But alas! For me it was only sad and distressing, and I said to myself: "O my lady, what violent prison holds you? What unworthy place detains you, and so deprives me of seeing you? This causes me such ex-

92

treme anxiety and pain that hearing the delightful harmony of the resonance of the sweet sound of the instruments cannot in any way please
me, but on the contrary, they augment my suffering. Alas! when Orpheus
went into the underworld to rescue the fair Eurydice, he sang so sweetly
that his sweet voice (with the melody of his harp) has such power that the
wretched souls forgot their painful woes. But even if Orpheus with his
nine muses were to try in my presence to sing deliciously, it would still
be impossible to diminish the travails I bear."

In such thoughts, not being able any longer to endure the excessive internal pain which agitated and tormented me, I pretended to have found a
messenger who was leaving for my country. And so, feigning that I intended to write, I had an acceptable reason for going away. But Quezinstra
was well aware that I had devised this feigned dissimulation only in order
to be alone so I could complain and lament, and so he followed me and
sought diligently to console me. But I told him that such a long stay distressed me too much, and that if he was at all desirous of helping me in
my urgent need, we had without delay to set out in search of the lady I
desired with such affection. He replied: "Guenelic, since I see clearly that
remaining in this noble city only distresses you the more, I do not wish to
put off our departure. For as you know through long experience, I have
always been solicitous and attentive to doing everything that I deemed
likely to satisfy you. To give you clear proof that I have a irrevocable resolve to persevere, whenever it pleases you I am prepared to say farewell
to ask the duke's leave and permission to depart."

On hearing this I responded with great happiness in my breast that my
desire was promptly to request the duke's permission to leave the following day.

Love complaints exchanged by the two companions.

Chapter 5

Talking in this way and turning our steps toward the palace, we encountered Zelandin, who greeted us with a warm welcome and a
smiling face. He wished to explain to us the cause of his great joy, which
was unlike him. He began to tell and amply declare to us that his father
the duke was making sumptuous preparations for a fitting reception for
all the lords who were his relatives and allies, together with the knights
his subjects, to whom he had sent a very express and general command to
notify them that they must not fail to be present in this city on the day of
the rites to be celebrated at the great festival which was to occur within a
few short days. "On that day milord has decided to make me a knight. On
that occasion he has arranged a tournament which will last three days.

The first day's victor shall have as a prize a half-dozen marvelously handsome and swift horses, which in races have always won and carried off the victory. The second day's winner shall have a sword of inestimable value, for it was long ago forged by Mulciber, the goldsmith and armorer of the gods, for the conqueror Hercules. The victor of the third day shall choose among the congregated and assembled virgins the one who pleases him most, excepting only milord's daughters, my sisters. O! How fortunate he who shall win victory, for it shall make him worthy of perpetual praise."

As soon as we heard these words, I perceived that Quezinstra was overjoyed by this news, wherefore I had little or no hope that we should depart, for as I could see, the words narrated by Zelandin had more power to retain than the lodestone has to attract steel. Because I was sure that leaving would cause him no less vexation than staying caused me, I did not wish to importune him. Therefore I decided to tolerate and put up with my misfortune by means of patience, so far as it was in my power to do so, in order not to distress the man who was trying so hard to please me. And so, with anxious difficulty, which could not have been more extreme, I restrained myself, not changing my countenance, with a greater desire to weep than to listen to such remarks which seemed to me too long and wearisome. Presently Quezinstra, who had well understood the distress I was suffering, fell into a sadness no less great than his earlier delight. For that reason, extolling the duke's praiseworthy undertaking, by fitting and honorable means he found a way to be alone with me, and then he said: "O Guenelic! I have no doubt that your heart is greatly oppressed and burdened with sadness because of your fear that I might try to persuade you to delay our departure on account of the news we have heard, which you should not fear, for I am ready to leave when it pleases you to do so, although the departure will cause me the most acute and bitter regret that could ever abide or lurk in my heart. For I want you to know that if I were certain it would not displease you, I should be completely desirous of seeing the assembly of noble knights that is to take place in this city; and even more I should aspire to be one of their number in order to follow in the valorous footsteps of my predecessors; and I should hope to demonstrate with rather good success what I can do, if the opportunity offered itself. But my cruel fortune will not allow such felicity to be accorded me; rather, it will use all its power to offer me adversities and bitter poisons, making me a perpetual fugitive without ever permitting me to return to my father's home."

When he had uttered these words, he gave himself up to continual weeping, and showed himself no less woeful than the son of Thetis lamenting the death of his dear friend Patroclus.[21] Seeing that he was led

---

[21]Achilles, the son of Thetis, was the lover-companion of Patroclus who was killed in battle. See *Iliad*, Books 17ff.

to such an extremity because it was not in his power to perform knightly deeds, although I myself needed comforting as well, I said to him: "Quezinstra, I am surprised to see you consuming your life in weeping, effacing your manly and pleasant face, seeing and considering that you have always been so prudent and are able to endure patiently every adversity. Why, then, are you so tormented and pained by the fear that has come over you that you will not be received back into your father's home? Don't you know that it often happens that when one thinks oneself farthest from felicity, one recovers it? Just as vessels, thinking they are safe and sound after having traveled over various seas and dangerous marine gulfs without succumbing to any peril, founder just as they are approaching a port, so too many people who think themselves wholly without hope of salvation end up in sweet and tranquil security. And in the same way many people are tortured and tormented by great afflictions on account of numerous calamities and misfortunes, just as you are, but afterward live in great happiness and sovereign contentment, as I hope you shall. For that reason I beg you in the name of our true friendship and our common pilgrimage to take heart, restoring your spirit's strength, and through discretion and constancy, mitigate your bitter pain. For my part, in order not to distress you, I am content to delay our departure so as to satisfy your ardent desire."

Putting an end to his lamentations, Quezinstra replied: "Guenelic, just as you are astonished by my anxieties and distress, I am even more astonished by the efficacious remonstrances you can formulate so appropriately to cheer up someone else. Nonetheless, it is not in your power to free yourself from the perils and torments to which you have succumbed, but continually trouble your sad and woeful life with weeping, tears and sighs. All the same, as I see it, since your understanding is not so perturbed that you have not the mental capacity to clearly discern what sort of life would be best for you, it seems to me that just as you entered into love through imagination, through prudence you could withdraw from it. Phoebus is new again since you last saw Hélisenne. You must know that the sun warms as it sees, according to the maxim of Avicenna, a marvelously knowledgeable philosopher;[22] amorous passion does the same, warming us when we find ourselves looked upon by the splendor of our beloved's eyes. But I am persuaded that when the person to whom we are inclined is not before our eyes, all passions can easily be forgotten."

When I had heard these words, I promptly replied: "Quezinstra, you

---

[22]Avicenna (abu-'Ali al-Husayn ibn-Sina), a Persian physician and philosopher born in 980 C.E., whose thought was largely based on Aristotle, and to a lesser extent, on the Neoplatonic philosophers. His works were translated into Latin and ignited the revival of European Aristotelianism that culminated in Scholasticism. Aquinas and other schoolmen cited Avicenna, and Marguerite Briet probably knew of him through their writings.

may be certain that it is not merely difficult but impossible to temper one's inclination toward the things that delight us, because habits established in the soul are moved with great difficulty. And you must believe that remembering a few past pleasures has a great power of keeping lovers captive; the pains and travails they endure have only the effect of augmenting their love, for true lovers confronted by torments and death, remain perfect and unwavering. In your view, when the beloved is out of sight she is forgotten by the heart. But you are gravely mistaken in this, for there is no distance in space, nor any length of time, which could in any way dispossess me of the memory of the lady for whose sake I have endured such extreme sufferings. For everything that comes before my eyes, whether waking or sleeping, represents my lady; and no matter where I am, in thought and in the place where my understanding lies, I contemplate no one but Hélisenne. You may be sure that I am burned and consumed by an even more excessive ardor when she is absent than when she is present. Consider then whether you have ever read or heard of anyone in love who died in the presence of his beloved; but through absence, a number of lovers have perished. How great is love's power! It wins dominion over every man and every woman, and even the gods have been subject to it. We read that Jupiter transformed himself in divers ways for the sake of love: one time into a bull for Europa; another time into a shower of gold for Danae; for Leda into the form of a white swan, and for the mother of the hero Hercules into the form of Amphitryon.

"Bright Phoebus was overcome by love for Daphne by means of the golden arrow, but that fair lady cared not for him because her heart had been pierced by the leaden arrow which inclined her to severe refusal. Nevertheless she was so beleaguered by Phoebus that she could no longer resist him, and as a final recourse she began to beseech her mistress Diana, who, having heard her prayer, transformed her into a laurel tree.[23] Seeing this, the god gave her the dignity of remaining ever green, and in memory of his beloved, adorned his head with verdant laurel branches.

"Mars, the warlike god of battles, fell in love with the goddess Venus, to the detriment of her husband Vulcan. And this same goddess loved the beautiful and gracious Adonis so excessively that despite her divinity, when she saw that her beloved was dead, she did not fail to weep and mourn. To perpetuate his memory she sprinkled her beloved's blood, of a beautiful color; from it grew a flower of a color like that of blood, and this flower is called Adonis. In addition, the fair Aurora, who illuminates our world with her radiant light, loved Cephalus to the disadvantage of Procris. It would be tedious, and difficult as well, to tell about the invin-

---

[23]This is a variation of the story usually told about Daphne, in which the river god, Peneus, and not Diana, changes her into a laurel.

cible power of love; and if celestial examples are not enough for you, you clearly see daily in our own hemisphere the rampant expansion of its power. It subjugates powerful lords shining with the titles, opulence and wealth of milady Juno. Resistance would be futile for those who pursue the studies of the goddess Pallas,[24] for through natural inclination we are subject to love. And so you would be greatly mistaken to think love blameworthy, for what is commanded, celebrated, and honored by everyone without being reprehensible can be neither condemned nor detested. Nevertheless, you must be forgiven for this, for one easily depreciates what one does not understand. But if you once understood the blessed joy of love, and how delightful are its pleasures, you would risk any danger to enjoy them. Since it exceeds my powers to express to you the mellifluous sweetness and delight of love, without consuming as much time as the Greeks did at the siege of Ilion in the expectation of the predicted bloody victory, I wish to put an end to these remarks, for I see Phoebus returning all tired out."

When I had uttered these words, Quezinstra briefly replied: "Guenelic, so far as I can understand, in the hope of victory you lovers who are afflicted with this lasciviousness want divinity to be attributed to your obstinate insolence, not recognizing that your love is no more than a bitter passion and that all your acts are useless and cowardly. If this essence of love is worthy of such great commendation as you claim, why do you not always praise and extol it? On the contrary, you often condemn and depreciate it, and according to your whim you treat it now as a god, now as a vain dream, depending on whether the lover is happy or unhappy. And when his desire is satisfied, love is worshipped, venerated, and thanked as a god, and he thinks his happiness proceeds from love. But the lover who is refused, saddened, and angered assigns love all the fault and blame. From this I conclude that you lovers are usually out of your minds. You say that because I don't understand the blessed joy of love I want to denigrate its power; I should prefer to be thought ignorant of such sensual pleasure (which I deem slight and of short duration) rather than to suffer excessively long and bitter trials in order to participate in it, without being able to hope for any good result. Consider what the Trojan did for Helen, Achilles for Polyxena, Marc Antony for Cleopatra, Leander for Hero, and Demetrius for Lamia. Countless are those who because of this sensuality have ended their lives; to safeguard against this, one must avoid idleness, for people who are deprived of activity are more subject than others to this passion. On this topic the poet of Mantua[25] says that

---

[24]Pallas is one of Minerva's surnames, which the goddess adopted in honor of her friend, Pallas, whom she accidentally killed. The name Pallas in early Greek means young girl or virgin.
[25]Virgil; see *Aeneid*, Book 4.

the queen of Carthage, being idle in her chamber, weeping and sighing, complained of excessive love to her sister Anne."

Our conversation was not yet finished when Apollo began to hide his head, and the departure of the daylight moved and compelled us to withdraw to the palace where the evening meal was already finished and people were beginning various games and relaxing diversions. But as soon as Zelandin caught sight of us, he had one of his footmen take us into a room to have our meal, where we were abundantly provided for. After talking for a while, our eyes grew heavy because we had been so long awake, and we decided to retire in order to repair our nocturnal weariness. But I could not find tranquility or peace in my heart, for a terrible and frightening vision suddenly presented itself to me. I seemed to see my lady Hélisenne in bed alongside me; she was violently agitated by a deathly illness, and looked so anxious, lamentable and trembling that I thought the daughter of Erebus (whom the naturalists call the ultimate terror)[26] held my lady's delicate limbs in her icy grasp. While I was sleeping, my soul was disturbed by this vision, and I was reduced to such a state that had I not been awakened by Quezinstra, I should have been ready to visit the realm of Minos.[27] I rose from my sleep as anxious and distressed as it is possible to be, and began to narrate my dream to Quezinstra, who tried diligently to comfort me, saying that I must not be so distressed by strange dreams. "For most often, nocturnal visions foretell the contrary result; and sometimes seeing oneself vexed, harmed, and illtreated is a sign of future happiness. Dreaming of weeping, or of being seized by Atropos, signifies that one's lucrative business will prosper. And dreaming of sating the belly with mellifluous and delicious foods, and being in sensual delight, demonstrates anxieties and heartache with bodily languor. Therefore I beg you to abandon this fear, and not believe in false imagined things." Quezinstra spoke to me in this way, but the more he tried to console me, the more upset I grew. And so I replied: "O, how wretched I am! I clearly see that such a dream is a sure presage of something sinister, whereby I am completely deprived of my saving hope; for there is no one who has not sometimes seen or understood some truth through dreams. Hercules, the learned astrologer and demigod, always paid careful attention to his dreams. Alexander of Macedon, Caesar, Brutus, Cassius, and Hannibal were informed of their final ends through dreams. Speaking of dreams, Cicero recounts in his book on divination that when Queen Hecuba was pregnant with the handsome Trojan shep-

---

[26]Probably a reference to Hecate, whose parentage is vague but sometimes attributed to Erebus (Tartarus). She was an underworld goddess who was often associated with sorcery, death, and, especially in the Christian tradition, evil.

[27]Judge of the dead in the underworld.

herd,[28] it seemed to her in her sleep in the depth of the night that she was giving birth to a blazing and bloody torch that was burning and consuming the noble city of Troy. The queen told king Priam about this vision, and he was extraordinarily perplexed and fearful, for at the same time Timethes, his bastard son, who was a great augurer and very expert in the art of astronomy, predicted that a child should shortly be born through whom the city of Ilion would be destroyed.[29] Calchas, the archpriest of the temple of Apollo, spoke similarly, saying the noble city would be reduced to ashes by fire coming from Greece.[30] The final conclusion drawn by the king was that the child should be immediately delivered and hidden in death's shadow. But the too compassionate mother had him secretly brought up, and this later resulted in her being the cause of the complete extermination of her relatives and land, which Asia and Europe still mourn. When I reflect on all these things, it is hardly astonishing that I am filled with internal distress. For on the basis of these examples I do not consider dreams to be vain illusions. And moreover, what appeared to me should be termed more a vision than a dream, since I saw the true image just as I might see it when awake, and this is something different from a dream, which represents itself in the figure of another image without revealing the identity of the people involved. For that reason I can assume that what appeared to me will come true. Consider then whether I do not have cause to be very distressed and afflicted. Alas! I am enduring such great travail and tormenting pain that unless I find some relief, my sad and woeful life shall come to an end."

After I had ceased speaking, I remained as if dead; my wrathful soul withdrew to the hidden vital powers, leaving my body destitute. Then Quezinstra, moved by charitable pity and compassion for me, sought through gentle comforting to call back the aching and virtually errant spirits, and said to me: "Guenelic, as I see it you are terribly agitated and upset by your continual distress. And so it is hardly surprising to see you in such great tribulation. It is not that I wish to deny that dreams sometimes bear true meaning. To those who eat soberly and properly, Nature provides great imagination and gifts. If the movement is slight and unimpeded, not only the imagination remains free, but also the mind's power to link perceptions, so that sleeping people discern similarities among these images. Sometimes the mind is so disposed that in sleeping it argues and composes verse and syllogisms. But if more vapor is released, as in those accustomed to stuff their stomachs, only transmogrified, inaccurate, and disordered phantasms appear. However, since I know you are a

---

[28]Hecuba was the wife of Priam, king of Troy, and the mother of Paris.
[29]These seem to be the attributes of Aesacus, the son of Priam by his first wife, Arisbe.
[30]Calchas was a seer who accompanied the Greek army in the Trojan War.

man of noble sobriety, I take your dreams to contain some truth. For that reason I am of the opinion that you should describe this vision to some augurer or seer to gain a clear knowledge of your future, and this should be easy enough to do. For I well recall hearing Zelandin say, among other things, that outside this city lives a very ancient man who is extraordinarily expert in the art of astronomy. I suggest you consult him concerning this doubtful misfortune." When he had said these words, I was somewhat comforted, hoping to gain certainty on the subject about which I was in doubt.

She who long ago was the cause of Procris's death was beginning to circle round and light up the goddess Cybele when I began to lift my weary and tormented body from the feathery bed. Then, as soon as we were dressed, we went to the domicile of the astronomer of whom Quezinstra had informed me. My tongue ready and my mind open, I immediately described to him the nocturnal vision that was the cause of my anxiety, humbly beseeching him to tell me what such a thing signified. By means of his certain sidereal knowledge, he told me that before Phoebus had twice returned to the house of the Ram I should see my much-desired lady alive. These words, uttered with discernment and discretion, lent me an indubitable belief. After having thanked and satisfied him, both in words and in acts, we returned with much joy and spent that day in greater pleasure and amusement than we usually did. The time of the solemn festival was already approaching, on which day all the princes who were the duke's relatives and allies, together with all the knights who were his subjects, assembled in the following manner:

Preparation for the princes' tournament.

Chapter 6

The first to arrive, with a very sumptuous, very magnificent, and very rich cortege, was Alcinas, king of Boetia. Afterward came Silperis, the king of Athens, in an exceedingly noble and splendid company, followed by Federic, duke of Locres. Afterward followed Librius, count of Phocides,[31] Philibert, duke of Foucquerolles, and then after him the count of the desert land. Aemery, count of Merlieu, Mabran, lord of Courval, the lord of Teuffle, and Baltasar, lord of Housen also made their appearance. Afterward came an innumerable company of knights who, in order to avoid prolixity, I shall forbear to name. The king of Boetia and the king of Thebes, who were close relatives, were received with great honor and re-

---

[31]Marguerite Briet spells this and other characters' names in various ways. To avoid confusion, we have tried to make the spelling consistent throughout.

spect, the former being joined through matrimonial property with Phenice, the only daughter of the duke of Locres and the niece of the duke of Goranflos, who was resplendent with unusual beauty. After the honorable reception of the kings, princes, and great lords, it was time for the evening meal; tables were promptly set up, at which the kings and some of the princes sat down, and were sumptuously served. Then after the tables had been removed, the knights and ladies moved on to the dancing, in which they took delightful amusement until Thetis began to light up the middle of the celestial hemisphere. Shooting stars, falling through the air, were urging weak mortals to take their desired repose when delicacies were brought into the hall with wines no less delicious than the one Jupiter is served by Ganymede. After the collation was over, all the guests were conducted to their chambers to rest. Quezinstra and I, like the others, retired, not to sleep, but only to continue our usual conversations. I wanted to speak about love according my custom—for the amorous flame ignited my desire with such great force that all the power of Neptune would not have been able to extinguish the most minuscule part of it—but Quezinstra was hardly suffering any less, not for a similar reason, but on account of the extreme internal distress that agitated him because he was unable to perform knightly deeds. And so I was forced to keep silent, for in view of his great pain, it was not an appropriate or propitious time to speak of love; and because the nocturnal shadows are very suited to mourning and sadness, he could not find peace or tranquility in his heart. Although I tried to cheer him up with friendly reminders, he spent part of the night formulating painful laments. Nonetheless, between the third and fourth watch his eyes were constrained to close.

Early-rising Lucifer[32] already smelled the palace doors opening, for they were strewn with redolent roses. Then commenced the whinnies and cries of the Apollonian coursers which had fed all night on fragrant ambrosia, and were already harnessed to the refulgent chariot. And so all the splendid and flaming stars were sinking in the west when I rose from my bed, where the night had passed in a brief slumber. We conversed casually as we dressed; then we proceeded to the temple where immediately afterward the kings and princes assembled to hear the divine service. When this was done, Zelandin was made a knight in the presence of the princes. Then everyone returned to the spacious hall where, as one might imagine, a marvelously sumptuous dinner had been set out. Afterward, all the guests left the duke to prepare and ready themselves in order to go begin the tournament; it was decided that the king of Boetia's men and the duke of Goranflos's men should hold the tournament against the others. By common consent, Federic, duke of Locres, was elected leader of

---

[32]The planet Venus; see Part Two, Chapter 9.

those on the inside and the king of Athens was elected for those on the outside.[33] As both sides were getting ready, the duchess left, accompanied by the queen of Boetia and a large number of ladies, and modestly entered her pavilion, which was draped with gold-embroidered silk, on which was represented the whole course of the Zodiac with the movement of the star-bearing sky, a marvel to see. It was also a singular pleasure to contemplate the beauty of the ladies, who were resplendent as much because of their natural beauty as because of their accoutrements of gold, scarlet, and precious gems. Juno herself could not accumulate so many riches as were seen in the attire of these angelic princesses. While we were absorbed in looking at them, Quezinstra turned his eyes away from all the others in order to contemplate the gracious beauty of the fair Phenice. Then, when he had observed her for a time, he began to accuse heaven of ingratitude because it had not adorned our country with such a beauty, and turning toward me he said: "O, Guenelic! If you have carefully examined the quality of this lady, you will be able to see that God and nature have put all their efforts into creating her. Here Venus would lose the prize of the golden apple, for the superior beauty of this lady could not be sufficiently expressed without invoking the aid of Calliope, whom I beseech to aid me with her eloquence in order that I may properly describe her to you. Look at her hair shining with brilliant color that makes her look like Apollo. Consider the amplitude of her fair forehead, with the lovely eyebrow that adorns it. Note the radiant light of her green eyes, more sparkling than any stars, the shape of her gracefully long nose, the fresh color and fair complexion of her face, the plumpness of her rosy cheeks, the daintiness of her mouth, and the way her coral lips reveal a treasury of oriental pearls when she smiles. Look at the delicate whiteness of her crystalline bosom. See the form of her little breasts that look like two rosy apples. I can go no further, for her exquisite attire conceals the perfection of her noble shape, which can be perceived only by the imagination. But in conclusion, I say that the celestial council is impoverished by not having anyone so refulgent as she." When I heard these words spoken with great affection, it seemed to me not the time to keep silent, and so I replied:

"Quezinstra, I beg you to put aside every passion that might affect your judgment, and form in your mind images of this lady, descending part by part and judging her; then perhaps you shall find heaven not so avaricious in bestowing its benefits on the maidens of our homeland. The praise you shower on this lady makes it appear that God, heaven and nature had deprived us of every celestial gift."

Then Quezinstra said: "I understood you as soon as you had uttered

---

[33]In other words, the inside team defends its turf against the besieging outside team.

these words; but if you are willing to consider the question yourself, I am happy to let you make the judgment. Be careful that the desire for truth does not depart from what you say."

In order not to prolong my suffering, I promptly said: "Certainly I do not wish to deny that this lady is endowed with great beauty so far as the comeliness of her face is concerned, but as for the rest, she is inferior to someone I know; and so I beg you not to try to exalt or extol foreign women in order to deprecate those whom we know and who do not deserve to be condemned. If this lady pleases you so much, you can seek her love without diminishing the honor of others."

He immediately responded: "Guenelic, be assured that the superior beauty of this lady has compelled me to utter the truth, without my judgment having been troubled by some blind desire that has taken control of my sight; for you must believe that I am resolved always to remain far away from love's arrows, which so indiscriminately and cruelly wound so many people."

As soon as he had said these words, without delay I replied: "Since your praise of this lady does not proceed from your having been affected by some amorous desire, I beg you to abandon such talk, for since you do not want love to obtain domination and lordship over you, you must not persist too long in contemplation, for that could easily make you fall into the difficulty of a man who by love's power was compelled to pray to the goddess Venus and beg her to make the image he had made come to life.[34] And so I wish to warn you that you must beware of the first steps. I understand very well that people of a melancholy complexion, such as you, are not so easily inclined to love as others are.[35] For because of this predominant humor, your habits and nature make you somewhat hard. But if you are once captured, you shall never extricate yourself; for melancholic people, because of the sluggishness and slowness of the earthy humor, are more likely to risk death than to abandon love. Choleric people are only too subject to love, because of the impetuousness of the warm humor; and while they are more willful and rash, they also escape more easily."

---

[34]The reference, of course, is to Pygmalion.

[35]In medieval physiology, the body was thought to contain four types of fluids or humors: blood, phlegm, choler, and black bile. The one that was dominant supposedly determined the character and health of the individual. A person might thus be sanguine, phlegmatic, choleric or melancholy.

Chivalric exercises.

Chapter 7

As soon as I had finished speaking, the duke arrived with some of his intimates, and climbed into his pavilion, which was so sumptuously adorned that everything around was illuminated by it. It was a beautiful sight to see the prince in his rich and triumphant garments; he was seated on a throne decorated with costly and exquisite precious stones, and resembled the lord of heaven handing down his final decisions in the celestial council. Soon after he had arrived, the duke of Locres appeared with his noble entourage of princes and knights all in armor. The king of Athens, accompanied by all his men, drew up his ranks in very fine order. Then the tournament began. The king of Athens lowered his lance and spurred his horse; the count of Phocides came to meet him. The king broke the count's lance and the blow threw the count violently to the earth. Next the king attacked Philibert, to whom he gave such a blow that he knocked him over his horse's rump. Then on all sides the knights moved forward furiously, and the Duke of Locres as well, who with great impetuosity confronted the lord of Teuffle, in such a way that the violence of the blow brought both the knight and his horse to the earth. Then with a similar thrust he struck another knight, whose shield and breastplate did him no good, for the duke's sword pierced them and reached the knight's flesh, and his extreme pain caused him to faint.

Zelandin the new knight sought to emulate the duke, and he showed himself worthy of his origins, for he was expert in martial arts, as if he had long been accustomed to practice them. When he saw the king of Athens, who was so strongly attacking the men within, he decided to joust with him. Because his lance was broken, he took one that was intact from one of his knights. Then with all his strength he attacked the king, who was riding toward him precipitously, and they clashed with such violence that they both broke their lances, striking each other with such fury that the king was thrown over the hindquarters of his horse; but it was Zelandin's misfortune to be hurled to the earth in a dead faint, along with his saddle, because the girths had broken. Zelandin remained for a long time in this syncope and swoon, and when he began to breathe, he said: "O God, what tormenting pain I feel!" He said this because of the sharp pain he suffered from his right arm being broken in his fall. Then with great haste he was taken up and carried outside the ranks, and seeing this, the duke immediately sent a young footman to find out what had happened. For his part, the king of Athens was extremely sorry about the misfortune, because he was afraid that his opponent's life might be in danger, and this caused him such distress that he wanted to remain at the tournament no longer. And so he named the duke of Foucquerolles chief and leader of his men. Then he went away and started toward the populous and celebrated city. When he had arrived there, he refused to stop at any place until he had been conducted into Zelandin's chamber. Zelandin was suffering such pain that he had taken refuge in his sad bed. He was attended by several surgeons who were preparing medicines that could heal him and make him well again.

For the present I shall leave this story to narrate the warlike proceedings of the noble knights, among whom the duke of Foucquerolles was performing great feats of arms. For he was attacking and knocking down everything he met, and having put his hand to his sword, he was striking right and left, so that nothing remained in front of him. On this account his men urged one another on, so that they fought vigorously. The duke of Locres tried to resist him; but his resistance did him little good, for the duke of Foucquerolles, with the help of the count of Merlieu and the lord of Housen, fought so hard that their opponents could not withstand their assault, but in order to avoid them were compelled to flee, wherefore the duke ordered a retreat, and everyone drew back. But the duke, who had succumbed to great distress because of his son's accident, inquired of the surgeons who had taken care of him, and they assured him that in a short time they would bring his son to a good convalescence. The duke immediately commanded the duchess to go to visit him, which she did, accompanied only by her two daughters, Zelandin's sisters. They found him very weak, but his pain was beginning to decrease. Each of the ladies said some words of comfort to him, giving him hope of a prompt recovery. Then after a while, fearing they were tiring and disturbing him, they left. But as soon as they had gone, Zelandin sent a footman to bring us to him so that he might, according to his custom, converse familiarly with us; but Quezinstra wanted very much to excuse himself, for he desired only to be alone in order to resume his sad complaints. Nevertheless, considering that no excuse would be acceptable, and that Zelandin might be annoyed with us, we obeyed his command, and went to his chamber. When we had arrived there, we discreetly offered the appropriate, customary salutations; then we asked him how he was, and if the surgeons, by means of their remedies, had not made his pain less intense. He replied that he felt some relief; then he immediately began to talk about the tournament and asked us which of the knights we thought Fortune had granted such felicity that he had won that day's victory. The instant he uttered these words I was sure my companion suffered a terrible interior pain, for his paleness showed it clearly; he began to grow cold, and his tongue became mute, which indicated extreme anxiety. Wherefore, pretending to have some business to attend to, he tried as best he could to take his leave. But Zelandin, who was not aware of the reason for his distress, said to him: "Quezinstra, for what reason are you now so silent? Why don't you tell me your opinion on the subject I asked you about? What new thing has happened to you which agitates and troubles you so much, as your pale face shows? If you are in need of something, tell me what it is, and as much for the sake of honor as for your benefit I shall provide it, as you may believe without my having to swear to it."

After these kind words I spoke up and said: "My honored lord, since you desire to be informed and completely understand so as to be amply sure whence proceeds my companion's distress, I shall be so bold as to reveal to you the secret of his heart, which I know to be so burdened that for the present, he would be unable to express it to you. But because between us there was never anything concealed, I shall declare the pure truth to you as he might do it with his own voice. To give you a clear knowledge of it, I want to inform you that the extremity in which he finds himself proceeds from the magnanimity of his heart. For when with your humane good will you kindly asked him who, in his opinion, had best performed in the tournament, your words transfixed his heart with such vehemence that he suffered no less pain than Hecuba when she saw the overthrow of Ilion.[36] For it made him recall that in his adolescence he was trained in such arts, being a man descended from a noble family with ancient origins. But blind and unstable Fortune, who daily persecutes the virtuous, led him into such misfortune that although he was blameless, he was expelled from his father's home. Hence it is hardly surprising that he finds it grievous to be exiled from his country and to have to abandon the society of the noble persons who procreated him and brought him into the light. Alas! it is very difficult to patiently endure such misfortunes, especially for those who aspire to live in a noble way in order to perform manly deeds worthy of praise, as I am sure Quezinstra wishes to do. Because he has no hope of being able to do so, his disappointment is so violent that it is not possible for him to temper it. And so, milord, I have divulged to you the cause of his regret, that through understanding it you may judge that he is not sad and dismayed without reason."

As soon as I had completed my faithful statement, I perceived that the young prince was moved to compassion; and then, with courteous urbanity he began to speak as his natural precepts and true nobility taught him, and said: "Quezinstra, I am extremely sorry that you did not earlier inform me of your misfortune, rather than keeping your grievous afflictions concealed and secret. For had I been informed of them, it would have been an opportunity for me to envisage the most suitable means for aiding you.

---

[36]The wife of Priam, king of Troy, and mother of nineteen of his children. In the *Iliad* she survives the sack of Troy and the loss of her husband and nearly all her children.

However, it is still not too late to do what can be done, and I assure you that I shall be attentive and vigilant in pursuing your interest and honor, and by experience you shall find that my words will not be different from my acts."

These mellifluous and gentle words gave Quezinstra some comfort, and he thereby regained the power of speech of which his excessive distress had deprived him. Thus he said: "Certainly, milord, I cannot conceive how my pusillanimous manhood will ever be able to offer you the due and fitting thanks your great generosity deserves. The way it seems to me at present is that if I were to devote the whole of my life to that task I should never succeed in fulfilling it. Nevertheless, I trust your good nature so much that I believe you will bear with me and also consider how inept I am."

The two companions are dubbed knights.

Chapter 8

A pollo, with his flaming locks, was returning home when, after having begged Zelandin's permission to leave him, we went away. When we arrived at the palace, we took our meal with some gentlemen. Then we immediately retired to our chamber, as much to converse as because the court was void of any sort of amusement, because of Zelandin's accident. We withdrew into our secluded rooms, talking of various things; stealthy sleep crept over us so much that it forced our weary limbs to seek the benefit of the desired repose; wherefore, to repair our nocturnal weariness, we got into bed.

Phoebus was already leaving his oriental domicile, driving away the nocturnal shadows in order to set free the reddening light, when we began to wake up. Then we dressed with great haste in order to go to the palace. As soon as we arrived there, we saw the duke, who, accompanied only by two of his closest gentlemen, was going toward his son's chamber. He found his son in a better state than he had expected, which caused him great joy. So he began to tell him that he had been so dismayed by his misfortune that the preceding tournament had ended without the knights daring to engage in any relaxing exercise. To this Zelandin replied: "Milord, I very affectionately beg you that out of consideration for my injury, from which I hope shortly to recover, you do not diminish the grandeur and sumptuousness of your court or prohibit the knights' delightful amusements, for that would cause me a distress more grievous than that of my body's infirmity." When these words were said, the duke soon wanted to go away; but inspired by some divine power, as it seems to me, he first asked Zelandin which of his gentlemen he desired most to keep him continual company. This seemed to Zelandin a very propitious beginning for his efforts to help Quezinstra, and so he said: "Milord, there is no company I should find more pleasant than that of these two young foreign gentlemen, because I find them modest, discreet, and superior to all others in their sovereign eloquence. But I am very displeased by the sadness of one of them, which proceeds from his not being able to perform knightly deeds as his predecessors always did; for I have learned from his companion that he is descended from a very noble family."

The duke replied: "Surely, Zelandin, I find it very agreeable to see this young gentlemen conversing with you, for I am persuaded that they are of noble lineage, just as you say, for although I have had scarcely any intercourse with them, on several occasions I have taken delight in contemplating their modesty and manly behavior. But I wonder what misfortune could have led them into such an unhappy state. I recall that when I first asked them about their homelands and the reason for their journey, they replied that it was only youthful curiosity, because they desired to visit a variety of lands."

"Ah, milord," said Zelandin, "you must not be astonished at that, for it is not the custom of wise and discreet persons to so lightly discover their secrets, which should not have come to my notice, had it not been for the pallor of his face, which indicated to me his interior pain. And when, upon my insistent request, his companion revealed it to me, I promised him that I should not fail to aid him. And so, milord, I beg and beseech you to agree to make him a knight; satisfying this noble desire of mine shall be no less praiseworthy for you than pleasing for me, because the time is right and nobility desires it."

The duke, persuaded by the urgent requests of his son, immediately told him that not only should his petition be granted (that Quezinstra be dubbed a knight), but to please him the more, he had decided to confer the same honor on his companion Guenelic. This decision was soon put into effect; for in the presence of his son and some of his gentlemen, we received from the duke's hand the order of chivalry, which was more pleasing to Quezinstra than was to Philip of Macedon the judgment of that child who, because of the great feats he accomplished, was called the Great.[37] Nor was Antiochus more pleased by Demetrius's victory.[38] As soon as these things had been done, the duke left his son in order to go to the temple to hear the divine service. When it was over, he returned to a spacious hall where tables were set up and covered with delicate viands of

---

[37] Alexander the Great.

[38] There are a number of men by the names of Antiochus and Demetrius who were members of the Seleucid dynasty, which won Syria and much of Asia as its share in the empire of Alexander the Great. The dynasty lasted from the end of the fourth century until the final loss of their territories in 129 B.C.

the sort which might have appeared on the tables of the noble Roman Lucullus. The great and sumptuous banquet finished, the noble princes and knights of the duke's company went away to begin to prepare themselves.

When we had retired to our chamber, Quezinstra began to talk joyously, and he said to me: "Guenelic, if you knew how happy I am that we can now count ourselves knights, I am sure it would give you great pleasure, although I am certain that for your part you aspire only to your lady Hélisenne, and had no desire to be granted the honor which has been given you without your having asked for it. Nonetheless, it should be acceptable to you, and you should be more grateful for it than if you had obtained it by entreaties, for a gift that precedes the request should be particularly esteemed. But it may be that the excessively puerile concerns that occupy your mind deprive you of good judgment; and *if such is the case*, you might not properly discern the light from the shadows, which would be a reason you might prefer wretchedness to glory, for that sensual love sometimes makes men pusillanimous. Wherefore it is feigned by the prince of poets Homer that the Phrygian, in battle with the Greek, avoided mortal peril by means of the goddess Venus, who, encircled and surrounded by a golden cloud, invisibly drew away her servant and set him down in her splendid and fragrant domicile. But you should understand that this shows nothing other than the pusillanimity of Paris, who, before he gave himself up to that unrestrained lust, was equal in strength and virtue to his brother Hector, the most warlike knight in the world. O, how strongly should be condemned and despised that Trojan shepherd for having thus become so effeminate and full of ineptitude! That should be an example to all modern gentlemen, and I have desired to remind you of it so that the love you have for Hélisenne might not destroy you.

On the contrary, you must be a true imitator of manliness in order that your manly activities might come to the notice of your lady, who will hold you in greater esteem, as Queen Guenevere did Lancelot of the Lake, on whom love had a very different effect than on that unfortunate Trojan, for he accomplished many warlike feats in order to be praised and exalted by his lady. You should follow his example. I am very sure that at first you will find the military art a little foreign, because you have not been instructed in it, having been completely occupied with the literary arts. Nevertheless, you will have to be guided and governed by observing those whom you shall judge to be most capable in these practices, and begin with good, virile courage, for the man who begins with temerity ends wretchedly."

Quezinstra faithfully admonished me in this way, and I replied: "If I ever was or am obliged and in debt to anyone, it is to you, and in great measure, because you admonish me regarding what you know to concern my honor and welfare; you deserve great praise for this, because it is no less a virtue to teach than to learn. But what distresses me is that I see you so fearful and afraid that cowardice and tenderness are taking up residence in my heart. You think this because I am under the conduct and power of the god of love, for whom you have no esteem, considering him inept and puerile. But I fear and dread that in the future you will repent and regret the small esteem you now have for love. Aren't you afraid you will succumb to the calamity that struck bright Phoebus, of whom you have so often spoken to me? Since I have not told the cause from which his love proceeded, I want to narrate it to you now. It happened because Phoebus was excessively proud of having conquered the great Python,[39] and for this reason he scorned and despised the god of love, telling him he did not deserve to bear either bow or arrows in his presence, but should hand them over to him, as to someone of marvelous strength. In this way he told Cupid that as his inferior he should humble himself before his sublimity. Cupid was greatly insulted by these proud and audacious words, and told him that he would soon make him feel the force and power of his arrows. And he did so, for without delay he flew up toward Mount Parnassus. When he had arrived there, without delaying or fearing to offend the divinity, with one of his arrows he transfixed Phoebus's heart, and the wound remained virtually incurable. This example should be sufficient to prevent you from further disparaging this sublimity, to whom should not be ascribed or attributed Paris's error, which I believe not to have proceeded from this source. For as I see it, in every case love makes a man prudent, eloquent, magnanimous, assured, cheerful, discreet, and generous; therefore I entrust myself entirely to his power."

As I was saying these words, Quezinstra began to look at me, and smiling, he said: "You do not always display all these qualities, for often when you are so woeful and anxious and sad because of this sensuality you are neither prudent, nor discreet, nor constant in the way you are now showing yourself to be."

Talking in this way, we went out of our chamber. As soon as we were in the street, we saw a very large company of knights who were going toward the place designated for the jousting, where the duke and duchess were already present. While we were taking delight in contemplating them, looking around me I espied a footman who, after having greeted us, told us he bore Zelandin's command that we should prepare ourselves with arms and horses, and that when we were ready, he would have these brought to us. We made the following response: "My friend, we are more obliged than we can say to milord your master for the benefits we receive from him, and we beg you to give him our very humble thanks. There-

---

[39]Phoebus (Apollo) killed the holy Python to avenge his mother against Juno, who had pursued her before she gave birth to him.

after, bring us the horses as quickly as you can, because we are afraid we may enter the tourney too late, since I believe it has already begun."

As soon as he heard these words, the footman left us, and with scarcely any delay, sent us two white horses, marvelously handsome and powerful, along with arms that were also white. We promptly began to ready ourselves, and setting out toward the tournament, I began to speak in this way, addressing myself to the goddess Venus:

The young knight's feats of arms.

Chapter 9

"O illustrious goddess, whose planet is one of the most refulgent of all the stars not fixed in the firmament, and which is named Venus because it comes to all things! (Sometimes it is also called Hesperus, Vesperus, or Lucifer, that is, light-bearing.) O marine star and planet daily preceding the morning sun! I believe you shone over my nativity, bringing to my conception an amorous influence and a totally sensual constitution. O holy goddess whose name I invoke, favor me by speaking on my behalf to the one who tempered his proud and severe eyes to acquire your benevolence. I am speaking of Mars, the god of battles; I am completely confident and hopeful that for your sake he will grant my humble request." When I had uttered these words, I no longer feared the mutability of unstable fortune. On arriving at the tournament, which had already begun, we paused for a while to contemplate the duke of Foucquerolles, who was exceeding the other knights in magnanimity of courage, so that nothing stood in his way. He cut down knights and horses with such fury and impetuousness that he spent the tournament throwing his adversaries back on the barriers, although the duke of Locres made it his duty to defend them. Quezinstra immediately spurred his horse and met the lord of Teuffle riding toward him; he gave him such a blow that he knocked both his opponent and his horse to the ground, and without breaking his lance, he went on to furiously attack another knight, whom he seriously wounded. Then he threw himself into the midst of the battle, performing marvelous feats of arms. And I, close behind him, was so favored by the goddess's lover, whom I had so humbly called upon, that I incurred no shame. Seeing this, the men on the outside lost their advantage, which greatly angered the duke of Foucquerolles. Taking a new lance, he rode toward Quezinstra, who also took a new lance, and they gave each other such blows that Quezinstra was stunned and about to fall. But the noble duke's horse, which had been in the midst of the fighting all day long, was not able to withstand the violence of the blow, and so the duke was downed along with his horse, and he remained a long time on the green grass. When he was able to do so, he quickly rose and withdrew beyond the ranks, extremely vexed, as is natural and customary in noblemen when they see themselves surpassed in virility, and he was as angry as he could be. The count of Merlieu came up to him and presented him with a powerful horse whose master he had just defeated. Then the duke began to be more cheerful, hoping to vindicate himself. So he confronted Quezinstra, saying to him: "Knight, prepare yourself for a joust, for it would grieve me excessively if you were to be the victor today without really deserving it." Quezinstra had no intention of refusing this challenge, but more ardent than a Lybian lion he exerted himself with all his strength, so greatly that the duke was thrown to the ground a second time. The clash of their lances reverberated even in the pavilions, making such a noise that it seemed some huge ship, blown by the violent and horrible Boreas had suddenly collided with a reef or rock. Then the ladies said: "God eternal! Who is this knight who has knocked down the duke of Foucquerolles, who earlier made everyone flee him, but who now has met his match?"

That is what the ladies said about Quezinstra, who had so seriously wounded the duke that the extreme pain he suffered did not allow him to speak or use his voice. But when he was able to speak again he said: "O God above! What a mighty knight! What a furious lance I have just encountered!" Then he was asked whether he wanted to get back on his horse, but he replied that it was urgent they should carry him as quickly as possible beyond the ranks, for he felt he should not be able to stay in his saddle. Hearing these words, some of his men immediately carried him away. But for the present I shall cease speaking of him in order to narrate Quezinstra's incredible feats. When he had taken his sword in his hand he performed so many chivalric deeds I could hardly recite them all, for he wrought such havoc among the men on the outside that any of them could consider himself fortunate if he avoided the fury of his enormous blows. The count of Merlieu made it his duty to resist him, but this did him no good, for in the end they were all defeated. Then the duke sounded the retreat, and the tournament was over. Both sides went off to remove their armor.

When the kings and princes had returned to the palace, they began to talk about the unmatched and inexpressible prowess of the new knight, and they all agreed that he resembled his courageous prince more than a simple knight, since no one was found comparable to him in warlike feats, and that he was worthy of being accorded great honor. The duke, seeing that everyone was extolling Quezinstra, called one of his knights and commanded him to go to our chamber to tell us that we must immediately come to the palace. As soon as we had heard this message, we went there, and were received with no less benevolence than Cicero by the Roman people when he returned from exile. Soon afterward the tables were set up, whereon we were so opulently served that it is unlikely that the wedding feast of Peleus and Thetis, at which the celestial goddesses debated the contentious question of who was the most beautiful, offered more delicious viands, with wines so excellent they equalled the nectars of the gods. When the sumptuous meal was over, the pleasant harmony of the sweet sound of musical instruments began, which harmonized with such melodious resonance that had Orpheus, Amphion, Thamyras and Dardanus been there, they would have suffered great sadness at being unable to make music so beautiful. While the knights and ladies were taking delight in dancing, the kings and princes were talking about the duke of Foucquerolles, who was lying grievously wounded in his chamber. They were considering which of them should be elected leader of the men on the outside for the following day; finally, they consulted and decided that it would be the king of Athens, who refused to accept the office, because on the first day he had been so unfortunate as to wound Zelandin. Nevertheless, he was urged so strongly to accept that he could no longer refuse. When this decision was made, a rich and superabundant collation of delicious preserves and wines was brought in, and afterward everyone retired to his chamber to rest.

However, Quezinstra and I went first to visit Zelandin, who welcomed us warmly and kindly; and among other things, he told us that he was extremely happy that we had begun our military careers honorably, for he had been given an ample account of them. Quezinstra replied: "Milord, if we have done anything worthy of praise, the honor is yours, for without your favor we should not have been received into the order of chivalry. Wherefore we offer you all the sempiternal thanks our present low rank makes possible, but not such as befits your dignity." With that, because of the late hour, we bade him good night. When we had retired to our secluded chamber, Quezinstra began to talk and to thank the divine power which had so favored him on that day. I responded only briefly, because I was greatly tortured by the violence of love, and awaited the end of this festival with great longing to set off on our pilgrimage to find my desired Hélisenne. Seeing how I felt, my companion put an end to his talk, fearing I should find it tedious. But a little while after we had gone to bed, the shadows and silence of the night, the vapors from my stomach, and the unaccustomed lassitude overcame my feelings so much that I fell soundly asleep.

Tithonus's oriental palace was already beginning to open in order to light up the world when we started to get ready. Beginning our early morning talk, we went to Zelandin's chamber. After we had greeted him, he began to address us and speak on a variety of subjects. Meanwhile a knight came in, nobly offered us his salutations, and then said: "Knights, to inform you of my reason for coming here, you must understand that at the command of the duke of Foucquerolles I have come to ask you on his behalf to agree to come to his chamber that he might be able to become better acquainted with you, for your knightly magnanimity has given him such a strong desire to know you that after yesterday's events he never ceased to ask about you until the duke, who had come to visit him, informed him on the subject."

Quezinstra replied: "Knight, I assure you that we are extremely obliged to the magnanimous prince, whose courteous good will desires to make the acquaintance of such poor knights as we, who are nothing in comparison with his highness. And so it is not reasonable that he should humble himself so far as to ask us, since he can exercise complete prerogative and authority over us, as over men who wish to be called his perpetual servants, and we are at his disposition."

So saying, we started out toward the prince's domicile, and did not stop until we had been led into his chamber, where we found him seriously indisposed. Nevertheless, he accepted and received us with great joy, and after we had exchanged salutations and greetings, he questioned us no less prudently than gently about our situation. We promptly and cleverly replied, without telling him the reason for our travels. He immediately understood, through the sublimity of his mind, that we wished to keep our business hidden and secret; and so he left this subject and began to say: "Noble knights, whoever you are, you are worthy of sempiternal praise on account of the incredible feats of arms you performed at yesterday's tournament. Because of the modest nobility I see in your persons, I am extremely pleased with your honor and usefulness, and I should desire that fortune might be as favorable to you today as yesterday, were it not for one thing I shall not conceal from you: should you win the victory, you will be able to choose among the maidens the one who pleases you best. On that account I am moved by an excessive anxiety, fearing that you might deprive me of the count of Merlieu's daughter, whom I love so fervently and cordially that if I were the possessor of as many treasures as Midas ever was, I should prefer to lose them all rather than give up my hoped-for reward."

When he had said these words, Quezinstra replied: "Milord, every blessing or honor a man receives in this low world he should attribute to the sovereign of the heavens, without being so ungrateful as to suppose that this honor results from his own merit. Hence, considering the happiness that it pleased the supernal goodness to give us yesterday, I humbly give thanks in my heart and in my words, and no praise that one might offer me will make me succumb to the labyrinth of presumption, which wish to avoid as much as I can. As for that which concerns you, I see no cause for alarm; for it may be that the dispenser of all good things has de cided to give this day's victory to someone else. But moreover, if I were to be so fortunate as to be granted a second day's victory, I assure you that you should not be deprived of your beloved. On the contrary, I should wish to make you her true possessor, and it would lie in my power to do so, for I have been told the victor can have the maiden he chooses or give her as a present to a prince or knight, as he wishes."

As soon as Quezinstra had finished speaking, with a joyous face the duke said: "O noble knight! You may be sure the promise you have made me pleases me more than would the conquest of all the land of Asia; for I have such great esteem for your courage that I have no doubt you shall return victorious. And now, if you wish anything I have the power and ability to give you, you must not delay telling me what it is. And out of appreciation for you I am willing to offer the same to your companion."

The end of the tournament
and the victory of the young knight.

Chapter 10

At these words we did not fail to thank him very humbly. Meanwhile, the dinner where we would be richly served was being prepared. After we had eaten, we begged the duke's leave and returned to our chamber. Then we immediately began to prepare ourselves, and with great haste we went to the tournament. After we arrived, opponents did not delay coming toward from all sides, among them was the king of Athens, the leader of the outside forces, who began first and attacked the count of Phocides with such impetus that he knocked him to the earth. Then he attacked another knight whom he struck so hard he bowled over both man and his horse. Seeing that, the duke of Locres assaulted him furiously; nonetheless, had the king's lance not broken, the duke should have landed on the ground like the others. Then the king took his sword in hand and performed such feats that it would be difficult to narrate them.

Elsewhere, Quezinstra joined the ranks, fighting with such prowess that everyone held him in awe; for he strove in such a way that those who saw him advancing toward them imagined themselves already on the ground. The duke of Locres, seeing such marvels, was filled with joy, and aided him as much as he could. They inflicted such losses among the outside forces that had the latter not been supported by the king of Athens and the lord of Housen, they should have been quite unable to endure the onslaught. But these two men resisted very strongly, and indeed the lord of Housen attacked me. We dealt each other such enormous blows that we were not able to sustain them without being unhorsed. However, we remounted without delay and were about to recommence our joust when Quezinstra, who was going through the ranks, cutting down knights and horses, came between us, and hence we were separated. The king of Athens was extremely annoyed when he saw his men being routed in this way, and so he took a new lance and rushed toward Quezinstra, who had prepared himself to receive him. Anyone who wished to write an account of the courage and magnanimity of the two champions would find it necessary to beseech not only Calliope, but all nine of the muses to provide a style suitable for describing their inestimable valor, which could not be expressed by human mouth. For they were moved by such a force that they not only made the earth tremble, but by their fury they made Apollo grow pale. Their encounter made such a horrible noise that it seemed Olympus and Ossa had crashed together.[40] The king's blow struck in the middle of Quezinstra's shield, piercing his chain-mail all the way to the flesh. For his part, Quezinstra hit the king in the middle of the breast and wounded him slightly. Their lances broken, they took up their swords, striking so furiously it seemed they could easily have split the highest mountains in icy Scythia. In their invincible courage, each of them gave and received so many blows that their shields were punctured and their armor pierced in several places. For a long time neither could win an advantage over the other, and no one could say who would prove superior; but finally the king could endure no more. Still, fearing the shame of being defeated, he conceived a subtle ruse, and as they drew back to catch their breath, he said: "Noble knight, since we are so evenly matched in strength that we shall be unable to reach our goals without killing each other, which would be an irrecoverable loss, I propose we have our armor removed so we can test our strength by wrestling; that would be more pleasing for the ladies than to see us cutting each other to pieces in this way." He said this because he was extraordinarily expert in that art. Although Quezinstra saw clearly that the king was about to be defeated, he graciously agreed. Their knights drew back on both sides to give them room, and stopped to watch them.

Right in front of the ladies' pavilion they began to grapple with their hands, arms, and legs, using all their strength. The king found Quezinstra to be an opponent of marvelous strength and great endurance, and so he came at him from all sides, like those who are besieging a tower and set up their devices all around to bring it down, and then begin their assault, first from this side and then from that, depending on where they think they have the best advantage. Nevertheless, in spite of the king's resourcefulness he was not able to gain the upper hand over Quezinstra.

---

[40]Mount Olympus in Thessaly was considered to be the home of the gods; Ossa is a neighboring mountain.

They fought so hard one might have imagined it was Hercules and Antaeus struggling against each other.[41] Nevertheless, after a long time, they separated for a moment to catch their breath, and then went back to it, making use of every wrestler's trick and effort they could think of.

The king, seeing he could not gain an advantage over Quezinstra, was greatly vexed, for he had never found a man who could hold out so long against him. So he strove with all his might, and so cleverly that he made Quezinstra stumble. Quezinstra nearly fell, but through force and nimbleness he avoided doing so, and then he settled himself firmly on his feet. In great wrath mingled with recklessness, he began to harass the king and press him very hard. Then, pulling the king toward him, Quezinstra pushed him back so harshly that he fell violently face down on the ground. Because the king was a large and powerful man, when he fell the impact was as great as that of a great tree falling in a violent wind or great storm. Everyone present was astonished by the king's fall, considering that he was so experienced in this exercise that up to that time he had never encountered his peer or match. The king was so shaken by his fall that he was unable to get up, and so his men tried to carry him away to dress his wounds; but because of the extreme pain he felt he began to cry out, saying: "Don't touch me, you will make my pain worse!" And then, he went on in this way: "O Eternal God! What a knight is this whom I have met! I am convinced it must be the god Mars, come down in human shape from the Olympic manors into this terrestrial and inferior region." While he was saying these words, the retreat was sounded, and an opulent litter was brought for the king. Thus everyone went away.

Not long after we had arrived in our chamber and taken off our armor, the duke of Foucquerolles sent for us. But Quezinstra excused himself, saying that a messenger from our country had come to communicate something of great importance to us, and it was necessary that we remain, but that we should not fail to visit him on the following day. With that the [duke's] messenger left. Then Quezinstra informed Zelandin that he was in some pain from his injuries, and Zelandin sent him the most knowledgeable and expert of his surgeons. The surgeon gave Quezinstra certain ointments to diminish his suffering, and told him that he would be completely cured within a week. After he had left and we were alone again, Quezinstra, who was no less happy than if he had won a battle victory on Olympus itself, began to say:

"Guenelic, we must indeed render thanks and eternal praise to the Sovereign Governor of the heavens, whose power informs all the universe, and offer up our victorious arms in his holy temple, since we have

---

[1]Antaeus, a Titan giant, was almost invincible in combat because he became stronger each time he was thrown to the ground. Hercules vanquished him by holding him in the air.

triumphed over such a noble assembly. We should no longer fear Fortune, who has been so adverse to us, for she will make us famous if we persevere in valor. It has never been thought good that the human spirit should always prosper; for in prosperity a man's strength cannot be so clearly demonstrated. Alexander the Great would have been praised incomparably had Fortune sometimes opposed him. Fortune has not been adverse to us, as we can now divine, in order to consume us, but rather to continue us in the habit of true valor in order to exalt us in triumphant fame and to attribute immortality to us. Atropos could not prevent from perpetually enduring the noble Scipio, chivalrous Camillus, victorious Caesar, triumphant Augustus, whose names are still flourishing, and this ought to produce great effects and emotions in noble hearts that believe that the true judge of heaven has not adorned the first ages with men so warlike that he does honor later times with similar valor. It is said that the beginning is more than half of all things. Therefore because our beginning in the military art has been so felicitous for us, we have only to persist without lapsing into idleness; for no reward of valor was ever accorded an idle man. Hence Juno sent Iris down from heaven to tell the powerful Agamemnon that every enterprising man must avoid idleness. Thus we must remember the misfortune of Hannibal, whom the ancients honored in prose and verse for the victories he won in Ausonia;[42] but after he allowed the wise Fabius to divert him and make his men slumber in Capuan delights, he never again enjoyed any success. I have told you all these things because I never want to fail to recall your honor and usefulness, for I desire them as much as my own."

Although these words were so ably spoken that they exceeded Virgilian eloquence, they lacked the strength necessary to move my will in any way. Nevertheless, I good-naturedly replied: "If it were possible for me to accommodate my will to yours without suffering a pain more acute than a violent death, I should strive to do so; for I have so much affection for you, because of your exemplary valor, that I would find it hard to express. Thus it is not necessary to consume time with a great wealth of ornamented and adulatory words, for since we first became friends my affection must have been evident to you. But concerning your point about martial feats, to which your heart is completely devoted, I assure you I praise and laud such a desire, but it rather displeases me that you seem not to have found a more convenient place than this city in which to exert yourself in these matters. For that reason it is as delightful for you to stay here as it is distressing and tedious for me; and that is why I cannot pattern my will on yours. I desire to investigate and search many places to find Hélisenne, and in doing that we should not fail to encounter various

---

[42]Ausonia is a poetic name for Italy.

adventures, and the idleness you detest so much would not accompany us. And so I beg you to abandon all worries that might cause you distress and trouble regarding our departure."

When I had said these words, I fell silent. Then Quezinstra saw clearly that my fear of prolonging our sojourn was making me extremely despondent. So he applied a remedy for my anguished suffering no less gently than prudently, by telling me that what he had said was not intended to make me despair of carrying out my desired enterprise, but only by way of fraternal exhortation; and he promised me that whenever it pleased me, he would prepare to depart.

While we were talking in this way, the kings and princes who were in the palace were taking delight in talking about Quezinstra, and they all agreed he was the flower of chivalry. The king of Boetia told the duke he thought we must be very high-born, for our nature and our manners, magnanimity, and gentility showed it clearly enough; on the basis of these virtues one might conjecture that in the future we should gain great honor. The duke replied: "Surely my opinion is not dissimilar to yours, and I am delighted that they have come to my court. But I am sorry that your fellow king cannot be here in the palace because of the bitter pain I am told he is suffering because of his fall. The duke of Foucquerolles is also unable to be present, for he has not yet recovered his strength and health, and that dismays me, for I should like them to be here with me. Nonetheless, I shall not fail to send for the knights so that the prizes may be distributed."

So saying, he ordered a knight to go to us and tell us that we should come promptly to the palace. The knight responded: "Milord, I believe that at the moment they are not able to come here, for I have heard in Zelandin's chamber that Quezinstra is slightly wounded, and in addition they wish to stay in their room for this day in order to give their weary limbs a little rest." The knight's words excused us from having to go to the palace until the next day, when we did not fail to go there.

Soon after we had arrived in the spacious hall, a knight came up to us holding in his hand a marvelously beautiful sword. After he had bowed to all present, he came to address the noble Quezinstra. With an eloquence equal to Cicero's, he began to speak in this way: "Very noble and valorous knight, whose admirable virtues are incredible and unparalleled: certainly, if I did not recall the ancients' maxim that said that praise should be delivered only after one's death, I should seek to praise and extol your singular prowess. But to avoid having the vice of adulation attributed to me—a vice all men of sound understanding flee like the plague—I have decided to abstain from doing so. Thus, knowing the exiguity, debility, and humbleness of my style, I should rather be silent than offer crude commendations, and so I shall hand over to you the fine sword you have won through your inestimable valor."

Quezinstra accepted the sword with the greatest joy; then, contemplating it and turning toward me, he said: "O, victorious sword, whose master was once so full of strength that no one could challenge him! He was the son of Alcemene,[43] and he put to death the seven-headed Hydra in the swamps of Lerna. He defeated the great lion, and then the Maenalian boar in Arcadia. He tracked and conquered the Parthemean hind, which had golden horn and iron hooves, and with his arrows he killed the Harpies of Stymphalos, near the Arcadian lake. He slit the throat of the mad fire-breathing bull that was in Marathon. He broke the horn of Acheleus, who transformed himself into various shapes. The tyrant Diomedes and the cruel king Busiris were killed by him. Antaeus the giant, the son of the Earth, was vanquished by him in a wrestling match. He stole the golden apples of the Hesperides by killing the dragon who was guarding them. He deprived Geryon, the giant with three bodies, of his cattle. He took the Amazon queen's girdle. Cacus the thief, the son of Vulcan, spitting fire from his mouth, felt his hand. He killed with an arrow Nessus the centaur, who was carrying off his beloved Deineira. He delivered Hesione, the daughter of Laomedon, from a monster. Troy was overthrown by him. He supported the heavens on his strong shoulders while helping the powerful Atlas. He tamed Cerberus, the three-headed dog, and chained him up. And in this way he inspired terror in all the inhabitants of Pluto's realm. O eternal God! I should be happy indeed were I to receive the smallest part of his prowess."

Quezinstra said such words to me, and considered himself fortunate that such a sword had fallen into his hands. While he was taking delight in saying these things, the duke, in order not to deprive him of the third day's prize, had all the maidens assemble so that he might choose the one he found most pleasing and delightful. Several of the maidens greatly desired to win Quezinstra's good will, as much because of his prowess as because of his sovereign beauty. For that reason, in a state of hope mingled with fear, they were awaiting the decision of his heart, just as litigants listen to the judgment and definitive sentence issued by their judges. But Quezinstra, wishing to keep the promise he had made to the duke of Foucquerolles, had secretly decided to choose the count of Merlieu's daughter. Still, he seemed to hesitate a moment; then, after having reflected and remained silent, he looked around, and when he had espied the maiden, he uttered these words: "No one should be surprised if I delay in choosing one of you, noble maidens, for you are all so full of gifts of grace and nature that, as I see it, each of you deserves an illustrious and

---

[43]Hercules.

magnanimous prince. Nevertheless, since it pleases the whole noble assembly that I should do so, I shall address the daughter of the noble and illustrious count of Merlieu." So saying, he approached her, and then, holding her refined, white hand and smiling sweetly, he said: "Most illustrious nymph, I beg you not to be sad that I have been so audacious and bold as to choose you, even though I am only a poor knight and a nullity in comparison with your sublime nobility and the great wealth of your family. Nevertheless, I have not done so with the intention of diminishing your estate, but on the contrary, in order to increase it; for I am determined—if you agree—to give you to the noble duke of Foucquerolles as his wife. He will accept you, I believe, with a joyful heart, because of your exceptional beauty, nobility, and virtuous prudence."

At these words the lovely maiden blushed, and there spread over her fair face a color like that of the noble scarlet on white ivory, which made her all the more beautiful to those present. Then she broke her sweet silence, and opened her mouth which was tinged with vermilion like the rubicund clouds when the sun hides itself, and in a soft voice more harmonious than the chords of Orpheus's lyre, she spoke these words: "Victorious knight, although in your courteous kindness you are pleased to say you are of low estate, that is a reason for thinking you are of very noble descent, for your grace, beauty, and eloquence manifestly demonstrate it. Wherefore I am willing to grant that it is very likely you could find a lady incomparably more endowed with corporal beauty than I am. But it seems to me that for the present your intention is not to concern yourself with love; for your valorous heart aspires to accomplish praiseworthy deeds, and your noble spirit desires to understand supreme things. But nonetheless you have not desired to give up [your right] without judiciously seeking to join me through matrimonial conjunction with this man whom you consider of a rank comparable to mine. I shall freely agree to this marriage, if paternal authority does not have other plans for me; for I could not exempt myself from daughterly obedience."

The maiden was greatly praised for her courteous and gracious words. The count of Merlieu was sent for, and he joyfully consented to a marriage that allied him with the duke of Foucquerolles. It only remained to find out how he felt in order for him to come to the palace to take possession of the prey he had so long pursued. Quezinstra and I promptly offered to announce the news to him, and so with great haste we went to his home, and he welcomed us no less warmly than Menelaus welcomed Ulysses when he was meditating and planning the destruction of Troy. And so he began to speak in this way: "O my unfailing hope! O unique healer of all my travails, by whose means I am led to consoled happiness! How true what we read about Elvidius, the philosopher and noble senator, who declared before the whole Senate that true friends are the instruments of fortune! You corroborate that conclusion, for through the fulfillment of your promise I see clearly the purity of your intentions toward me, and therefore I consider myself fortunate and happy. For no greater blessing could be conferred on a man than to have a companion as beautiful, modest, discreet, and prudent as the one your prowess has given me. Thus I am so pleased that I no longer feel any pain, and I no longer fear any ill fortune. I am not afraid of dying today, since I have attained what I most desired."

This said, he had a robe of scarlet velvet brought to him, because he wished to go immediately to the palace. Then, as soon as he was dressed, he left in the company of several knights and ourselves, his body refreshed and his soul elated. When he arrived at the palace he was received with great honor by everyone present. Various games and amusements were immediately begun; only the count of Phocides looked sad and anxious in the midst of the general joy, because he loved the maiden very much, and was not happy about this marriage and did not cease complaining about it. Quezinstra learned of this, and went up to him to admonish him, saying among other things:

"Noble Perseus, the son of Jupiter and beautiful Danae,[44] saved the gentle nut-brown Andromeda from a perilous serpent, a sea-monster ninety cubits long, and thereby justly won the maiden's love and the right to succeed to her father's throne. But Phineus and his adherents, through temeritous presumption, tried to disturb the royal wedding; as a result, several were killed, and others changed to stone. Wherefore, considering this, you ought to be careful not to disturb and hinder marriages, for fear the supernal Governor might justly put a miserable end to your life. I have said these things to you in a familiar way, illustrious prince, in order to dissuade you from trying to protest this marriage; for that would be neither noble nor legitimate, and it could cause you great grief."

When the count of Phocides had heard these remonstrances, considering that he could do nothing about it, he dissimulated the pain he felt in his sad heart, and did not let it show in his face. He tried to make it seem he took these modest and gentle words in very good part. So Quezinstra said that in his opinion and judgment he[45] was willing to be totally governed by prudent reason. While he was saying these things, everyone was

---

[44]Neptune demanded that Andromeda, an Ethiopian princess, be sacrificed to atone for her mother's irreverence. Perseus saw the girl chained to a rock by the sea and rescued her. Her uncle, Phineus, interrupted their wedding because Andromeda had been promised to him, although he had not tried to save her. A battle ensued in which Perseus killed his rival and finally the couple was married.

[45]The French text is ambiguous, or perhaps corrupt, here. A preposition could be missing—"he said 'to' Quezinstra"—since, given the context, it makes more sense for the count to say this to Quezinstra than for Quezinstra to say it to the count. We have left the

occupied with recreation and worldly pleasures, and so the day was passed and spent.

The wedding feast and the fruition of love.

Chapter 11

A t the hour when Phoebus has his golden-reined steeds brought outside his lofty house, Neptune's trumpet calls the ocean back to its place, and shortly afterward the princes and knights awoke from their lazy slumber. For they were urged to do so by the harmonious and jubilant notes issuing from the joyful throats of little birds. When they were all triumphantly appareled, they went to the lodgings of the duke of Foucquerolles, whom they found richly attired in a scarlet robe trimmed with gold and ermine. Thus he left his lodgings with the noble company. For her part, his future spouse was honorably accompanied by ladies of sovereign beauty and nobly adorned. The maiden was dressed in a robe of azure blue, embroidered with subtle needlework, and embellished with a prodigious number of large oriental pearls; on her head she wore a magnificent crown with so many diamonds, rubies, carbuncles, sapphires, emeralds, topazes, and chrysolites that she was surrounded by a great splendor. She was so resplendent with Venus-like beauty, grace, and eloquence, that glances from her green, sparkling eyes could have attracted an adamantine heart and subjugated it under Cupid's empire.

The noble company left in very beautiful procession. When they arrived at the temple, observing the ceremonies customary among the ancients, they were solemnly married. Afterward, they returned in the same way they had come. They were led into a spacious and beautifully decorated hall, where a sumptuous nuptial banquet had been prepared, which included more dishes than there were at the ancient wedding of Peirithous and the fair Hippodameia. When the meal was over, the sound of harps and musical instruments was heard; I dare not say they exceeded the harmonious sound of Apollo's lyre, fearing Marsyas's punishment.[46] Several young knights were trying to persuade me to dance, and it was fitting that I should respond to their urging, although my anxious, sad heart was not in accord with such solace. But in order to show myself courteous and capable of noble civility, I had to put on a happy face to dissimulate the unbearable internal suffering that cruelly tortured me.

---

subject of the verb "was willing" ambiguous to keep open the possibility that Quezinstra makes the statement about the count.

[46]Marsyas boasted that he could play the flute as well as Apollo, but lost a contest with the god. He lost and Apollo had him tied to a tree and skinned alive.

Alas! Delicate bodies can grow all too weary and painful when they are deprived of the sight of their beloveds. Alas! trying to cheer them up by games and amusements only augments their sufferings; for to the person in pain fire is a mortal threat: the soul cannot be cooled by such delights, which are only suitable for relieving corporal ills. But there I was in a place where everyone was intent on soothing pleasures, some dancing, others going to sit near the fair ladies in order to contemplate them and entertain them with amorous talk. Some of the princes armed themselves to go joust; the new bridegroom refused to go along, for he was far more interested in the nocturnal joust. When supper time came, the meal was no less opulent than pleasant with gracious and modest conversation, and they all enjoyed themselves until it was time to retire. Then the queen of Boetia and some other young ladies led the bride to her chamber, where she was put to bed. Soon afterward the duke came in; for him, the day had been tedious because of his intense desire to enjoy the fruition of love; and for this reason, he quickly had himself undressed and went to lie down next to his sweet beloved. Some of the young princes intended to go visit them, and as they were carefully investigating and searching out a way they could enter, they espied a half-open window, which allowed them to get in. As soon as one of them was inside, he opened the door to the others, and so they approached the lovers' bed, and urged and prodded them to get up. So they discovered that the nightgown had been torn through force and violence; apropos of which one of the young princes said that an inquiry ought to be made in the interest of love. "For such excesses must not remain unpunished; it is not forbidden to hunt rabbits, but we have to prevent the enclosures from being broken." Everyone heartily agreed, and they insisted that the young lady be interrogated under oath to determine who had perpetrated and committed such excesses. All pale and white, and lowering her eyes, she said that her nightgown had been torn as she was getting undressed. But this excuse was not accepted; for in any event, the delinquent and suspect person in the case had to be interrogated. Commissioners were named, both to interrogate the husband and to inform him of the day on which he would be expected to appear [before the court]: "the following day, at eight o'clock in the morning, in order to respond to the declarations, requests, and demands that might be made in his regard; and the fair lady along with him, as she had concealed a miscreant." Then they appealed to the court of love, where the trial is still pending and undecided. In such amusements the young princes diverted themselves, and then they left and allowed the bridegroom to enjoy his beloved. Although his passion was great in breaking down the door and the walls, it must be supposed that he afterward showed himself courteous and tender. And so everyone went to bed.

From the ocean had not yet risen the racing horses whose surging Apollo's son cannot restrain, when I speedily arose and dressed. Then, walking about, I began to think about the desired departure. Soon afterward Quezinstra awoke, marvelling at such great haste, and so he asked me the reason. I responded: "It is not the custom of Cupid's servants to sleep profoundly; rather, they always detest sleep. For lovers continually and without cease ponder and think about various ways to satisfy their affectionate desires; wherefore you must imagine that my thoughts are totally occupied in searching land and seas to find the lady the sight of whom has the power to restore sweetness and tranquillity to my wretched life. Believe that if Jupiter, the sovereign of the gods, wanted to beatify me and take me up into the supernal residence, as of old he did the noble Trojan Ganymede, I should not consider that felicity comparable to the sweetness and delight I could receive from familiar enjoyment of the eyes and the dulcet conversation of my much-desired lady."

On hearing this, my companion sweetly began to smile, and he said to me: "Surely, Guenelic, since you deem the fruition of love so delicious, I am not surprised that you are willing to risk any peril to enjoy such bliss. Therefore I promise you that promptly, and without further delay, I shall ask the duke's leave to depart, in order to satisfy your desire." Saying these words he quickly rose and dressed. Then we went to the palace, where all the nobility was present, enjoying themselves in various gay conversations. Then Quezinstra, desiring to please me, approached the duke and said to him: "Milord, the time has come when we must leave. Therefore, after having obtained your highness's permission, we shall depart, giving you all the thanks in our meager power, and not such as befit your sublime highness. But by means of your civility and clemency, you shall put up with the limited powers of those who will perpetually keep a ready memory of the benefits you have conferred on them, and neither distance nor time shall ever cause us to forget you. And as the years go by, the more we shall gain a true knowledge of your civil life and noble customs. But since our time is short, we shall humbly take our leave."

I saw that on hearing these words, the duke was somewhat moved, and he said: "Noble knights, I beg you to tell me the reason for your sudden departure. Is there someone at my court who has through folly or temerity provoked your wrath? If that is the case, tell me about it, and I promise you that the offense shall not remain unpunished, for it shall be given its just desert. But if it is rather that you want to leave my court in order to honor another court with your presence, this shall cause me great shame. For you must be certain that nothing you ask of me shall be denied you."

Quezinstra replied with great humility: "Noble prince, I assure you that nature has made us such that we shall always wish to be obedient to your highness, and we should desire to remain forever at your court if the urgent necessity of doing otherwise did not move us; for it would be too painful to us to be absent from this honorable court, which is the home of all nobility and the refuge of all virtues. How difficult we shall find it being far away from so many valorous knights! But if our bodies are deprived of this pleasure, our minds shall never be. And if the sovereign Governor of heaven and the general Arbitrator of the whole world permits us to complete our journey, we shall not fail to return to this renowned city in order to dedicate ourselves entirely to your honorable service."

When the duke had heard our ultimate and irrevocable decision, he looked very sad. But seeing that we said that our departure was so necessary, he did not wish to insist that it was otherwise, considering that no one should be so importunate as to ask for something it is not legitimate to grant. To give us clear proof of his good will toward us, he ordered a large quantity of money to be brought to us to pay for the things we might need on our journey, for which we accordingly thanked him. Then we went to the lodgings of the king of Athens, who was not yet healed, and we found there the duke of Foucquerolles, who offered us no less than the duke of Goranflos. After we had taken our leave of both of them, we went to Zelandin's chamber. He was more distressed than anyone by our departure. For when we came to say farewell, he was so troubled that he could not speak or make a sound, and he merely signified in his eyes the anxiety and sadness he felt in his heart. When he could, he spoke these words: "O Quezinstra, and you, Guenelic, tell me, whence proceeds your desire to leave so suddenly? Why are you weary and unhappy in this place, which ought to be so delightful to you? Consider that we have always cared each other, not in a servile but in a fraternal way. If you had been in a state of subjection, I should not be surprised if you wanted to free yourself from it; for nature cannot endow a man with anything better than liberty, and whoever deprives himself of it I do not esteem to be full of wisdom. But since you have resided here you have never been deprived of your freedom. I cannot imagine for what reason you desire to leave in such great haste. We replied immediately to these words, giving the same sort of excuse we had given the duke; and in addition we assured him that we should soon return, which cheered him somewhat. We embraced him warmly and said a sweet and friendly farewell, and then we went away.

Before we set out to sea, the good duke commended us to the protection and discretion of a merchant who was leaving for a distant country. As the sail billowed under the wind, I begged the divine clemency to moderate Eolus's ferocity and pacify Neptune. The wind was favorable to us. In a few days we arrived at the island of Cythera, which in olden times was propitious to navigators, as Strabo says in his geography.[47] In that isle

---

[47]Strabo was a Roman writer, historian, and naturalist of the first century B.C.

was constructed in ancient times a temple dedicated to the honor of the goddess Venus, as its inhabitants told us. I venerated and worshipped the place in remembrance of her on whom all my hopes rested. There we were able to see the place where the Phrygian first enjoyed Leda's daughter,[48] and was granted the fulfillment of the promise Venus had made him. In that place flourishes a plant which grew from the tears of that fair lady, which is called Helenion, and has the property of preserving ladies' beauty; it also has the power of moving men's hearts to love. We were on the point of picking some to give to the ladies of our country, but considering that it is apt to stimulate love in men's hearts, we put off doing so; for my part I already felt myself sufficiently weighted down by love's unbearable burden, which my companion wished to avoid.

On leaving this island we intended to head in the direction of the great city of Troy, but Aeolus's ferocity was so great that we were driven to the right, despite our desire to go to the left, and we were swept toward the coast of Africa, which is now called the Barbary coast,[49] and we passed by the islands of Crete and Rhodes on our left. From that point, the violence of the winds carried us into the Carpathian[50] sea and into the Pamphilian sea, where the gulf of Sathalia is, near the Turkish shore. Finally we found ourselves in the vicinity of the isle of Cyprus, where, once the sea had calmed, we made a stop to rest and refresh ourselves. Then we went back to sea, and fortune was so adverse to us that we were carried into the Lebanese[51] sea off the city of Sidon, which is in Syria. This is one of the greatest countries of Asia major; in the east, it has the great river of the Euphrates; in the west, Egypt and the Mediterranean sea; on the south coast, the Arabian sea; and on the north, Armenia and Cappadocia. It is divided into four parts. The first is called Syria of Mesopotamia, situated between the Tigris and Euphrates rivers, and there is the great ancient city named Edessa.[52] The second is Celosyria, in which is found Antioch, where Saint Peter was first a bishop. The third is called Phoenician Syria, and it is so named after Phoenix, the son of Agenor and the brother of Cadmus who founded Thebes, and who was the first inventor of the characters and forms of writing. And the fourth is called Damascan Syria, in

---

[48]Paris and Helen.

[49]A fairly precise itinerary is suggested, though the use of "left" and "right," rather than "north" and "south," seems odd. Guenelic and Quezinstra intended to sail northwest toward Troy, but were blown southwest, passing between Greece on the right and Rhodes and Crete on the left. Being blown around the Mediterranean was a convention of Greek romance, but Marguerite Briet seems determined to give these wanderings some trackable course in the real world.

[50]Probably an error for "Carian sea," Caria being a city on the coast of Turkey.

[51]"Mer libienne."

[52]Possibly a reference to Odessa, though it lies on the north shore of the Black Sea, far from the location given in the text.

which is found the city famed because of Saint Paul's conversion; it is situated near Mount Libanus, from whence springs and issues the very holy river Jordan. Thus we arrived in the port of Sidon, situated in one of these parts of Syria, still wanting to see the place where Paris, also called Alexander, took the lady who was the cause of all Asia and Europe being in commotion,[53] and so we set out in that direction. Without further wandering or diversion, we proceeded so expeditiously that we arrived in the port in which Prothesilaus left the ruins of his young life.[54] Attracted by the antique form of such a great city, we decided to inspect it all. There we saw the river, in ancient times called Panthus, that divided the city into two equal parts. It is said that the Tiber, which flows through the middle of the Rome, is similar to it. Contemplating it, and our desires being satisfied, we noticed a tomb which I recognized as that of Hector[55] because of certain words inscribed on it. Nearby was another on which words had also been engraved, and on reading them we could conjecture that it was the tomb of that Ajax who ran himself through with his own sword. Then farther on we saw another, at a considerable distance from the first two, and on this one it was written how, for the repose of Achilles' soul, the royal maiden Polyxena, who was of exceptional and resplendent beauty, had been immolated on this sepulcher by the hand of Pyrrhus, shedding her virginal blood as a sacrifice. After examining all these things, and the wind filling our sails, we went next to the Hellespont, which is so named because the virgin Helle was drowned there.

In a short time we sailed into the port of a very beautiful city, which was then named Eliveba,[56] where we decided to rest because we were extremely weary and worn-out by our long voyage. When we had arrived there, we conceived a desire to have a look at it. It was very well constructed and built, and fortified with large warlike and defensible towers. Several temples had been erected there with sovereign art; and in particular there was one as renowned as was formerly Apollo's oracle in Delphi. We went into this one, because of its beauty, and with hardly any delay a young woman came in; she was of surpassing beauty and richly adorned. With her was a large number of gentlemen and ladies, and she appeared in this place with such magnificence that she seemed to me the image of the splendid and brilliant lady Diana surrounded by her fair nymphs. All of them showed her extreme honor and reverence, which demonstrated that she held sway and power over the land.

---

[53]Helen's abduction by the Trojan prince Paris sparked the Trojan War.
[54]Prothesilaus was the first to leap onto the soil of Troy at the landing of the Greeks, although he knew that he would be killed.
[55]The most valiant of the Trojan warrior; he was killed by Achilles.
[56]Thought to be a palindrome of "Abbeville," Marguerite Briet's birthplace and home.

The liberality of a regal princess.

Chapter 12

While this lady was modestly contenting herself, she lifted her eyes with noble gravity; looking around, she caught sight of Quezinstra and me. Then she began to look at us attentively, and remained a long time without taking her lovely eyes off us. Then when she arose to leave the temple, she summoned one of her knights, and expressly commanded him to inquire who we were and what the reason for our coming there was. The knight, wishing to carry out his mistress's command, approached us, and as he had been enjoined to do, carried out his mission by courteously asking us where we were born and why we had come to that city. We replied in the same way we had earlier replied to the duke of Goranflos. As soon as he had heard our response, the knight left us to make his report; but the lady did not find it sufficient. For avid and eager to sate her eyes with new sights, as it is truly women's nature to be, she immediately sent the knight back to us, and he told us that milady commanded us to go to her palace, for she wished to learn more about us. When we heard these words, we obeyed her command without delay. When we were at the palace, we found the lady in a beautiful hall so richly tapistried it was marvelous to behold. After we had bowed and greeted her in a suitable fashion, she gently questioned us, and through her clever eloquence, she carefully persuaded us to agree to reveal our condition to her and give her a clear understanding of it. Because she thought some enmity on the part of the prince or some other misfortune was the occasion of our voyage, she generously offered us her possessions, saying that her will was so constituted that she desired that all unfortunate gentlemen should be warmly received in her city. For she had a singular desire to gratify and please nobles and virtuous people, who, she said, sometimes have more tribulations than others.

As soon as she had finished speaking, Quezinstra replied in this wise: "Most illustrious princess, since your highness has stooped so much as to kindly inquire into our low estate, it is only right that you should be informed. For if we occult and conceal anything from you, you might deem it to proceed from our great presumption, since you have so distinctly inquired into it, and moreover, we are perpetually obliged to your highness for the offer you have so liberally made us. For that reason, milady, I wish to tell you and make clear to you the reason for our voyage, which on my part is nothing other than to seek out and pursue adventures in the world, and also to accompany my companion here, who is toiling for another reason. But you will excuse me for not explaining it, since it is not right to divulge a friend's secrets."

The fair lady then said to me: "My gentleman, I am sure you will not delay telling me the cause of your travail, any more than your companion has." In a low voice and with shame I promptly replied that lord Love was to blame. Seeing how I changed color, the lady imagined she had importuned me too greatly; therefore, with sovereign wit, she began to praise the amorous enterprise, saying that love sometimes stimulates his servants to undertake laudable works until they are held in great esteem and repute by all, and especially by their ladies. For that reason she advised me to persevere, and to toil and suffer for love, in order to gain more esteem than I should by leading an idle life.

After this, the servants began to set the tables, where we were served so copiously and with viands so delicate they had the power to make people recover appetites they had lost for any reason. After the sumptuous service, milady wanted to go enjoy herself in the beautiful, pleasant, and delightful gardens. But news arrived that caused her excessive anxiety; it was that a powerful admiral with countless ships was coming to lay siege to her city. Hearing this sad news made the lady so anguished and woeful that it would be difficult to describe her bitter pain. For in the presence of some of her knights and ourselves, she began to weep and cry, with grievous laments and exclamations, and among other things she said:

"O fortune, blind and unstable stepmother of felicity! Nursemaid of unhappiness! Cruel enemy of tranquillity! Instigator of death-dealing wars! Adversary of repose! Leader of adversities! Alas! why do you want to persecute me so cruelly? O accursed and hateful fortune, how many clever minds and excellent persons you have stained and brought low through your variation and your lack of consideration! Alas! See to what distress and bitterness you have condemned me; wherefore I have reasonable cause to accuse, detest and vituperate you. Thus I must in justice blaspheme against Atropos, for not having deprived me of life before I succumbed to such a vexation. O! How happy I should have been if the sovereign of the heavens had allowed it to happen that the unfortunate day my mother brought me into this transitory and mortal world a violent whirlwind had carried me off to some deserted mountain, or I had been drowned in the marine currents and hidden by the shadows of death. Alas! I am certain that if this cruel man were to realize his iniquitous goal, which is to overthrow and totally destroy this very flourishing and populous city, he would be so irritated and angry with me that I cannot foresee the contumely, opprobrium, and insults that I should have to endure. Therefore I can conjecture that because of my persistent and continual woe, my sad and painful life shall prematurely end."

Continuing her tears and moans in this way, the lady tormented herself so much that everyone present took pity and felt sorry for her. They did all they could to comfort her, reminding her that the city was so strong and warlike that it would not be in the power of its enemies to take it by assault, and hence there was no cause for such despair, but on the contrary one ought to be hopeful, considering that the city was equipped with a great multitude of people well-suited to martial exercise, and by means of whom the enemies might be repulsed.

While this was being said, I was as distressed as if I were navigating with a frail and leaky vessel the tempestuous seas of Scylla and Charybdis. Seeing that it was impossible for me to leave, I was so afflicted by cruel tribulation that it would be difficult to express it. Seeing this, Quezinstra led me to the place that seemed to him most secluded and silent. Then faithfully, with judicious and well-intentioned arguments, he gently comforted me, saying: "Guenelic, I beg you to try to mitigate and temper the bitter pain that so continually tortures you. Consider that if we were to let ourselves be troubled by every misfortune that occurs in this hemisphere, without the virtue of patience having the power to overcome the passions by which we are agitated and persecuted, matter and cause for despair should come along every day. For there is nothing in this wretched world that one can take as a secure foundation. You see this noble lady, who is so opulent and rich. Fortune has been favorable to her thus far, and has exalted her, but now, through its variable mutability, Fortune seems to want to embrace her with all its force, and then suddenly, through an unforeseen calamity, prostrate her and bring her down. Nonetheless she will have to restrain her wrath and show herself to be strong. For if anything good came from our laments, complaints, and weeping, and if our sad thoughts could thereby be purged, then tears would be more precious than oriental gems.[57] But since tormenting oneself is a pain endured in vain, without the expectation of any good result, we should prudently avoid such lamentations."

Through such words Quezinstra hoped to console me. But I was so outrageously vexed that I took no comfort from them, and in anger I furiously uttered these words: "O gods so vigilant to my detriment! O times prompt and ready to cause me harm! Alas! Where am I being led? O Lachesis and her sisters! If to others you are bitter and cruel, to me, wretched as I am, you would be most pleasing, though you bring about

---

[57]The French text seems self-contradictory here: "Car, considerant que aulcune utilité ne vient de nostre lamenter, plaindre, et larmoyer, par lequel se expulser povoit nostre dolent penser, plus appréciées seroient les larmes que gemmes orientales." We have taken more than the usual license in translating what we take to be the intended sense.

the dissolution of the weary and amply numbered[58] body, in which all the immobilized members oppose the vital forces; when the body can no longer bear them, its life ceases. Alas! There is no body in the world more care-worn and weary than mine. And thus it should dissolve." I spent my time in uttering such words accompanied by hot tears and a multitude of sighs. If the day was bitter for me, the night had no rest for me. Faithful Quezinstra was so seriously disturbed by anxiety that it seemed to him he felt the sadness of my soul and the misery of my body. He tried assiduously to comfort me with kindly and gentle words.

At the hour when toward the east fair Aurora began to appear, driving away Lucifer[59] and the other stars, which according to their custom remain longest in the sky, we began to get up and dress. Then, anguished and woeful as I was, I moved my care-worn and sad body, and we went to the palace, where the mistress was already present, sitting on a magnificent seat, in no less majesty than Juno [when] she sits in the celestial council. Then she began to address her knights in her sweet voice; they fell silent, and she uttered these words: "O faithful men, you understand very well why this admiral—a scoundrel and a wicked man—seeks to persecute us and finally reduce us to total ruin and extermination. It is nothing other than my refusal to be joined to him through the bond of marriage, to which I should not consent even if he were the master and peaceful possessor of all the world, as much because of his customary actions as because of his advanced age, which is not in any way suitable to my flowering youth. And so, having considered all these things, you are faithful people who are attached to my honor and welfare; such a marriage would be no less vexing for you than it is distasteful and displeasing to me. You should also fear that you might be ruled and governed by an ignoble prince who might institute iniquitous and evil laws, whereby you would succumb to such great heart-sickness that you would find it a very painful thing to endure. For that reason, out of magnanimity of heart, each of you should be persuaded to preserve and guard this fair city, which, if it were destroyed, would scarcely ever be able to repair such a loss."

After she had said these words, everyone present responded with a single voice that they were determined to vigorously defend the city, and that they hoped to drive the enemies away. While they were saying this, the admiral arrived with five hundred and sixty ships, and landed in the port, which was called Hennerc, and at once they spread out their sails, hoisted their flags and standards into the air, and set up several tents and pavilions, among which was that of the admiral, which was marvelously

---

[58]"Fourny de nombre."

[59]Here, Lucifer is Venus, or the morning star.

rich and sumptuous. But meanwhile, the city-dwellers were arming themselves, and came out in very fine order. Seeing that, the enemies were struck by admiration at the sight of the great multitude of knights; none of them was so audacious or vigorous that he felt no fear. Nevertheless, recovering their spirits, they took to their arms, and there was a marvelous conflict and a deadly battle. The city-dwellers showed very clearly that they were astonishingly warlike, for they began to press and injure their enemies so cruelly that their violence forced their adversaries to retreat, and the admiral's forces could not have held out much longer had his brother, who was very skilled in the military arts, not arrived. He began to urge them to recover their strength, and thus they made much work for the city-dwellers; there was an extraordinary shedding of blood on both sides as the execrable battle continued. Apollo began to decline; wherefore everyone, weary and worn, began to leave, and the men from Eliveba returned to their city.

The assault on the city, the imprisonment of Guenelic, and his deliverance.

Chapter 13

After the bloody encounter, the enemies tried daily to make several assaults, which the city-dwellers strongly resisted. Quezinstra was a great help to them, as he clearly manifested his marvelous valor through incredible feats that made him known to the whole army. But sometimes I was taken for him, since I bore similar insignia. One day, as the enemies were attacking with all their strength, hoping to completely destroy the city, which they were unable to do because of the [city-dwellers'] courageous defense, and especially because of Quezinstra, who persevered in such magnanimity that no one could resist the vigor and strength of his arm, for the force of his blows was so great that they made everything tremble, even the stars. The city's knights, seeing such an astonishing sight, were marvelously cheered, and determined to aid him as much as they could, so that they would have made their enemies flee, had it not been for the admiral's brother, who offered a vigorous resistance, and urged his men to defend themselves in a manly way. But their resistance would have been of little use had it not been for the misfortune that happened to me, which was this: by freeing and separating myself too much from Quezinstra, I got so far advanced among the enemies that I could not avoid being taking prisoner and led away. Quezinstra was so distressed by bitter, stinging internal pain that his vigorous courage failed, since he was more concerned about my death than about my capture. And so without delay he left and went back within the city, and the others followed him. But when he was in his chamber, no longer able to endure the extreme suffering that oppressed him, he lay down in his sad bed as a last refuge, and there began to give vent to grievous laments and sad regrets, which he continued assiduously without anyone being able to encourage or comfort him.

Thus my faithful companion was tortured and woeful, thinking me more likely dead than alive, for he did not know that I was in the magnificent pavilion of the admiral, who began to ask me questions on various subjects, which I could hardly answer because of the distress I felt. But meanwhile a knight came in who in a loud voice testified that I was the warlike knight who was continually wreaking such havoc on them, saying my white insignia clearly demonstrated it. Then at the admiral's command I was immediately led away to a dark prison which much resembled a place reserved for those who have committed the crime of lèse-majesté. Thus I began to pitifully complain, raising my voice so much that I could easily be heard a great distance from the place. Then in a trembling voice I said: "O unfortunate and miserable Guenelic, what sinister and envious fortune has brought you to this place? O my lady, whom I so much desire! I see clearly that the heaven, the stars, the winds, the water, the earth and all the elements are conspiring to destroy our great love. Alas! At this time I feel myself totally destitute of my saving hope, whereby I am so violently afflicted that it is not possible to find any suffering comparable to what I am enduring: neither that of Erysichthon, who in his exorbitant hunger ate his own flesh, nor that of Calydonian hunter,[60] whose cruel mother put an end to his life by means of the fatal firebrand, nor that of Pelops, whose avaricious father presented him to the gods to be eaten, nor that of Pelias, whose daughters were persuaded by Medea to cut him to pieces; all their pain taken together is nothing in comparison with mine, for death, which came suddenly for them, was their ultimate and final pain. But woe is me! I can foresee that the end of my suffering shall never come."

Lamenting and weeping in this way, I complained and exclaimed, whereby I was soon almost out of my senses, my courage destroyed and stunned by unbearable suffering. But when the hour came at which Tithonus shows himself, distressing news was brought me, for the prison guard, crying out furiously, came before me and said: "Leave this place, you wretched creature, and come to receive your final punishment, to which you are condemned; for on the preceding day, the admiral and his men consulted and decided to put an end to your life, which has been so damaging to us. For as I have heard, an infinite number of knights have

---

[60]Meleager.

died at your hands." These words entered my heart with such great vehemence, because of the anticipation of death, that I was no longer able to hold up my feeble members, and I fell down as if dead. Then, after a time, when I had recovered some of my strength, I was surrounded by cruel officers, who hurled against me every insult they could think of. And then, on the way to the admiral's tent, which was a fairly great distance away, I began to speak and said:

"O poor unfortunate man, yesterday you detested your sad and painful life and desired death, which you did not imagine to be so close to you. O sovereign governor of heaven, whose justice and clemency are virtues peculiar to you, see my innocence, for your supernal goodness knows I have not deserved such a punishment. Do not withhold your grace from me, any more than you have from many others. You allowed the legislator Moses to pass sheltered through the perils of the sea. You also delivered the innocent Hebrew woman from the fire prepared for her. To Jason you granted a fortunate return. You saved Leander so many times. To Phrixus you sent a golden sheep to swim under the sea-waves. You kept Europa on the bull. You guided Arion on the dolphin. You did not deny the hero Hercules the descent into Pluto's realm. You exalted the builders of Rome to the supreme heights of the sovereign empire. You delivered Cyrus from the countless multitude when he was exposed to be devoured by wild beasts. Therefore since you have granted your mercy to so many people, may it please your benevolence to succor me; and do not permit me to give up my being through such an unfortunate and premature death. Alas! If only before I went to visit the kingdom of Minos I might be granted such bliss as to contemplate the lovely face of my lady, I should be eternally content; or if at least I might be drowned in the sea and afterward my body, floating on Neptune's waves, might arrive in a place where I could be found by my dear lady Hélisenne, as of old Alcyone found her beloved's body, and the youth of Abydus was found by his beloved Hero.[61] Had that happened, I am sure my sweet beloved, seeing my remains, could not prevent some liquor from flowing from her celestial lights.[62] And although pallid and frightful death would render my body pitiful and broken, she would not hesitate to repeatedly kiss my pale and deathly face, whereby I conjecture I should still be able to feel some pleasure from my beloved." This said, I fell silent for a while, and then I continued: "Alas! when I think it over carefully, I should not want such a thing to

---

[61] Alcyone married Ceyx, son of the morning star, who drowned at sea. Hélisenne suggests that it was Alcyone's body that was found by Ceyx, but it seems to have been the other way around, and we have rephrased the text to reflect this. Abydus was the home of Leander, who was drowned as he swam across the sea to visit his beloved Hero; she found his body and (like Alcyone) threw herself into the waves.

[62] That is, she would have shed tears.

happen, for perhaps my death would cause hers, because her delicate and loving heart would be overcome by excessive and bitter pain, would be unable patiently to endure and sustain such a misfortune, and thus I believe the spacious sea would serve her as a sepulcher. And so the death which has been prepared for me will be happier than the one I imagined, for the premature death of such an excellent lady would be too great a loss."

Expressing such piteous complaints, I approached the admiral's pavilion. But the knavish and wicked people who were conducting me were derisively laughing at what I said, and mocking me, and they said to each other: "I believe this man has lost his senses, seeing that he knows himself to be near his end, and yet he cannot forgo speaking of his love." Saying such things, we were soon in the presence of the admiral, who commanded, as soon as he had laid his cruel eyes on me, that I should be promptly led to the designated place where I was to be decapitated. Then, without further delay, I was taken away. But it seems to me that some divine power inspired the admiral's brother to insist on the contrary, and addressing his words to his brother, he said: "Milord, I am most astonished that you wish this valiant and warlike knight to die; in addition to his courage he possesses such natural beauty that I have taken a singular pleasure in looking at him, wherefore I should be greatly saddened by his death, which he has not deserved. I am certain your men urged and pressed you to put an end to his life; but I say this advice is iniquitous and unjust; and you should not be so credulous, but first carefully consider and reflect, and then pronounce your sentence and conclusion."

When he had said these words he fell silent. But the admiral replied in this way: "Brother, I beg you not to try to persuade me to preserve this man's life, for he has daily injured and oppressed my knights to an extent that would be incredible for anyone who had not seen his admirable deeds, which surpass those of all other knights. And so when I consider that he alone would be as harmful to us as the powerful Hector was to the Greeks, I would not for anything in the world acquiesce to your importunate request. Therefore I beg you not to urge me again to consent to his being freed; for you must believe that to ask for what is not suitable, and to grant what is not legitimate, is a manifest wrong."

The admiral's brother was outraged by these harsh words, and in great anger he said: "Milord, I see clearly that a faulty opinion has as much power over you as a good and well-founded reason, and this causes me extreme concern and distress, considering that such a prince should not behave in this way. On the contrary, he should be slow to anger and willing to listen, with unfettered judgment, mature counsel, setting aside passion and keeping his eyes on justice. But since you are far from these praiseworthy conditions, I shall separate myself from you. You shall see that after you are deprived of my aid, your enemies will easily be able to consume and confound you, for you know that in many assaults and conquests of cities you have had extreme need of my help. Nevertheless you are resolved to be so ungrateful that you will do nothing to thank or please me; and you accuse and blame me, saying that I importune you too much and that my request and supplication is unreasonable, because you imagine the great prowess of this knight might be too unbearable for us in the future. But in order to free you from this fear, I am happy, if you agree, that this war should terminate and come to an end through hand-to-hand combat between the two of us; this will be very advantageous to you, my brother knight. For you see clearly that this city is so warlike that it will be difficult to satisfy and fulfill your ardent desire without losing a countless number of knights. Moreover, you are not certain of being the victor; wherefore you should not defer the carrying out of this enterprise of mine, especially since you know that I am rather experienced. If the eternal Creator permits me to prevail, it will be a deed that will win me perpetual praise. If it happens that I am defeated by this knight, I shall not deserve vituperation, considering that no one more valorous than he can be found. And so I beg you to think over this proposal, and then to tell me your decision. If it is in conformity with mine, all that remains is to send some emissary or ambassador to the lady to find out if she is willing to agree."

After he had attentively listened to and reflected on these persuasive remonstrances, the admiral's resolution was somewhat shaken; he remained taciturn for a time, without uttering a word. Then, turning toward those he deemed the most faithful, he asked their opinion. They assembled and moved off a bit, where they consulted and debated for a long time. Their conclusion was that the proposal made by the admiral's brother's should be put into effect, for it was the best and most expedient way to reach their goal without consuming time in this vexatious war. They all told the admiral that he should not refuse his brother's request, since he made it so fervently, and that they had no doubt that he would be the victor in this battle. They said this because he was a knight of marvelous valor and had performed many feats.

As soon as they had pronounced their decision, the admiral called his brother to him and said: "You have so persuaded me by your continual urging that I am constrained to grant your request. Thus it remains only to find out whether the lady will consent to your plan, and I leave that task to you." Turning toward me, he[63] said: "Knight, I have such esteem for your valorous magnanimity that I believe you would sooner expose yourself to the peril of death than do anything that might tarnish your

---

[63]The context suggests that it is the admiral's brother who now speaks.

137

splendid reputation. And so once we have received your word of honor as a guarantee, I shall not hesitate to allow you to return to the city. You shall present our proposal to the lady, as I shall now clearly explain it to you: if she desires to terminate this odious and distressing war, she can do so, on the condition that you or one of her other knights is willing to undertake the [single] combat as I have described it. If it happens that her knight is the victor, we promise to lift the siege of this city and never again cause them any trouble, and moreover, if she agrees, we shall be perpetual confederates. If it happens that the gods give me the victory, we shall be able to do as we like with her and with her city, without her having any right to protest. That is our final resolve, which you may report to her."

When he had finished, the iniquitous people who had led me there said: "Milord, if you wish to be very sure of his promise, make him promise by the faith he owes his beloved, which he would not ever wish to break, for he has such great affection for her that no matter what fear of death he might have, he has never stopped talking about her."

These words made the admiral's brother laugh, and he said to me: "Since you are such a perfect lover, I want no other promise than the faith you owe your lady."

I replied: "Milord, you should consider yourself certain on that account, for rather than break that faith I should expose myself to a peril greater than the winding passages of the Cretan labyrinth. Since it is my good fortune that you allow me to go announce this news, after receiving your permission and leave, I shall depart to carry out my mission."

Saying these words, I departed, having discarded and shed the greater part of what lay heavy on my heart, and I said: "O sovereign and exalted God, how can I thank you? Words would not suffice, since you are the creator of wisdom; neither would real thanks,[64] for you are the lord of all. To offer you the life you have preserved for me would be nothing, for you are its creator. But not to succumb to the detestable vice of ingratitude, I shall every day assiduously present my sacrifice in your holy temple." Saying such words, I joyously went on my way with a certain hope of attaining my desired contentment.

When I arrived in the city, I could scarcely move because of the multitude of people that crowded around me. They said: "Here comes the knight we had thought dead, concerning whom the flower of chivalry, who is his companion, is so excessively vexed." One of those who said this went to tell Quezinstra the news, and he was so overjoyed that he awaited my arrival with more desire than the ladies of Greece awaited the arrival of their husbands. When I was finally led into his chamber, he gave

---

[64]"Reales." Real (substantial, actual) as opposed to "mere words."

me a welcome as magnificent as it was warm, and we could not refrain from shedding a few heartfelt tears. After some gracious and gentle discourse, I explained to him the reason I had come. Promptly and without delay, we went to the palace, where the lady was present with a great number of knights. Then, with due and fitting reverence, we greeted her, along with the noble company, who were all astonished by my arrival, for they thought I had been execrably cut down in battle. But when they saw me, they were extremely happy, and especially the lady, who kindly asked what misfortune had befallen me that had caused my absence. I explained everything to her as modestly as I could, without holding anything back; then, I began to tell her about the admiral's proposal, as I had been enjoined to do, without exceeding the bounds of my express charge. When she had heard everything in detail, she remained extraordinarily pensive; then she began to tell her counselors that it was very urgent to discuss this affair to be sure that they made the right decision. The most experienced and wise began their consultations immediately, and remained for some time without arriving at a decision; then as a final resolution they concluded and said that if the foreign knight wished to undertake the combat, the lady ought not to refuse him; and that they firmly believed he would obtain the victory.

As soon as they had said these words, the noble lady, who surpassed all the others in beauty and good sense, addressed herself to Quezinstra, and said to him: "Noble knight, you have heard the decision of my people, who have clearly shown their confidence in you. For my part as well, I believe without a doubt that if your magnanimity is willing to agree to take charge of this matter, that the enterprise will be carried out to your honor and benefit as well as mine; but I do not dare to ask this of you, considering that you are not my vassal or subject, and therefore you are not obliged to do my bidding. However, were I so fortunate that some divine power inspired you to do so, I should consider myself perpetually obliged to your nobility."

Quezinstra was as attentive to the angelic princess's words as the queen of Carthage was to the lamentable memories of the pitiable Trojan.[65] He replied in this way: "Illustrious lady, be assured that the kind welcome and honorable treatment you have given us has had such an effect on my heart that I am extremely distressed by your present calamity and misery, from which to liberate you I should risk a peril greater than that risked by Hippomenes in undertaking to race against the virgin Atalanta.[66] So when you wish you may order me, your knight, to be ready and

---

[65]Dido, listening to Aeneas's account of his travails. Cf. Virgil, *Aeneid*, Book 4.
[66]Atalanta, in an attempt to avoid marriage, agreed to run a race with each of her suitors. She won every race until she ran against Hippomenes, whom Venus had helped by provid-

prepared tomorrow at whatever hour they shall be disposed to meet me. Have no fear because your enemy provokes you, but remember what the queen Semiramis wrote to the king of India: battles are won by valor, not by words."

As soon as she heard Quezinstra's response, the lady wished to promptly send a messenger, but I told her that it was fitting that I should without delay return as I had promised, for I should rather die than break my word. But before I left, I fervently beseeched Quezinstra to allow me to fight this battle, which he would not allow me to do, telling me that he believed I had enough vigor in my heart and enough strength in my limbs to undertake it, but that since he was more experienced than I, the outcome would be more certain. On hearing these words, to please him I did not persist in my opinion, and thus I departed. When I arrived in the admiral's magnificent pavilion, I made an ample report of what I had been ordered to tell him. But as soon as his brother heard my report, he asked me why I did not undertake the combat myself. To which I replied: "I should very much have wanted to do so, but to satisfy the desire of one of my companions, who was even more desirous than I, I did not insist in order not to incur his indignation." The knight did not inquire further, and he said nothing more about it until the following day, when the two knights arrived in the place where the single combat was to take place.

The combat of the two champions to put an end to a war.

Chapter 14

Apollo was speedily driving his great chariot down toward the tail of the supernal lobster,[67] lighting up the middle of his sphere by his violent heat, and ripening all the terrestrial fruits, when the two valorous knights came together, at the assigned hour, in the presence of many people. The admiral's brother was richly armed and was mounted on a powerful and fast horse; it was descended from one of Mars' horses and an elephant. Quezinstra had no arms other than his white ones, but one of the lady's relatives had presented him with a horse that was descended from Pegasus. It was wonderful to see the exceptional magnanimity of the two knights, whose valor was so great that the tongues of a thousand poets could not express it. For each of them showed himself to be full of enough bravery to confront the proud, vain, and cruel god Mavors, who

---

ing him with three golden apples. He threw the apples in front of Atalanta during the race, and because she stopped to pick them up, she was defeated.

[67]That is, toward the constellation Cancer.

nevertheless inspired great fear in the marvelous giants.[68] While the whole assembly, on both sides, was extolling the valorous air of the two champions, they were moved by such vehemence that the frightful sound they made when their lances met was no less than that made by Jupiter's blacksmith Vulcan, the maker of thunder and lightning. It seemed old Saturn had been thrown from his seat along with the whole frame powerful Atlas supported. The warlike Quezinstra struck the knight in the middle of his shield with such force that he penetrated all the way to his flesh, and this blow knocked him to the ground. Quezinstra's shield was struck in the same way, and he could not avoid falling. But he got to his feet first, and took his good sword in his hand and rushed toward the knight, who had quickly risen, and gave him such a blow on the right arm that he made him sink to one knee. For his part the knight gave an extraordinary blow to Quezinstra's helmet, and tried to strike again, but noble Quezinstra with great agility leapt to one side and was not hit. The blow fell on the ground, so hard that the sword could hardly be pulled out. Meanwhile, courteous Quezinstra waited until the knight had pulled out his sword. Then, they began to give each other such violent and enormous blows that they chopped their shields and their armor to pieces and pierced it everywhere. For a long time no one could tell who would be the victor, which caused great fear in those watching on both sides. But the extreme distress and fear I felt exceeded that of all the others. The battle was long, and the knights were so weary and worn out that at last they could do no more. Nevertheless, Quezinstra did not seem as tired as the admiral's brother, who, covering himself as best he could with what remained of his shield, no longer did anything but endure, so that a blow Quezinstra gave him on the helmet split and separated it into two parts, and wounded him severely; the helmet fell to the ground, and the knight fell along with it. Because he had lost a great deal of blood, he could not get up; when the noble Quezinstra saw this, he went up to him and helped him rise. When the admiral's brother considered the gentility and courtesy of his adversary, he said to him:

"O victorious knight, it is indeed time that I cease to try to resist you, and that I put myself entirely at your mercy. But since it has so pleased the immovable heavens, your inestimable valor, accompanied by benevolence, makes me consider myself fortunate to have been defeated and overcome by the bravest knight in the world, whom I do not wish to refuse to obey, with the assured resolve to forever persevere in your happy service." To this Quezinstra replied: "Milord, I assure you that I am overjoyed to have tried myself against such a valiant knight as you. For I can

---

[68]Mavors is an epithet for the god of war Mars. The reference is to the "gigantomachy" or war between the gods and the giants in Greek mythology.

rightly call you the flower of all those whom I have encountered since I began to exercise the military art. If through your benevolence you offer to dedicate yourself to serving me, you may be certain that I shall not fail to offer you the same; for it would not be in my power to remunerate you for the great and singular pleasure that you have provided me by saving from death my companion, whom I love no less than myself. And so I consider myself perpetually obligated to you, as if you had preserved my own life."

Then, hand in hand, they went to the pavilion of the admiral, who had gone away because he could not endure any longer the anxiety that troubled him, because of his fear that his brother might die in this battle. But when he saw him, although it was very hard for him to bear his being defeated, he was still somewhat comforted, and gave Quezinstra a fairly warm welcome. Then he said: "Knight, I see clearly that the gods are not favoring proud hearts, but on the contrary, strike them down and oppress them, as I see in my own case, for I thought no one could resist my power, which I thought to be invincible. I intended to totally destroy this city. If my cruel and evil intention had been realized, I had decided to cause the lady continual distress by accusing her and tormenting her in diverse ways, even though her purity and sincerity had never offended me; for one should not be astonished or ascribe the fault to her if she refused me. At present, reasonable considerations force me to say that she would have been mad to acquiesce to my request; for a man so aged, weak, and broken as I am is not suited to her gentle youth." On hearing these words, Quezinstra began to smile, and said nothing in reply. Meanwhile surgeons were summoned to apply some medication to the wounds suffered by the admiral's brother, whom they found to be seriously injured. Nevertheless, he was not in danger of dying. They wanted to examine some small wounds Quezinstra had sustained, but he told them that he had to return to the city, where there would be ample time to apply some ointments to help him heal. And so without delay they said farewell to the admiral and his brother, who was very distressed to be so grievously wounded, and cursed his ill luck, more because his wounds prevented him from going with us than because of the extreme pain they caused him; for had it not been for that, he had resolved to accompany us in all our adventures, good and bad. But considering that he could do nothing about it, he had to be patient.

So we returned with light hearts; for Octavian's[69] return from Egypt was not more joyous than our return to the city, where we were wel-

---

[69]The adopted son of Julius Caesar, who defeated the rebellious Antony and Cleopatra at Actium, near Egypt. After the victory, he changed his name to Augustus and made himself emperor of Rome.

comed and received with great good will. And thus we were shown more honor than the Greeks ever showed the magnanimous son of Thetis.[70] When we were on the palace steps, the lady came out and approached us. When she stood before us, she embraced us warmly and, almost in tears, she said: "To which of you I am more obligated, I could not say; to you, Quezinstra, for having been my true protector and defender; or to you, Guenelic, for the sake of whom more than for any other reason this was undertaken; for after you were taken prisoner, your companion was so anxious that he could not in any way be consoled until he was sure you were out of danger. Therefore I can well imagine that he performed this deed as much to restore you to liberty as because of the pity and commiseration that moved him on seeing me in such a calamity."

Saying such things, we went into the hall; then the surgeons were promptly summoned to treat Quezinstra. When they arrived, they applied to his wounds medications that would alleviate every pain, no matter how acute. When this was done, the knights, ladies, and maidens began to disport themselves, and they passed the day in all sorts of amusements and delightful pleasures. Then, at the hour when Somnus[71] urges all our tired limbs to take their repose, we retired to our chamber. Thus the body was granted the slight repose that the brief space of the night offered us.

The departure of the knightly companions, the lady's gifts, and new adventures.

Chapter 15

Sorrowful Procne[72] was already beginning to announce the arrival of fair Aurora when the admiral lifted his siege, and he and his men went away from the city. That same day we decided to put our affairs in order so we could soon leave, for love was spurring me on with such great vehemence that I was continually urging and prodding Quezinstra to depart as I desired; and I did so until finally on the third day we said farewell and took our leave of the noble princess, who gave us many gifts. In particular, among other things, she made us a present of two marvelously opulent rings, and as she presented them to us, she uttered these words: "Quezinstra, see this ring, which I give you, not for your honor or valor, but as a faithful reminder of the lady who will never forget you, as long as she lives." Then, turning toward me, she said: "Guenelic, I beg you to accept this little gift in the same spirit as I give it to you; for it is no less a

---

[70]Achilles.
[71]The Roman god of sleep.
[72]Procne was transformed into a nightingale.

virtue to graciously receive than to generously give. If it pleases you to give it to your beloved, that will delight me, thinking that when you see her wearing it, you will perpetually remember me."

To these gracious words we modestly replied: "Milady, we read that it is necessary to drink only a little of the liquors of the river Lethe in order to forget things past; but we should consume the river altogether before our memory of you would fall into oblivion. And for that reason, milady, you may be sure that you may consider us your loyal and faithful servants in perpetuity." After we said this, she approached us and laid her head on our shoulders, at the same time kissing and embracing us. Then, saying farewell to her, we left her very sad and pensive.

Thus we departed the city of Eliveba, and when we were at sea, our sail to the wind, we passed Rhodes and the kingdom of ancient Saturn. But we were heeled far over by the violent blowing of the winds Eurus and Notus and the surging waves filled our whole galley, so that the mast leaned under the weight; seeing us one might have thought we were at the antipodes. Still, through the favor of the one who saved the great father's ark from a similar peril, we arrived at an island rather well-suited for resting and refreshing our weary and weakened bodies—which we did. Afterward, we set out again on the sea, and in a short time we were in the city of Athens. Then we came to the city founded by the man who at Pallas's command sowed the dragon's teeth, from which were born knights armed and ready for battle.[73] Having left that place, we went to lofty Mycenae, of which we examined every part. Afterward, we sailed into the port of a little city named Basole, where we decided to remain for some time to refresh ourselves. But we had stayed there no more than three days before I began to be vexed by the special yearning I had to see the lady in search of whom I should have willingly ventured as far as the burning waters of the underworld.

Thus I was accompanied by a desire that continually urged me on; wherefore it was impossible for me to prevent the anxious distress hidden in my heart from revealing itself in my face, and I soon showed it there, so that Quezinstra saw it clearly and said to me: "Guenelic, I am amazed to see that you are hesitating to unveil and declare your thoughts to me. Don't you know that your happiness would give me as much joy as it could give you? If you think otherwise, you are very far from the truth, and whether one should put one's trust in experience, I leave for you to decide."

I promptly responded: "O dear friend, I have always known you to be a

---

[73]Cadmus the Phoenician founded Thebes; he was instructed by Pallas Athene to sow half of the teeth from a dragon he had killed. The other teeth were given to King Aeetes, and it is from these that the knights sprang forth.

faithful, discreet, and gracious friend; but what has prevented me from expressing the desire I have to depart is the fear of importuning you. But since through the subtlety of your mind you have understood my travail, you shall succor my sad and weary life as you see fit."

On hearing these words, Quezinstra immediately made preparations to leave the next day, which we did. For as soon as Apollo began to show his fair head, we once again set out upon the sea-waves and were carried to the island where the fugitive Diomedes left his bones. Thence we passed by Manfredonia and the perilous promontory of Ancona, along with the stormy channels of Pesaro, and came to the ancient city that was the fearful refuge of Caesar's legion.[74] Having departed, we came to the city of Lubio.[75] Meanwhile we were informed that we were quite close to another city which was being besieged because of a rebellion of its people against their prince.[76] This city, which was called Buvacca, was inhabited by perverse and iniquitous people who did not want to obey or have any superior; for on account of their overweening arrogance they thought no one could conquer them. When Quezinstra had listened carefully to this report, he urgently sought to persuade me that we should go to the host assembled before the city, and offer our service to the prince so that we might perform deeds worthy of being remembered. Considering his request virtuous, it did not seem right for me to delay its fulfillment, although I found it very hard. But to satisfy him I concealed my feelings and said that such a proposal did not displease me. As soon as I had said these words, we began to prepare ourselves, and we left [Lubio] to join the prince's forces, which were no more than four miles away. Hence we arrived there in a short time. But before we were allowed into the presence of the prince, we were questioned by several people who wanted to know what we were doing there and what we were trying to learn among them. We replied that what motivated us was nothing other than our ambitious desire to serve the prince in some way that was agreeable to his highness. Then we were conducted to the tent of the magnanimous lord, who, on being informed of our intention, willingly accepted us into his service. From that day forward, continual assaults were made on the city, at which Quezinstra and I did not fail to be present, and we comported ourselves with such valor that we won the prince's entire good will. He urged

---

[74]Manfredonia is a seaport on the Gulf of Manfredonia on the Adriatic coast of southern Italy; Ancona is another seaport farther north along the same coast. According to Secor, the "ancient city" is probably Rimini, which Julius Caesar occupied at the beginning of the Roman civil war.

[75]Possibly modern-day Lugo, about fifteen miles west of Ravenna on the Adriatic coast.

[76]The text reads: "laquelle estoit assiegée par la rebellion que les habitans avoyent faicte à leur prince." The succeeding passage makes it clear, however, that the prince is besieging the city in order to crush its rebellion against his authority.

us to continue to persevere, promising us that our services would not remain without suitable reward.

The siege of the city went on for a long time without our being able to completely destroy it. But one day we attacked it from all sides so vigorously that they could not resist us, although they tried as hard as they could. But Quezinstra performed such feats of arms that everyone was afraid of confronting him. For by the violence of his blows he made as much noise as Boreas does when entering swirling clouds and colliding with the humid air gathered in them, wrenching from the hands of the Cyclopes[77] the forged thunder and lightning bolts before he has presented them to the thundering son of Saturn;[78] in such a fury, he wrought havoc on the enemies. Seeing this, the prince began to exhort his men, telling them that on this day they might easily conquer their adversaries if cowardice did not prevent them from doing so. Urged on in this way by their prince, the knights began to take courage, and following Quezinstra's example, they fought so valiantly that the arrogant city-dwellers could no longer resist them. It was horrible and frightful to hear the laments and moans of the dying, of which there was a countless number. This enormous and execrable battle lasted so long that finally more through Quezinstra's prowess than anything else the city was subjugated and taken. In truth I can say that the victories won by Hannibal in Ausonia were nothing with respect to this one. They [the prince's forces] entered victoriously into the city. You may be assured that neither Agamemnon's prey[79] nor the conquest of Colchis was anything in comparison with the one I am telling you about. It seemed to me I was in Priam's city or in that of the Saguntians,[80] because of the lamentable vociferations and pitiable feminine howling that redounded to the Empyrean heavens.

Nevertheless, at Quezinstra's urging, the prince had published and announced that upon pain of death they must cease to harm them any further. Then he made the survivors congregate and assemble. When they were present, he began to look at them with an eye that was no less cruel than that of Hector when he set the Greeks' ships afire. Then in a bitter voice he said to them:

"O you scoundrels and wicked men! You may be sure that I have been informed by my ambassadors, whom I have several times sent to you, which ones among you were inveterate and hardened in their offenses and did not want to extirpate or abolish their ancient and customary rebelliousness. And so, considering your manifest iniquities, it is very urgent

---

[77]One-eyed giants who serve Vulcan.
[78]Jupiter.
[79]The city of Troy.
[80]Priam was king of Troy; Saguntum was sacked by Hannibal in 219 B.C.

that the rigor of justice and odious vengeance fall upon rebels who are not afraid of offending their lawful lord. Therefore, after consulting with my faithful men, you may be sure your wickedness will be gravely punished." On hearing him utter these words, the poor vanquished people were thrown into an extreme perplexity as they awaited the ultimate decision of their prince; after having listened to his men's various opinions, he settled on that of an old knight who said that he did not counsel the prince to put them to death, for death would put too rapid an end to their suffering. Therefore that punishment would not be so painful as giving them a difficult and tiring life, such as they would have if given over to perpetual servitude under some cruel galley-master, to labor on the seas. They would then be like beasts in the forest, suffering continually under the heavy blows which would, as is customary, fall on them without cease. This sentence would have been executed at once, had it not been for Quezinstra, who, moved by an internal compassion, addressed himself to the prince, saying:

"Milord, although these city-dwellers in their mad temerity have presumed to take entire control and government over themselves, tried to deprive you of your hereditary right, and thereby have deserved a very heavy punishment, nevertheless it seems to me that clemency should be preferred to rigorous justice. You should recall the victorious Julius Caesar, who, after having attracted and reconciled most of his enemies through liberality and prodigal gifts, decided to conquer the rest through courtesy and clemency and readiness to pardon, whereby he prospered so greatly that he carried his victorious eagles, in spite of the Roman Senate's severity, right up to the Capitol, and made sacrifices to his city's protector, Jupiter. I have desired to remind you of this, illustrious prince, in order to urge you to extirpate all inflexibility from your noble heart, so that this virtue of clemency, which well befits your noble highness, might find there its accustomed place of residence which through wrath has been occupied by rigorous severity." Quezinstra fell silent, and the prince remained pensive for a time. Then he began to reign in his wrath, and this allowed him to articulate these words: "Valiant knight, your speech is so restrained that the judgments contain more than the words, which produce such a great effect on my heart that for your sake I am prepared to completely abandon my former appetite for revenge, although these perverse and iniquitous people have committed and perpetrated a grave offense through their obstinacy. When I consider that they have been overcome through your inestimable valor, however, it seems to me reasonable that you should be permitted to do whatever you wish with their lives and possessions, and I freely grant you this. If you want something else, do not hesitate to inform me of it, without any fear of being refused anything you may request."

The gentleness of a prince toward his subjects.
With the sequel to the adventures of the two knights.

Chapter 16

On hearing these words, Quezinstra was marvelously happy and tried to offer the prince due and fitting thanks. Then, addressing the city-dwellers, he first remonstrated with them, urging them to abandon their proud arrogance and never rebel against their prince, who had restrained his wrath by preferring benevolence to stern vengeance, which should move them to be perpetually faithful to the supreme clemency and gentle kindness of this man who was their lawful lord. On hearing these words the city-dwellers were incredibly overjoyed, as people to whom their freedoms were restored, and who had earlier thought themselves condemned to the most severe punishment—which indeed they deserved on account of their sedition. But seeing that they had obtained clemency through the noble Quezinstra's intercession, they remained prostrate at the feet of their prince, and did not rise until they had said these words:

"Magnanimous prince, since it has pleased your highness to extirpate from your noble heart the rightful wrath you had conceived for us, and to accept the leniency of pardoning us, despite the grave offense we committed against your nobility, we must conclude that your natural instinct and true gentility moves you to act in this way. You also show you remember what the Holy Scripture testifies and says: that they are blessed who are poor, for they shall be granted mercy.[81] And by this one can understand that there is nothing more fruitful for the achievement of a happy life than to forget the vexations one has suffered. In this case we have clear evidence that these evangelical words are graven on your heart more firmly than they could be engraved on metal.[82] For considering our iniquities, it was not to be supposed that we should ever find peace or reconciliation with your highness, but your civility has won out, and it has been so powerful that it has mitigated and finally destroyed your ferocity, for which you deserve perpetual praise. For among the gifts and graces of the body and the soul, that single proper and peculiar virtue is ascribed to Caesar Augustus, of whom (as I see it) you are a shining example. Wherefore, given these considerations, we can deem very fortunate the people who live under such a prince's authority. And so, having obliterated every

---

[81]Cf. Matthew 5.3: "Blessed are the poor in spirit, for theirs is the kingdom of heaven"; and Matthew 5.7: "Blessed are the merciful, for they shall obtain mercy."

[82]Secor's text reads "metail," which Cotgrave defines as "Messlin or masslin; wheat and rye mingled, sowed, and used together." We assume this is either a variant spelling of "metal" or a misprint for "medaille."

sort of arrogant rebellion in our hearts, we have decided to begin faithful service, and to persevere in it. If we act otherwise than our mouths have said, we beseech the supernal divinity to make all splendid daylight harmful to us as long as we live, and when we are dead, may our wretched bodies be the bestial nourishment of cruel animals, and may our spirits wander forever in dim, dark shadows, never finding peace or repose. We are certain that because of our past knavery you will be inclined to suspect us of something sinister, but the pleasing service we hope to offer your highness in the future will clearly prove that we have completely returned to the true light of reason, from which we had for a time strayed far away."

After they had ceased speaking, the prince had them rise and said nothing more to them, other than that they should take care that their words not be uttered through deceptive dissimulation, and that they were in accord with their subsequent acts. When he had said this, addressing us he embarked upon various discourses and arguments to which we replied as modestly as we could. That day was spent in such conversation. But the following day, the prince desired that laws be established which were later esteemed as highly as those of Lycurgus.[83] They were so well observed by the inhabitants that they perpetually preserved true concord and singular affection among them. A few days later, our sojourn there growing tedious and painful to me, I began as usual to seek to persuade Quezinstra that we should depart forthwith; he did not wish to tarry, but rather, to satisfy my ardent desire, he promptly agreed to take leave of the prince and bid him farewell. Wherefore, without delay we went to a richly decorated hall where we found the prince with some of his intimates. After bowing to him, Quezinstra began to speak:

"Most victorious and virtuous prince, the divine will has been inclined to grant you such grace as to subdue the arrogance of the rebels, and return them, moreover, to true uprightness, in which I may presume they are determined to persevere. This gives us great joy because of the warm welcome your nobility has given us, which we are not able to recompense by a service befitting such a great benefit. To do so a thousand years would not suffice. Nevertheless there is no lack of good will. For you may be certain that we had resolved never to leave until you had brought this vexing war to an end. But since you are now free of such trials, after having begged your lordship to grant us leave, our decision is to depart this glorious city."

On hearing this, the prince looked somewhat sad, and did not at first reply. But when he began to speak, he said: "Noble knights, for what rea-

---

[83]The legendary Spartan lawgiver (ninth century B.C.), who was regarded as the founder of the Spartan constitution and military system.

son do you wish to leave my court? Is your departure so urgent that you cannot postpone it a little? It seems to me that you should not separate so hastily from a prince who would very much like to learn your desires in order to satisfy them most promptly, which I feel myself obliged to do for you who have been my true protectors and defenders, and without whose support I should not have been able to realize my goal. Wherefore with good reason I may feel sad if I am deprived of the aid of those who would be my unique refuge if any of my enemies should have the temerity to try to invade me. Therefore, because of the extreme distress your departure might cause me, I should like to induce and persuade you to change your opinion; and I very affectionately beg you to do so."

After the aforesaid words, Quezinstra responded in this way: "O noble prince, if our will were not in the power of another, it would not be necessary for your highness to humble himself so much as to beg us, but you might give us commands which we should completely obey. But since remaining here is not in our power, it will please you to excuse us."

Then the prince said: "I see rather clearly that your intention is so firm that I should not be able to divert you from it without great difficulty. Nonetheless, since I cannot do otherwise, I very urgently beseech you, and on my oath as a gentleman I urge you, to tell me the reason why you are not at liberty."

Then, with a smile, my companion looked at me and told me that we could not honorably deny this request. Seeing this, and hanging my head with shame, I said that Love for a lady urged and spurred me to travel. When the prince heard that I suffered so much on account of sensual love, he began to utter these words:

"O Guenelic, the singular affection and ardent benevolence I have for you compel me to exhort you to forsake this deadly solicitude. Consider that it is not the action of a prudent man to follow sensuality and abandon reason, for we should not deserve the name of rational creatures if reason did not have a dwelling place in us. To show that you wish to conform yourself with it, pursue no longer this unrestrained lustfulness; leave off this immoderate madness that can very easily transform men as the companions of Ulysses were transformed.[84] So consider carefully the many infelicities, calamities, and miserable ruinations into which this inordinate passion has led the world, as both Africa and Europe testify. What caused the extermination of the Tarquinians? That banished madness. What caused the discord between Caesar and Pompey? That ill-considered bitterness. What made the Romans so cruel to the Sabines? That universal plague. What stained the imperial house of Claudius? That frivolous infirmity. What destroyed Antony and Cleopatra? That

---

[84]These men were transformed into swine by the sorceress Circe.

acute pain. What vanquished Hannibal? That common fury concerning which Siphax maintained he would sooner lose his faith than abandon it. What tormented Demetrius? That cruel anxiety. What led Nero, Caius Caligula, Catiline, and Sardanapalus to extremities? That devouring flame. What filled the lofty minds of Plato, Xerxes, Aristotle, Socrates, and Ptolemy of Egypt with infamies? That venereal ardor. If you don't believe all the ancient stories, you may read the modern ones. If you want to wander through the world, you shall see clear examples of it. And so consider for yourself that from love proceed only travails, tears, sighs, moans and torture of the body and mind. Therefore call back your thoughts to better uses. Abandon the cultivation of concupiscence, and recall that you are a man and not an irrational animal. Thereby you shall be able to free yourself from these useless passions that cause you so much anguishing travail. If you are so fortunate as to succeed in liberating yourself from them, you will then be able to occupy your generous spirit with the most supreme and lofty things, which at present it is not in your power to do. For you must believe that being in this lustfulness, you shall never be able to set yourself to anything virtuous or profitable. For because of your continual yearning to have the fruition and enjoyment of the one you love, you have expelled all other cares and solicitudes. If it were to happen that you became the possessor of your lady, perhaps your life would not be so sweet and tranquil as you think. For it is the custom of many lovers that after they have satisfied their desires, out of fear and terror of being despoiled of them, they guard them with great solicitude and care, and this care cannot exist without passion in the heart, and it is without order and reason. Therefore, considering all these things, and showing yourself to be virtuous, you must lower your sails in a more tranquil port. If you do not do so, you shall find it to be true that one who good counsel does not heed, shall have great suffering as his meed."[85]

Although the prince's persuasive arguments were marvelously penetrating, they still did not have the power to change my heart; rather, my desire to see my beloved Hélisenne ever augmented. Nonetheless, I replied to him in this wise: "Milord, I assure you that the friendly exhortations and remonstrances you have made me give me indubitable proof of the affection you have for me. If Jupiter's eyes vigilantly watched over the safety of the man who governed the world so peaceably for fifty-six years,[86] I deem your eyes no less favorable toward me. For that reason, your kindness obligates me and puts me in debt to your highness, whom I desire with singular affection to serve in some acceptable way. Since I

---

[85]"Celluy qui de bon conseil ne tient compte, convient que de travail abonde."

[86]Presumably Augustus, who first came to power in Rome in 43 B.C. and was emperor from 27 B.C. to his death in 14 A.D.

know our presence pleases you, if it were in my power to delay our departure I should willingly agree to remain. But you may be sure that to bring relief to my wretched life, my departure is most urgent and necessary. If you realized with what force love dominates and lords over me, I am convinced that out of kindness and humanity you would yourself urge me to leave. For I am certain your request arises in part only from your recollection of the misfortunes that have occurred in times past on account of Love. But consider that all lovers are not so cruelly treated in the service of their ladies as those you previously mentioned. Whence proceeded the warlike enterprises of Lancelot of the Lake, Gawain, the courtly Gyron, Tristan of Cornwall, Pontus, and many other knights, if not from their desire to serve love and to retain the good will of their ladies? Through their loyal service they have deserved to be written about to their triumphal fame. Thus they serve as an example to all their posterity. As for your remark that we lovers are so agitated, persecuted, and afflicted, I freely grant that one's desire remaining unsatisfied often causes one to suffer painful anxieties. But if the lover decided to desist from love on account of such woes, he would be greatly mistaken. For if from the outset a love is very strongly rooted in the heart, one would sooner endure any cruelty rather than give it up. The reason such variation is found in some personages is the different kinds of love. Some proceed through long and continual commerce and secret conversations. In such love affairs, out of sight is out of mind.[87] There are other kinds of lovers who love only in order to satisfy their unrestrained lustfulness. To such lovers often happens what happened to Amnon,[88] who so ardently loved his sister Tamar, but whose ardor was extinguished as soon as he had satisfied his desire. But the love affairs from which one can never desist are those that are awakened at first sight. For that signifies that the personages are not of different temperaments, and that the will of one of them can easily conform to that of the other, and such loves endure perpetually. For that reason, considering that my greatly desired lady won entire possession of me at the first glance, it should not be supposed that I can abandon my love. Since it is not therefore in my power to preserve my own life, I must search for the lady from whom I hope one day to beg complete remuneration of my past travails and hardships, for beloved ladies are not so cruel that they do not grant solicitous lovers the contentment of their desires."

After I had expressed such words, the prince no longer tried to insist on opposing my desire, for he clearly recognized that my irrevocable conclu-

---

[87]"Eslognement de l'oeil est oblivion de cueur."

[88]King David's son Amnon desired his sister Tamar and raped her; immediately afterward, "Amnon hated her with a very great hatred; so that the hatred with which he hated her was greater than the love with which he had loved her" (2 Samuel 13.15). In revenge, another of David's sons, Absalom, had him killed by his servants (2 Samuel 13.1-29).

sion was decreed and confirmed in me, and he was very sorry to see this. But since he could do nothing about it, he tempered his wrath. In consideration of the pleasing services we had done him, he rewarded us adequately. Then, after taking fond leave of him and of the nobles present, we went away.

FINIS.

Here ends the second part of the Torments of Love:
Newly printed in Paris by Denys Janot,
Bookseller and printer,
residing in the rue neuve Notre Dame,
at the sign of St. John the Baptist,
next to Ste. Geneviève des Ardents.

PATERE AUT ABSTINE

De Crenne.

The Torments of Love

Part Three

The Third Part of
The Torments of Love

*Composed by Lady Hélisenne,
Speaking in the person of her beloved Guenelic:
Including the death of the said lady,
after having been found by the said Guenelic her beloved.*

De Crenne.

Preamble

In my humble opinion, O noble readers, there is in this world no vice more enormous and detestable than the sin of ingratitude, which I deem the origin of all the others. For if the first man had not been ungrateful toward the one who is author of all—from whom he had received so many benefits—he would not have succumbed to the deadly, sinful fall whence proceeds the contamination of all his posterity. For this reason, and in consideration thereof, if it is possible for me to do so, I wish to prevent myself from being stained by the aforementioned vice. Hence, before going on with my effort to complete this work, I wish to thank the one from whom all blessings come, whose mercy has allowed me to put down at length in my writings what I had narrated to you briefly in my epistle; then, after praise rendered in the measure of my ability (trusting to him, who through his prophet Hosea, in the second century, said to the soul: *I will even betroth thee unto me in faithfulness*),[1] I shall commence relating to you further journeys made by Guenelic and Quezinstra. Then I shall show you the clever means by which Guenelic found what he so ardently desired. Thus I shall make you understand what caused the joy he felt to be converted into a very serious and cruel passion—considering which, you shall have even greater occasion to detest this abominable vice of disorderly love. That is presently the chief concern which spurs me on ever more to continue writing assiduously with such an ardent desire. For if I earlier exhorted you to learn the military arts to acquire triumphant renown, I am now more strongly provoked to urge you to resist your sensuality, which is a difficult battle to win. Saint Paul writes about this in the fifth chapter of Galatians: *For the flesh lusteth against the Spirit, and the Spirit against the flesh.*[2] But who shall offer the spirit harbor and favor if not Dame Reason? I did not choose to believe in her salu-

---

Hosea 2.20. Unless otherwise noted, we give the text of the King James translation for all quotations from the Bible. There are more biblical references in Part III than in the previous parts.
Galatians 5.17.

157

tary counsels, but totally repulsed them; and since that time I have been unable to call her back to me. Wherefore I beseech you not to separate yourself from her in any way, so that through her, sensuality may succumb and be vanquished. If that good fortune is granted you, you shall then be able to say what Saint Paul said: *I keep under my body, and bring it into subjection.* To that end I exhort the eternal divinity to grant you favor in this matter.

Guenelic persists in his adventures in search of his beloved.

Chapter 1

After having taken leave of the prince, we set out to sea and sailed to the greatly renowned Carthage. When we had arrived there, we visited every part of it. Thence to Valencia, Barcelona, Marseilles, Bordighera, Albenga, and Savona.[3] Soon afterward we arrived in Genoa, and there we entered the port and dropped anchor, because we were so weary that we had to rest. Entering the city, I saw a gentleman who had formerly been a friend of mine and an intimate in my own land. On espying him, I said to my companion: "Quezinstra, if memory does not fail me, I see there a gentleman who was often in our company in our country." So saying, we carefully approached him, and stopped to look at him. When we were certain, we went closer, and then very honorably greeted him. In turn, he observed us intently; and when he recognized us, with a certain affection and friendship, he asked us courteously and cordially why we had come to that place. I promptly informed him, not without tears, of my calamity, the account of which provoked him to tearful moans, and he said to me:

"Guenelic, you are not alone in having cause to lament, for I, whom you know to be of noble lineage, am at present, through the instability of fortune, a resident of this city, where I have to converse with arrogant people to whom every good custom is foreign. For although this land is rich, opulent, and beautiful, still it produces nothing but ungrateful children with whom no one of good spirit can be in accord. Nevertheless, since such is the will of the immutable heavens, I am eternally content with them. Henceforth, remaining as solitary as I can, I shall live in my

---

[3]The geography is "accurate" in the sense that the ports do come in that order as one sails north along the Spanish coast and around to the Italian Riviera. Thus after their tour of the Levant, Guenelic and Quezinstra now tour the Western Mediterranean.

house, which I beg you to consent to visit in order to refresh yourselves, making yourself at home just as you might do in your own hereditary domain. If you do so I shall consider it a great honor and a singular pleasure." On hearing these words, we thanked him as much as we could, and without refusing his offer, we went to his house. When we got there, we embarked upon diverse subjects and questions. Meanwhile, sustenance for the body was procured. Then, after supper, we were provided with an honorable repose.

Accompanied by desire, I passed the night in a brief slumber, for my intention was to not stay longer than a day in the city. But my ungrateful fortune, always contrary to my desire, did not allow my intention to be put into effect, because of a vexatious fever, by which I was so cruelly agitated that I expected nothing more than shortly to count among Proserpina's family. Seeing this, the good gentleman who had so kindly welcomed us wanted to do something to help me. With great haste he sent for a prudent and diligent physician, who used several means to completely evacuate all that was harmful to me, so that I was gradually set on the way to convalescence. Nonetheless, for a long time I was so weak that it was not in my power to begin the desired departure. Still, my customary affection continually spurred me on, and I said to myself:

"O Guenelic, what sinister event, what suffering, what destitution of health prevents you from going toward the lady you so much desire? Don't you know that there is no beatitude, felicity, or contentment that can surpass or even approach yours, if you are once allowed to be in her presence? How much happier would you now be to die rather than to live absent from her! And so you must labor to regain your spiritual strength and fortify your weak and weary limbs, as if you were certain that their labors would not remain without reward. Wherefore, fortunate shall be the travail, and felicitous the martyrdom that will lead you to such delight: you shall be strengthened and restored from all the hardships you have suffered, and thus you shall be brought into perpetual and infallible happiness. Therefore the fear of any peril, no matter how great, should not hold you back."

Imagining my hoped-for future boon in this way restored some vigor to me, and to augment it I strove to eat nutritious and substantial foods, so that by this means my strength, which had left me because of my illness, could more easily return to my limbs and drive out debilitation. This was not very difficult for me to do, for the greatest principle of healing is the desire to be healed. When I felt myself to have regained my former strength, I began to forget all the calamities I had suffered. At once, without any delay, after having warmly thanked the gentleman for all he had done for us, we prepared to leave.

Once we had set out again on our sea vessels, Aeolus granted us a favorable wind. In less than a week we came to an island that seemed a suitable place to rest. It was surrounded by very high rocks and forests; nevertheless, there were a few inhabitants, among whom was a man who shone with an admirable saintliness. He was so experienced in knowledge that the spring of Helicon and Mount Parnassus might well have owed their existence to him. Having learned of him, we greatly desired to visit him, which we did. After we had greeted each other and bowed, he began to question us to learn what urgent matter brought us to this place. He said this because it was the custom of those who lived in the environs to come to him to ask his opinion when they were in doubt as to what they should do. We replied that for a long time we had been searching all over the world to find something we desired. In doing so we had encountered so many trials and travails that we could have conquered the mountainous kingdom of Persia with much less trouble.

On hearing this, he asked us to tell him the reason for our travail. Then I felt a little timid, considering the man to whom I was talking; his gravity, true religion, austere life, and his continual occupation with virtuous deeds made me reluctant to divulge to him the reason for my journey. Nevertheless, after having hesitated for a time, without concealing any of my past and present anxieties, I informed him of them. He listened to everything with care, and then said to me:

Colloquy between a religious man and a lover.[4]

Chapter 2

"O, my son, I beg you, in order to more easily abandon this lustfulness, to consider how unreasonable, unhealthy, and dreadful it is to persist in something that damages the body and tortures the soul. Reflect on what you may gain by relinquishing reason, which every living man should follow, for a vain appetite. The philosopher Anaxagoras, asked why he was born, responded: "In order to contemplate the sun." Such a response should not be interpreted as meaning the light of the sun, but the power it has to lend to all creatures the splendor of understanding and virtue, which everyone should emulate in order to avoid offending divine clemency by committing or perpetrating sins. To avoid the latter, you should recall the wise words of Seneca, who said, although he was a pagan: 'If I knew that the gods would not have any knowledge or awareness of it, and that no man would know it either, still I should not sin.' Now

---

[4]Secor notes that most of the references in this chapter are probably taken from Chapter 5 of the anonymous *Petit Jehan de Saintré* and, to a lesser extent, from Caviceo's *Peregrino*.

therefore think about this pagan who detested vice so much; so much the more should we abominate it. And so I want to exhort you to resist this sensuality in order not to succumb to the vile sin of lustfulness. Follow rather the saying of Saint Augustine: 'Flee lustfulness that you not be tarnished with ill fame. Do not give in to your body's urging, so that with your sin you do not wound Jesus Christ.' On this topic Saint Peter admonishes us in his first epistle, saying: 'I beseech you as strangers and pilgrims, abstain from fleshly lusts, which war against the soul.'[5] The Doctors of the Church wrote several other things, and moreover, so did the philosophers. Among others, Boethius says: 'Lust is ardent in conjoining and fetid in disjoining, a momentary bodily pleasure and the destruction of the soul.' Because, my son, this sin is so vile and dishonorable, I exhort you to avoid it, and not to be so misguided and poor in wisdom. Let not your way of life be so unfortunate that you go toward your downfall in such extreme distress, but rather seek to be virtuous in resisting and doing the contrary of what your heart urges you to do. If you do what is within your power, God will not abandon you. Saint Paul cites the verse in the book of Joshua, in which He promises and says: *I will never leave thee nor forsake thee.*[6] And although He leaves us sometimes in pains or agitations—as He did Saint Paul, whose prayer He refused to grant when he asked Him three times to be delivered from the spur of the flesh and the persecution of the evil angel—nevertheless if through our fault or negligence He does not come to us, He will never fail to remain with us in His grace, which, as He replied to Saint Paul, must suffice us in all adversities, which are often necessary to humble us and make us understand that our own virtue is powerless without our Creator's protection. And so you must not marvel at carnal temptations, but think of the great merit of resisting them. In order to do so, invoke the name of Him who has not only comforted His friends in their tribulations, but has liberated them from these tribulations. Did He not preserve the ancient father Noah, who saved the human race in a little bit of wood? And also Lot, when Sodom and Gomorrah and other neighboring cities perished and were destroyed because of the enormous and execrable vices that reigned in them? Did He not favor and aid Abraham when He delivered him from the hands of the Chaldeans? Did He not save His son Isaac's life by delivering him from the sacrifice that Abraham, his father, intended to make of him? Was not Jacob saved from the hand of his brother Esau? Joseph was also saved by His providence from the hand of his brothers. Then afterward Moses and Aaron and the people of Israel were through His mercy succored and liberated from slavery in Egypt; and David from the hand of

---

1 Peter 2.11.
Joshua 1.5; quoted in Hebrews 13.5.

Saul, and from the hand of the giant Goliath. Afterward, Daniel was delivered from the lions' den, where he had been thrown at the command of the king and at the people's urging. Was not the good Judith delivered along with the Jewish nation, His adherents, from the hand of the powerful Holofernes? And Mordecai and the other children of Israel from the hand of Haman? The three children Shadrach, Meshach, and Abednego were also preserved from the heat of the fire, so that it neither burned them nor harmed them. Jonah the prophet was freed and brought out of the whale's belly where he had lived and remained for three days and three nights. And so many others He has preserved that the writings necessary to describe them would be too long. If you did not hope to beg His mercy because you did not feel you had in you the perfections found in the aforementioned personages, you should not for that reason abandon hope; for He has not only had mercy on the good, but, through special grace, He has converted the iniquitous and wicked. I presume you have not been a persecutor of the faith, as Saint Paul was before his conversion. You have not denied your God, as Saint Peter did on three occasions—and nonetheless he begged forgiveness. Mary Magdalen, who was called a sinner, was converted and afterward perpetually persevered in virtue. To the Samaritan woman He granted such mercy that the salutary water satisfied her. Wherefore, considering all these things, you must entrust yourself entirely to this divine clemency, having unshakable living faith that after having persevered so long in resisting, eternal God will make you worthy of his favor and liberate you from the perilous battle against carnal urges. If such felicity is granted you, the more you approach a mature age, the more you shall feel shame for having so long occupied your lofty and generous spirit with something so useless. Then you shall judge that continual languishing through such a passion, consuming the spirit without either utility or honor, may be equated with or ascribed to the vice of pusillanimity."

There this good and religious person ended his salutary remarks, which I cared little about, since the exercise of oratory has little effect on the deaf and dumb. The more he remonstrated with me, the more the memory of my lady Hélisenne inflamed me with ardent desire, whereby appetite dominating reason did not allow me to discern the truth. Then I said to him: "Certainly, I feel myself greatly obliged to you, and I thank you very warmly for your friendly reminder and paternal counsel, which I understand to be such that it would lend sense to those who had strayed from reason; to the ignorant, prudence; to the pusillanimous, magnanimity; to the lascivious, it would give the habit of continence. And if I thought the love I have for my lady was blameworthy, your most efficacious words would easily alienate me from it. But when I carefully consider that love for a lady so gentle as mine can lend the lover nothing but

162

modesty, the faculty of doing well and instruction in all good ways and customs, it would be distressing and painful to me to think of turning away from her love. For you must believe that the lover who seeks to acquire the good will of a noble and virtuous lady, if he persists in this, will be separated from everything vicious."

"First of all, [the lover] will guard against the sin of pride, for in order not to fall into the lady's ill grace, he will be more than anyone gracious, sweet, and good-hearted in order to avoid there being anything sinister in him that could be reported to his lady. He will recall the saying of Socrates, who said: 'No matter how good you may be, if you are arrogant everything is destroyed; your arrogance alone damns you.' The wise Thales the Milesian[7] also says: 'If you are abundant, rich, and opulent, if you have wisdom, nobility, and all corporeal perfections, pride alone, if it is in you, destroys all your virtues.' But if the true lover as I have described him were to be tempted by this sin, fearing he might displease his lady, he would think of death. Such a meditation has the power to humble us, remembering what the wise Chilo of Sparta said: 'If you are descended from a noble family, you should be even more noble in virtue, for the nobility of good morals is worth far more than the nobility of family; and nobility, no matter how lofty, cannot overcome death.' Therefore the true lover will expel and exile from himself the detestable sin of pride, and will keep by him the gentle virtue of humility, concerning which it is written in Isaiah: *For thus saith the high and lofty One that inhabiteth eternity, whose name is Holy; I dwell in the high and holy place, with him also that is of a contrite and humble spirit, and to revive the heart of the contrite ones.*[8]

"As for the sin of envy, the true lover will never be stained by it; for if it came to the attention of his lady, he might incur her indignation, since it is not an honorable lady's custom to love a man subject to such a vice. And so the gentle lover will wholly avoid this displeasing sin, recalling Plato's saying: "Flee envy, for envy is without love and dries out the body and makes the heart iniquitous and wicked." Therefore this abominable voice will be banished from the lover, who will associate himself with the noble virtue of charity. He will exercise it not only toward his friends, but even toward those who wish him ill, so as to win back their good will, and extirpate the hostility they may have conceived for him. By this means nothing will be said against him. Thereby he will accomplish what Saint

---

[7]Thales of Miletus is one of the so-called Seven Wise Men of Greece. Others are mentioned later in the text: Chilo of Sparta, Pittacus of Mitylene, Bias of Priene, Solon of Athens.

[8]The English differs considerably from the French in this case; the latter might be translated: "Thus speaks the sublime lord who lives eternally, whose name, though holy and exalted, nevertheless wishes to live with the humble in order to give him life through its grace" (Isaiah 57.15).

John Chrysostom urges: not only 'Do not hate your enemies,' but also 'Refrain from harming them; rather, do them good in order to bring them to charity by making your enemy your friend.' Thus the heart of the true lover will be sincere and pure, having been ennobled by this glorious virtue.

"As for the sin of wrath, it will never find a place in the heart of the true lover. If for some reason the lover occasionally finds himself weary and vexed, if the cause is nothing other than love, this is not held to be wrath, about which Saint Augustine says in one of his epistles: 'Just as bad wine spoils and corrupts the vessel if it remains a long time therein, wrath corrupts the hearts within which it resides.' And Cato says on this subject: 'Wrath hinders and puts out a person's eyes, so that he cannot see what is true.' Likewise Pittacus of Mytilene: 'Flee anger and wrath that they may not give you the cruel plague, for they are paths that make one stray from the straight road, and feed schisms and divisions.' On that head, when Plato was once asked what the perfect good was, he replied: 'Knowing how to restrain one's wrath.' Therefore I deem it a great blessing to the lover that he is separated from this vice and accompanied by the gracious virtue of patience, through which he can tolerate all adversities. On this topic Saint Gregory says very well: 'Our adversary the devil will be completely vanquished if our will or consent does not allow itself to be persuaded and tempted by wrath. Thus amidst the insults and contumely of our neighbor we take care not to hate him. And thus amidst the adversities God sends us, we take care not to complain.' Therefore since this virtue has such great power, love for a lady should not be condemned because it is the reason this virtue is acquired.

"As for the sin of avarice, certainly the noble lover is totally exempt from it; for in order to please his lady, he will seek only to be generous in every honorable way. Nevertheless, one must not fall into prodigality, for that would not show prudence. Therefore it will be only in licit and honorable matters that he will offer evidence of his liberality. He will detest the sin of avarice, concerning which the philosopher Bias of Priene: 'The man who is covetous and greedy is sorrowful and weeps more in losing than he takes delight in having. The more he amasses, the more he is enslaved and wretched.' The Scriptures also say: 'A greedy man's eye is not satisfied with a portion.'[9] Socrates also says: 'Do not be covetous, and you shall have peace of mind, and thus you shall be at rest in all places." On this subject the divine Plato also says: 'The thing that has given me the greatest joy has been that I have cared nothing for lucre, and I have had

---

[9]Here again the French differs considerably from the English (taken in this instance from the *Oxford Annotated Bible with Apocrypha*); the French might be translated: "The greedy man's eye is insatiable, and will not be satisfied with a portion of iniquity" (Sirach 14.9).

greater delight than having accumulated money; for I should have had anxious thoughts, and I have pleasure that grows as I acquire knowledge.' Therefore our gentle lover may call himself happy, since he will not be a slave to covetousness. Rather, through the fair virtue of liberality he will perform acts of mercy, by distributing his wealth to the indigent and needy; concerning which Saint Gregory says: 'I do not recall having read or seen that anyone ever died a bad death who had willingly shown mercy to others; for whoever does so has so many intercessors it is certain the prayers of some of them will be answered.'

"As for the sin of sloth, you may be sure that no lover will ever be slothful, for love continually prods and goads him to acquire or maintain himself in his mistress's good will, and that will free him from this vice. He will recall the poet Athenaeus's saying: 'Idleness is often venom in the thoughts of young people, for the bodies of the young are a special cause of vices.' For that reason Saint Bernard says: 'I have seen some madmen make Fortune their excuse, but you will hardly think a diligent person can be unfortunate.' Hence it is popularly said that everything is due people who are diligent and solicitous. Because this splendid virtue is very urgent and necessary in love, the gentle lover will keep it by him, and will exempt himself from the unhappy sin of sloth.

"As for the sin that consists in taking too great a delight in sating the belly and eating food in greater abundance than is reasonable, certainly the true lover is pure and clear of this sin; for he takes his refection so soberly that it is only sufficient to sustain life, following the saying of the Philosopher, who says: 'One should eat and drink to live, not live to eat and drink.'[10] The Philosophers also say that he who wants to acquire good sense and clear judgment should be sober in refection, and not take too much delight in the superabundance of exquisite viands. For as Saint Bernard says in his *Morals*: 'When this vice comes to dominate a person, everything good that one ever did is lost. And when the belly is not restrained by the strict rule of abstinence, all virtues are submerged in it.' Therefore since the lover will be freed from this sin, in him shall dwell sweet abstinence and sobriety, which constitute a flourishing virtue.

"As for the sin of lust, truly the lover will avoid it; for out of fear of distressing his lady he will not only avoid it in deeds but preserve himself from it in thoughts as well. But if love should constrain him to succumb to this sin with his lady, I do not wish to deny that this would be a vice; but nonetheless, since it leads one to avoid committing this sin with diverse persons, it seems to me one ought not to consider it so great a vice. For as I have already said, for fear of vexing his beloved lady he will stay away from all others, recalling what the wise Solon of Athens said:

---

[10]Plutarch attributes this ancient adage to Socrates.

'Through wine, dice, and associating with loose women and frequenting them, you shall always be unhappy and indigent,' for a man who is so lascivious that he cannot keep from associating with many loose women will, if he persists, lose, as the philosopher puts it, six things: the first is his soul; the second, his spirit; the third, his morals; the fourth, his strength; the fifth, his reputation; the sixth, his voice. Thus, since through his love for his lady, the lover is exempt from such a peril, we should not condemn such affection. For my part I love my lady with such a loyal love that if it were possible for us to join together in marriage, I should greatly desire it, for I want to remain with her forever." Then the good religious began to speak: "O my son, by your words I clearly see that you are wholly disposed to endure all extremities rather than desist from your amorous enterprise. Therefore, knowing that all the salutary exhortations and discourses I might pronounce would be vain and useless, I shall pass over them in silence. Because I feel compassion and pity for you, I should like to contemplate your physiognomy, by examining which I shall be able to tell you how your love affair will turn out. But to understand it more clearly, you must tell me the day and hour of your birth." I promptly told him. When he had heard my words, he remained pensive for a time; then, breaking his silence, he began to speak to me in this wise:

"O my friend, at the hour of your birth your horoscope was Aquarius; the sun was in the sign of the Lion; Phoebe[11] in the Scorpion; Saturn, in the Lion; Jupiter, in Aquarius; Mars, in the Scorpion, and Venus, along with Mercury, in the sign of the Gemini. This conjunction, in accord with the influence of celestial bodies, signifies that through venereal cupidity, you shall suffer extreme calamities. Even if you recover the lady you desire, you shall not enjoy her in peace; but rather, in order to compel you to give her back, an enormous tumult shall ensue, not without a great shedding of blood, which moves me to commiseration. But if you wish, you can still do something to avoid this. For although the constellation under which you were born inclines you in that direction and somewhat determines you, still you shall not be constrained or forced to act in this way, for everyone can make use of his power of free will. But certainly your vehement affection totally prevents you from accepting good counsel. Wherefore you shall suffer such extreme misery that meditating on your future woes causes me to be terribly afraid."

When I had heard these words, I was cast into an extreme perplexity, so that if Quezinstra's sweet eloquence had not labored to console me, the fear which so violently agitated me was powerful enough to deprive me of life. But after I had received some comfort from his mellifluous words, at

---

[11]Here, the moon.

the instigation of the holy man and Quezinstra I accompanied them to the homely table where were laid out viands such as he was accustomed to eat, which offered us a very sober meal. Then, with scarcely any delay, we went to bed with the firm resolve to leave soon.

After many travails Guenelic has news of his beloved.

Chapter 3

Fair Aurora was still abed when, after having bid the religious a gracious farewell, we set out on our way. We went along by the light of Proserpina[12] until Tithonus's beloved[13] began to grace us with her sight. We did not cease to travel along until the face of the shining day[14] began to diminish its brightness. At that time we arrived at a town situated in a quite beautiful place. But unfortunately for us no one in this town undertook to lodge visitors in their homes. For they were people who had neither charity nor love; on the contrary, among them reigned rivalry, sedition, and envy to such an extent that a few words with them sufficed to show they were worse than devils. Wherefore it was not surprising that we, as foreigners, noticed their iniquities, of which they gave us ample evidence. For they were so proud that no matter what our supplications, no pity within moved them to offer us lodging; instead, they derided and mocked us. For it was their custom to delight in provoking people to wrath. And so to make us angry they said to us: "Good sirs, please tell us about yourselves. Have you come to make war on the Macedonians? The Arabians? Or the Athenians? May you not find it tedious to recite your feats of arms." Then afterward, seeing that we remained silent, they said: "If you do not wish to recount your martial feats, tell us if you have come to see the beautiful girls of the isle of Cyprus; for your handsome white, delicate faces with such well-combed hair truly show you to be more suited to nocturnal jousts than to any other kind."

Quezinstra, hearing such things said, could scarcely restrain his anger. For when he considered that so much honor had been shown us by princes and great lords, he was very vexed to have to put up with these iniquitous people. For there is nothing so bitter as being offended by one's inferiors. So I said to him: "I beg you, let us leave these people, who are such wicked scoundrels their superabundant infelicity leads them to speak more from insolence than from a desire to learn. I see clearly that when we escaped Scylla's dangers we fell into Charybdis's perils. Though

---

[12]Here, the moon.

[13]Aurora, goddess of the dawn.

[14]The sun.

I thought no one was worse than the people of Buvacca and Genoa, the inhabitants of this town exceed them in malice."

Saying such things, we were going away when we perceived a lady looking out a window, and examining us with great care; seeing this, we thought it must be out of good rather than ill will, since women are commonly inclined to all sorts of kindness, courtesy, and clemency, for otherwise they forsake their natural condition. This consideration emboldened us to beg her not to deny us succor in our urgent need. But if the others showed themselves proud and arrogant, this lady showed herself even more furious, so much so that her cruel visage like that of the Medusa Gorgon[15] terrified me. Then she thundered in her voice full of horror and threats, and told us that she would rather see us die an execrable death than please us in any way, and that we should without delay leave her presence, for otherwise she would show us how great her displeasure was. After hearing what she said, before we left we said: "Madame, had we thought our request would be so disagreeable to you, you may be certain we should not have made it; but thinking that you were sweet and kind as ladies are accustomed to be, we made bold to do so. Nonetheless, if you say we have made a mistake, I concede you are right, for now our crude notion and feeble knowledge may be justly blamed and detested, since despite perceiving that you were so ugly, we failed to comprehend that perhaps there was no goodness in you." With that, we departed without further delay. As soon as we had left the town, we saw a little castle only a short distance away, and set out toward it. When we had arrived there, the gentleman who lived there received us very honorably, and began to question us on several topics, concerning which we recounted part of what happened to us, both favorable and adverse. He took special delight in hearing this. But among other things, we did not forget to tell him about the inveterate malice we had found in the people who lived in the town, and especially in the cruel lady who had so inhumanely rebuffed us and driven us away. As soon as the gentleman heard these words, he interrupted, saying: "Certainly I know very well the lady you speak of; she is so accomplished in all sorts of iniquity that the mouth can scarcely express it, the mind understand it, or the imagination figure it. Among other vices that reside in her person, that of detraction never leaves her, and she has exercised it in such a way that there is no memory of her being otherwise. Wherefore, without usurping the rights of others, she has acquired the reputation of a wicked-tongued lady, for a true or kind word never comes out of her mouth. So I wish to warn you that not only through her words but also through the effects of her perverse acts she has

---

[15]In ancient Greek mythology, the Gorgons were female monsters; Medusa was a Gorgon decapitated by Perseus; her head turned to stone those who saw it.

caused her reputation to spread to more diverse places than that of a valiant and magnanimous knight could be spread by marvelous feats of arms. Moreover, her cruelty has grown a great deal since the time one of her relatives had a disagreement with a very honorable lady, his wife, on account of certain matters that are concealed and not known to us. But in any event, his ire was so vehement against the noble and gracious lady that he made her life worse than violent death. For she has long been held captive in a castle named Cabasus. In order to increase her suffering and aggravate her torments, and also to satisfy his cruel sister—knowing that she delighted in doing evil—he put his wife in her custody, and I have since heard that she began to heap contumely and opprobrium on her. But nonetheless, as I see it the harm she has done her is nothing compared with what she intended to do. For no more than Hell is satisfied by swallowing up souls, this outrageous lady is not satisfied by carrying out her iniquitous desires. Wherefore the poor prisoner must truly desire to die. O, how great a disaster is the loss of such a lady! For you must believe that the evil-tongued lady is no more consummate and perfect in malice than the other is in gifts of grace and nature, so that because of her perfections and kindness (with which God and nature have singularly endowed her) all the gentleman and ladies of the region pity and long for her, as if she were their own relative. And in general, considering her condition, we all believe that it is certainly wrongly and without good cause that she is suffering such a calamity."

Epistle of two lovers who have not seen each other for a long time.

Chapter 4

The gentleman's remarks concluded, and having listened to them very eagerly, I requested him to tell me the name of that virtuous lady to whom fortune had been such a cruel enemy. He promptly replied that her name was Hélisenne. On hearing that name I felt like a creature who had escaped some marine peril, and who in great fear remains without breathing or consciousness. Nevertheless, when I had somewhat recovered, as honorably as I could I withdrew into a quiet place, where Quezinstra followed me. Then, in a weak voice, I said to him: "Dear friend, because idleness is not fitting in men of action, we must strive not to be negligent in this matter. Since things that have their origin in good counsel usually come out well, I ask what your opinion is, for it has always been very useful to me in my most important affairs."

Quezinstra replied: "O Guenelic, truly we must think and reflect on the means most suitable for liberating Hélisenne from this captivity. To aid us in this, it seems to me that you could not do better than to inform her of your arrival through a most faithful letter. Once informed, she will not cease to imagine ways to escape, not so much to recover her liberty as because of the ardent desire she may have to be with you. For if a man is ardent in love, you must imagine that the lady also burns, and that the ardor that dominates in one of them is not lacking in the other. But because the feminine condition is more apt to invent clever ruses than that of men, her advice could be very helpful, and she could give it to us by benefit of a letter."

As soon as I heard this suggestion, although it was late and time to retire, I did not wish to fail to begin my amorous writing, which went like this:

Letter from Guenelic

"It would not be possible for your Guenelic, sovereign lady, to discern which of two dissimilar things occupying his heart will gain an advantage. One of them is the incredible happiness he felt on feeling himself close to the thing which he has endured every travail to recover. And the other, which is very different, is the painful anxiety constantly troubling his heart because he is certain you are languishing and consuming your life in extreme misery and calamity; I[16] should rather die than to fail to set you free therefrom. My long service ought to offer you indubitable grounds for believing that. But before beginning this enterprise, I have wished to communicate everything to you by letter, as much to make you certain that I have been healed as to learn your opinion. For I am always willing to yield to your judgment, because it is wholly determined by discretion and prudence, and whatever you decide and counsel will be acceptable and agreeable to me. But if my faithful service to you is seen with any degree of benevolence, I exhort and beg you not to be parsimonious in writing letters to the man who desires so much to be in your presence; for if I am not very amply informed regarding your condition, I shall remain in extreme perplexity, fearing that the reason you are not writing may be that something sinister has befallen you, whether an infirmity of the body or a violent distress of the soul. For since ladies are fragile and of slight constitution, that might easily happen to you because you are held in such captivity and deprived of all consoling joy. Nonetheless I hope that in the future, if you remember my services, you will recover your strength; and that in order to set my mind at rest without delay concerning your condition, you will reassure me."

---

[16]Guenelic here reverts to the first person in speaking of himself.

When this amorous letter had been written and sealed, my mind was occupied with diverse thoughts, as I was meditating and thinking how I could consign them to my lady's lustrous, beautiful hands. Seeing that, and fearing continual concern would cause me to fall victim to some adverse malady, Quezinstra said: "I beg you to desist from these superfluous thoughts, which serve only to consume your spirit and dissipate your body. I am astonished at what moves you, seeing and considering that you are at present so near what you desire. In your opinion, is it so difficult to send your letter to your lady? You may be sure that we shall find some subtle means of doing so. And to please you, I accept the obligation of seeing to it that she receives it, wherefore you should feel certain joy and consolation in your heart." On hearing Quezinstra's promise, I had such a high opinion of his ability that with his help, I was in hopes of being able to realize the greatest part of my desires. Thus I relieved my heart of what was troubling and afflicting it, and we lay down to rest.

But at the hour when Proserpina is leaving her mother to return to the tenebrous realms of her husband, wishing to put our affairs in order and detesting sleep, I rose. To please me, Quezinstra refused to obey insidious sleep, and also arose with great promptitude; then vigilant and concerned with my desires, he occupied himself with several ideas, and among others he recalled that he had heard it said that the evil-tongued lady was in control of the castle of Cabasus of Madame Hélisenne. Therefore it seemed to him that in order to realize our goal there was no better way than through pretense and dissimulation to make use of the cruel lady's name, so that she might herself present my letter to my lady, who, having read it, would understand very well our clever and thoughtful ruse. When he had once hit on that idea, he put it into effect. The bearer being carefully instructed, he carried out his mission with great diligence and brought me a letter whose content went like this:

Letter from Hélisenne addressed to Guenelic.

"After having received your letter, dear friend, I was in danger of succumbing to the impediment faced by the Roman matron who, because of her anxiety on learning of her only son's death, could not die. And afterward, on encountering the said son, who was not yet dead, she died from excessive joy. Likewise I, who through assiduous and continual pain have not been able to reach the pain which is the end of all woes, although I have sought it by diverse means. But now that I have been informed of your arrival, my heart is filled with a certain joy so profuse that through superabundant delight, I have scarcely been able to prevent my feeble body being separated from my soul. But nonetheless, after a long fainting spell, a little vigor has returned to me, and this has allowed me to write this present letter, having an ardent desire that you be present here to recover the singular pleasure of seeing you, and also so as to express to you my opinion concerning what you desire so much to know. To satisfy our common yearning, I notify you that I have concluded that there is no means more suitable for communicating with one another the secret of our hearts than for you to come to this castle. When you arrive, come to the largest of the towers, in which I am held captive; there you will perceive a barred window through which we can talk, at least if you have armed yourself with a ladder suitable for reaching such a height. But you must not fail to come at the silent time of the secret night—providing it is very dark, and Diana[17] does not wish to grace you with her radiant splendor. So that through my fault you and I do not find our desires frustrated, I want to give you a more ample and clear description of the place. And to be very sure, you must understand that the aforementioned window looks out on the garden, and at that place there is a tree of such height that it exceeds the summit of the tower. Thus, since you have been well informed, you cannot use ignorance as your excuse. So I beseech and beg you that you not delay your desired arrival beyond this very night, when I hope I shall be able more easily to tell you more about my condition than I can by literary means."

After having read several times the letter I had received, because of the consoling ideas that occurred to me, I said to myself: "O Lord who granted Anchises' son such felicity when in Elissa's lap you rested in the form of Ascanius![18] Now I cannot thank you enough, for I see clearly that you have granted me more grace than to the man I have just mentioned, although he was your brother, for it is no less a virtue to preserve than to acquire. I have uttered these words because, despite my long absence, you have not permitted my lady's love for me to diminish. Therefore, all cares and trials notwithstanding, I am convinced that I am more loved by Hélisenne, and with greater fidelity, than any gentleman ever was by a lady. And because I do not wish to be ungrateful, considering, Lord Love, that from you all prosperity proceeds, I shall render to you all thanks, I shall bring you all honors, I shall lay before you every sacrifice, and I shall perpetually worship you. So long as my spirit informs my body, in every place where I may be, through perpetual testimony I shall proclaim your glory. And I shall commend your holy name to posterity, since you have made me worthy of your sweet favor."

---

[17]The moon.

[18]Anchises' son is Aeneas, with whom Elissa (Dido) fell in love after having heard of his exploits from Cupid, who took the form of Ascanius, the son of Aeneas and a Trojan noblewoman. The "lord" in question here is Amor or Cupid.

Guenelic finally speaks to his lady.

Chapter 5

These words spoken, I felt completely consoled by my secret idea, and said to Quezinstra that it was time to leave this place to approach the castle where my lady was a captive. As soon as I had said this, without further delay, we bade the gentleman farewell, thanking him for the good and honorable treatment he had so liberally accorded us. Then, when we had gone out the door, looking all around us we perceived the castle of Cabasus. What made us easily recognize it was that the gentleman had described its situation and how it was constructed and built. But as soon as I had glimpsed it, to myself I said: "O Guenelic! There is the place where your supreme contentment lies. There is your true joy, which Heaven has made for you. O how fortunate the pain that is followed by such a reward!" Saying these words, we approached the desired place. Seeing that a short distance away there was a beautiful, large forest, we set out in that direction to rest there, and also to find out if there was some agreeable place there where we could refresh ourselves a bit while awaiting the opportune moment. When we had gone a little way, we saw a house where lived people who were charged with preserving and guarding the forest. This place was propitious for us until the time had come when Somnus more forcefully assaults the human heart. Then, provided with what I needed, I promptly left and went to the designated place; when I arrived there, you may be sure my limbs were lighter than an autumnal leaf on the sapless branch. When I was near the window, I saw the lady who was the unique compensation of all my travail, who made me such a salutation as was never made by Jupiter to Alcmene, Venus to Adonis, or Deineira to Hercules, for her welcome was no less jocund than benign. I immediately felt such excessive joy that I forgot myself. In my contemplation, love bound my heart with such force I was unable to utter a single word. But what speech denied me, feelings and exterior movements manifested. On the other hand, I had certain proof that my lady was no less affected than I, for she remained in uncertainty in order to contemplate me. By some movements of colors I perceived her radiant eyes, whose pupils, errant and vagabond around the circumference, sparkled with amorous desire, like the rays of the morning sun reflected in a clear spring-pond. After having kept silent for a long time, my heart recovered its tranquillity and repose, and then I began to say such words:

"Madame, do not be astonished if I am so slow and tardy in speaking, for your presence—with the light of your eyes received by mine—has illuminated my heart with such intense ardor that the heat spreading into my limbs makes the intemperate and cold winter seem like hot summer. As for the alteration of the heart which is so painful for me to endure, just as the flames of a furnace in which the fire is too violent hinder each other at the entrance to the chimney, from my breast sighs depart in such great numbers that I am entirely deprived of speech. Yet I assure you that to express to you the force with which love dominates me, all the eloquent tongues of the Greeks and Latins would not suffice; for since love is incomprehensible, you must know that it is also inexpressible. My lady, since you know with what good will I have remained faithful to our love among so many hardships, woes, and travails, you must believe that my affection will endure in perpetuity. Therefore it remains only to find a suitable means of liberating you from this calamity and extreme misery in which you are held. Alas! If you knew how much pain thinking of your sufferings causes me, you should deem the love I bear you still more faithful and perfect than you do now. But nonetheless if experience cannot be trusted, I shall shortly show you how much your unhappiness vexes me, for neither fortune's variability nor the fear of death shall make me abandon my enterprise. But while awaiting the opportunity to carry it out, may you not find it tedious to tell me how you came to be moved to this place."

As soon as I had finished speaking, I saw my dear lady open her rose-like mouth to utter such words: "O Guenelic! You may be sure that the excessive love I bear you not only spurs me to obey you after having heard your words, but leads me to want to know your secret thoughts in order to realize them insofar as I can. And so, although the memory of what you have asked me to tell you causes me an incomprehensible affliction, nevertheless I will not fail to tell you what I can recall. In order to give you a more ample account, you must know that after you had given my husband certain proof of our love through your indiscreet pursuit, this caused me to be the object of so many opprobrious, insulting, and cruel torments that not being able to endure such disasters, with my own hands I sought several times to put an end to my life. However, several impediments intervened, and I was unable to realize my iniquitous and miserable intention. My husband saw that it was not possible for me to stop loving you, and that I was inclined to despair because I could have no joy. In order to prevent misfortunes, he caused me to be taken away. But, alas! If I were to try to express to you the extreme pain I suffered from my departure, you must believe that the rest of my life would not suffice; for since I left your city, I have not ceased to weep and cry. When I was conducted to the place where you see me, I was put under the guard of a lady who is my husband's sister. Thereby I understood that he had some internal compassion for me, and did not want to make me languish a long time. For I knew his sister to be so perverse, I imagined that being ruled and governed by her, my sad life could not last long. Wherefore I believed death would shortly deliver me from my misfortunes. But nevertheless my desire for death has been frustrated, for although my body is so delicate and tender, still it has not been able to dissolve, despite the bitter pains it has sustained, but rather my suffering soul, troubled by innumerable passions, has been retained in my body. For along with the bitterness I felt because of being absent from you, I was continually afflicted and cruelly persecuted, as much in deeds as in words. Among other things that caused the augmentation of my torments, that accursed creature treacherous to our love found a marvelous way to accuse me because she had been shown a book about my torments, which I had written down, in the hope that through this book you might be reliably informed about my tribulations. But alas! I believe they were not consigned to your hands, my dear friend, but to further aggravate my woes, my bitter fortune allowed it to fall into the hands of my cruel enemy, who by this means had clear proof of the unfailing love I bear you. Therefore she has not ceased to insult and upbraid me, and to persuade my husband to believe some evil spirit has inspired me to write this work, and that it would be a very beneficial thing to put an end to my life. Alas! If she had understood what a pleasure dying is to lovers who are separated from their beloved, she would not have been so prompt to want to arrange it for me; but through lack of understanding, and thinking to distress me, she gave me joy. But nevertheless, despite her constant urging, she was unable to make my husband consent to her desire. When she talked to him about it, in order to free himself from his concern he told her that he believed I was so weak that because of the pains and travails I suffered my life could not last long; wherefore he did not intend to try to shorten the little time that remained to me. When she heard that response, with furious rage she began once again to torment me, and she has continued to do so since I was shut up here, except for the past three months; but this discontinuation proceeds from the fact that she is busy tormenting other personages, against whom she has made some unjust accusations. By this means, since it would be impossible for her to persecute us all at once (because of the distance involved), she is in this castle only twice a week. And now she makes up for the time she thinks she has lost by being twice as hard on me. Because two days have gone by since she was last here, I believe she will come tomorrow. But since Fortune has so favored me as to allow me to have the delightful pleasure of seeing you, it may be that she has had enough of persecuting me. Wherefore the fear of the future woe perverse Fortune may cause me is not so depressing as it was in the past, for the memory of you, along with the hope of being soon delivered, will give me strength, so that all hardships will be easy for me to endure."

Narrative of the adventures of each of the two lovers.

Chapter 5 (continued)

While I was listening to such words, I was moved to such great compassion that the suffering of my heart caused my face to be watered with the flowing tears my eyes distilled. When I could speak, I said to her: "Alas! My good mistress, how has it been possible that your delicate person has been able to endure so many cruel and unbearable torments? Surely you should be listed in the Catalog of martyrs, and solemnly commemorated. But how can your husband have been so cruel, considering that you never received any delight from love beyond looking and talking? For that you have not deserved such a grievous punishment."

To these words my lady replied: "You must not be surprised at my husband, for at the urging of many wicked tongues he has been moved to torment me. For you must know that it was so often reported to him that you were maligning me that for this reason he was so perplexed and doubtful that he did not know which decision his judgment should take; whether he should preserve my life, or put an end to it. Be assured that had it happened, or were it to happen, that I arrived at the fifth and last stage of love, and that this came to my husband's attention, you must understand that he would not follow the example of the Greek who was deprived of his wife by the Phrygian. Despite the fact that she willingly allowed herself to be carried off, nevertheless she received no punishment; rather, when she returned to her husband ten years later, he kindly welcomed and accepted her.[19] In the same way Philip of Macedon patiently endured his wife's love affairs.[20] But I am very sure that such pity would not be granted me; I would be exterminated and brought to an end by the most cruel and ignominious death they could think of. Consider then in what peril my life was through the dangerous bite of the pestiferous tongues that pronounced what I believe was never uttered by your mouth. I imagine that sometimes your patience was exhausted with waiting, and for that reason you were not able to be as discreet as urgent necessity required, and so I assume you may have said some thoughtless things, not such as were told me by the false reporters, whom for decency's sake I refrain from naming. Therefore in order not to cause anxiety in our hearts, I shall leave this subject, begging you not to impute malignity of

---

[19]This refers to the story of Paris ("the Phrygian"), who deprived Menelaus ("the Greek") of Helen and thus started the Trojan War. When Menelaus entered Helen's chamber during the sack of Troy with the intention of killing her for having gone willingly with Paris, he was unable to execute his plan and instead took her home to Sparta.

[20]His wife, Queen Olympias, was infamous for her extramarital affairs; in fact, Alexander was often thought to have been fathered by Zeus rather than by Philip.

heart to me for having recalled your little faults, which I have mentioned only in order to make you understand the pain you and I have suffered because we did not know how to simulate and feign the contrary of what your heart and mine desired."

These words said, I replied as follows: "My lady, I see clearly that the false reporters have been the cause of our torments. If sometimes from impatience, as you say, I have indiscreetly pursued my amorous enterprise, for two reasons I must ask your mercy: the first is that excessive love constrained me to act in this way; the other is that I have suffered unbearable woes and hardships in your service."

As I was saying these words, she interrupted me, and said to me with a smile: "Guenelic, you have forgotten to mention what would more strongly buttress your case: it is the virile condition that when a man is not satisfied promptly, and as he would desire, he becomes annoyed and impatient, and this often causes him to exceed the bounds of reason. For that reason, if one were punished for so doing, there would be very few who would remain unpunished."

After such words, I said to her: "My lady, although such excuses as you provide for me may depreciate the male sex, nevertheless I do not wish to deny you this, for it suffices me that I am not deprived of your good graces. Thus I beg you not to speak further of something that could distress us somewhat. I should rather meditate and think on the most suitable ways of getting you out of this captivity in order that I might joyfully take you away."

As soon as I had said this, my lady began to form these words in her sweet voice: "Very dear friend, it seldom happens that excessively serene weather does not bring on storms; in the same way immoderate joys, if they are not tempered, are led into bitterness. I see by your face and behavior that you are filled with great jubilation, and it seems to you an easy thing to deliver me; and that notion proceeds from the ardent desire you have. But if you consider it well, you will see that in things that concern lives and honors, one must think and cogitate well and then make a decision and conclusion. Before I state my opinion, I beg you to tell me what has happened to you since you were informed of my absence." In response, to satisfy her desire, without holding anything back I recounted all the calamities and miseries endured in my painful and weary travels, and her compassion was perhaps greater than that of Scipio for Masinissa,[21] for I saw her lovely eyes wet with little tears that resembled oriental pearls, and these glorious tears consoled me for all my earlier sufferings. When my lady saw that I had finished my story, she said:

---

[21]Masinissa was a Numidian prince who fell in love with his captive, Sophonisba; Livy is said to have sent her poison to allow her to escape being taken to Rome by Scipio.

"I am well aware, O unique lord, comfort and salvation of my life, that because of your affection for me your life has always been without tranquillity or repose. But since Fortune has made me worthy of your presence, putting an end to my lamentations I shall describe to you the well-considered and thought-out means which seems to me most apt to realize our intentions. To divulge it to you, you must understand that if it were in your power to capture the good will of the man who is charged with guarding the nearby forest, it seems to me our ship would be near the secure and desired harbor; for that man is very intimate and familiar with the porter of this castle, and because of their accustomed conversations, he often comes to this place. Therefore, by means of his acquaintance, you can easily enter with him, along with your men; but you must await the opportunity. And so it is very important that you know first to come when the evil-tongued lady is not here, for as I already told you, I am certain she will shortly arrive. I have stated my whole idea and final conclusion to you, with the reservation nevertheless that if your opinion differs, I shall rely on your prudence."

When I had heard all this, I said: "O my sweet lady, moderator of all my travails, your discreet, mellifluous, and sweet words give me a delight that preserves me from all woe for the new joy—if I may with great effort offer praise befitting your wise counsel. But you, being the one in whom prudence and humanity reside, will excuse me with your customary benevolence. Because the goddess who had such pity on Orpheus that she agreed to restore Eurydice to him is already beginning to hide her cusp, I shall be compelled to separate from you.[22] But although I am departing with my body, I leave you mistress of my soul, and I beg you not to be distressed if my return is more tardy than you and I desire. Do not think the delay results from my malevolent fault, but rather from my desire to give our enterprise a good beginning so that a good end may follow."

Sweetly responding, she said: "Guenelic, I greatly praise this consideration of yours. Do not be afraid that your absence will be so sad for me that I cannot patiently tolerate it, since I shall be certain that it will be only in order to await the opportune moment. Therefore go in peace, and remember me." Then, after we had said a sweet and affectionate farewell, I left her.

---

[22]Proserpina is the goddess who restored Eurydice to Orpheus; the rest of the passage alludes to the moon, normally associated with Diana. Cf. the beginning of Part Two, chapter 3.

The lover's clever way of reaching his beloved.

Chapter 6

Back at the house where I had left Quezinstra, I recounted everything to him, and having heard it all, he told me that the ruse Hélisenne had thought of seemed to him clever enough to attain our goal. Seeing that the thing seemed not so difficult to him, I was overjoyed, for Caesar was no more content or happy after the battle of Pharsalia than I was then. And so I spent some time remembering Hélisenne. Later, when I saw the opportunity, I began to falsely dissimulate as I inquired and questioned the forest warden, asking who was the owner of the castle of Cabasus, and what sort of people resided there. He promptly replied that for the present there was no one there but a lady, who was held captive in extremity for some reason unknown to everyone in the vicinity. Then Quezinstra and I asked him if no one went there to visit. He replied that no one did, except for the lord's relative, who was not there to console the lady, but on the contrary to torment, afflict, and cruelly persecute her. At these words we said that this lady's unhappiness was a great pity, and that if it were possible to see her, we were prepared to risk every peril to do so. Then he replied that he often went there because of his friendship with the porter, who was to be completely trusted. We then begged him urgently to do us the great favor of helping us be worthy of being in the presence of this unfortunate lady. To which he promptly replied that the porter had an express order not to permit anyone to enter. It would be as difficult to get into this castle as it would be to undertake to restore all the pyramids of Egypt and the royal and populous city of Babylon, he said, and he would not want to take on a task so arduous. My great joy was then converted into a great anxiety, for these words seemed to me no less bitter than to Menelaus the report of his wife's rape. Seeing this, Quezinstra took me aside and said:

"Don't be too distressed, seeing that this man is in no way favorable to your desire. What obligation, what contract of friendship, what benevolence binds him to you that he should so easily agree to your pleasures? If you desire to know his final decision, you must offer him a rather large sum of money. If you do so, I believe without much resistance he will yield and obey your will. We read that the daughter of Leda was persuaded by her maids to submit to the Phrygian's pleasure, although these maids were deemed so faithful that they were virtually charged with being the queen's bodyguards—and especially by the king, Menelaus, whose relatives they were! But they were overcome through avarice, for there is nothing in this world that cannot be corrupted thereby. Therefore desist

179

from your foolish worries by making use of my advice." As soon as I had heard these words, I wanted without delay to act on this advice, and I did so. This idea was very useful to me, for this man, overcome by avarice, after some resistance agreed to take the money, promising to completely satisfy our desire. We decided that the next night, toward two o'clock, before fair Aurora arrived, we should go to the castle of Cabasus.

The night, accompanied by desire, did not allow me any rest. When the time to leave had come, we went to the desired place. As soon as the porter heard the voice of our guide, he promptly opened the gate. Astonished by the unexpected arrival, he asked the reason for such haste, since the hour was more suited and fit for repose than anything else. While he was uttering these words, we entered through the gate. Seeing this, the porter was terribly angered. Therefore he asked our guide whence proceeded this bold temerity of having brought men with him, and why he had done it. "Alas!" said he, "you have truly deceived and circumvented me, which astonishes me, for I had total confidence in you. I see clearly that this will cause my ruin and extermination, for if the lord's relative is informed of it, there will be no excuse that can save me."

Then we said to him: "My friend, desist from this fear which has come over you, and accept our intention, which is such that before we leave this castle, we shall deliver the lady from the captivity in which she is detained. See that you help us in this matter; if you do so, your service shall not remain unrewarded. But if you oppose our desires in any way, and you cause any upset or tumult, you had best prepare yourself with true contrition and patience, for as soon as people arrive I shall put a violent end to your life."

When the porter heard our words, considering that his life was in another's power without his being able to resist, he asked our guide if he knew anything about us, and if we were relatives or allies of the lady. He replied that he was ignorant of that, and that we were gentlemen he did not know, who had through clever arguments and continual persuasion seduced him by giving him to understand that we desired to see lady Hélisenne, and that through excessive credulity, he had been deceived. The porter listened to all this, and seeing that he had no choice but to yield to our will, he told us that he knew no way to help us in this matter, unless it were appropriate to break down the door of the tower. After saying this, he tried to go away, saying that to save his life he had to flee and never return to this country. Then, fearing that some trouble might thereby come to us, I forbade him to leave, and told him that he should not leave this place before we did. Then to satisfy him, we made him a present of a rather large number of coins, with which he was very content. Then without further ado, we were conducted to the door of the tower, which we immediately broke down. Entering the chamber, we graciously greeted my sweet lady Hélisenne, who said to me:

The unfortunate liberation of Hélisenne, and the end of Guenelic's love affair.

Chapter 7

"O Guenelic, I cannot conjecture what joy could be so great that it could surpass or even approach that which I now feel. O gods! What celestial influence has made me worthy of such beatitude? O felicitous presence! You bring me such great contentment that I cannot express it, for never Demetrius to Lamia, Leander to Hero, Jupiter to Europa, or Hercules to Iole, were as agreeable and pleasant as you are to me. If I thought happy the sight that was on the preceding days accorded me by means of the window, this one exceeds it by far in felicity, for I was very perplexed and fearful that I might not arrive at my future deliverance, but now through your providence I see myself totally liberated from my former travail."

After this amorous and sweet utterance I said to her: "O my unique lady, be assured that if my sight gives you pleasure, being in your presence is as delightful to me as ever Andromeda's was to Perseus, the Egyptian's to the victorious Caesar, or the fair nymph Hesperia's to Aesacus.[23] But because too slow a departure might harm us, my lady, it is proper to carry out our decisions and prepare ourselves for going away."

As soon as I had stopped speaking, my lady turned to an aged maid, who had served her with great fidelity. For this reason she said to her: "My friend, in order not to be ungrateful, I want to reward you for the good and pleasant service you have given me, and as recompense therefore I freely give you a rather large sum of money which you will find in my little chest; here is the key."

So saying, she presented it to the maid, who gratefully thanked her. Then the maid said to her: "Milady, I am very delighted to see an end put to your constant sufferings, but I am afraid that when it comes to the attention of milord your husband and his relative, they will cause me to suffer some injury; for they might suspect that I was privy to your secrets. You know they are precipitous in their wrath, and that they are likely to be cruel to their servants."

Then my lady replied: "My friend, you will be able to assure milord my husband and his relative that my friend Guenelic—for whose sake I have endured such grievous pain—entered the castle through a clever trick as

---

[23]Andromeda was chained to a rock, whence she was delivered by the hero Perseus; the "Egyptian" is Cleopatra, who, in order to speak to Caesar, had herself rolled in a rug and unrolled at his feet; and Aesacus was a son of Priam who fell in love with the nymph Hesperia on first sight. At her death, Aesacus threw himself into the sea.

well as by force, with the firm resolve of removing me therefrom; to which I made no resistance, for the lord Love, who holds domination and lordship over me, urged and goaded me to follow him. And so you shall inform milord my husband that if he desires a wife, he should find himself one; and that he has lost all hope of ever seeing me again, for I have no intention of ever being in his presence."

Immediately after this was said, we left the castle, going out through the gate where our horses were prepared and waiting for us. Having mounted them—not slowly, but with great and extreme haste—we began to ride away. But meanwhile some unfortunate influence of the heavens allowed the evil-tongued lady to be informed of what we were doing. This misfortune happened to us through a wicked and unhappy boy who had heard all our conversations in the castle. So, without our being aware of it, he had slipped away from us to make a full report to the cruel lady. Alas! Here was an occasion to convert our great joy into even greater bitterness, for as we were traveling through the forest, and were still only four miles distant from the castle of Cabasus, we thought we heard the loud sound of hoofbeats. My lady was very afraid, for mentally foreseeing her misfortune, she recalled and thought over all the things that could harm her. Hence she said to me: "Guenelic, I cannot guess whence proceeds the painful anxiety that has come over my heart. I am in extreme perplexity, fearing that this may be some presage of future ills, for the sound we have heard makes me afraid."

No less concerned and distressed than she was, I was beginning to comfort her when the sound became louder and louder. Soon afterward we perceived a great multitude of men who cried to us with one voice: "You are ravishers and not knights! Give us back the lady you have carried off or otherwise you shall be constrained by force to do so!" At these words my lady was afflicted with such a cruel pain that there could have been no greater. And so, in a very troubled voice she said to me:

"Alas! My dear friend, I see clearly that on this day when we thought ourselves so happy, thinking that it was the beginning of our perpetual beatitude, we shall be very unhappy; for it is obvious that we shall prematurely end our young days through a bitter, furious, and execrable death." When I heard these pitiful and lamentable words, although my internal pain was great, I did not let the torment my sad heart felt show in my face. To console her, I told her that she should be strong and courageous, for I trusted some divine power would preserve us from this mortal peril. So saying, I contemplated her face, which was pale and without color, so that she looked more dead than alive. Seeing that, Quezinstra and I decided to have her dismount and rest under a tree, fearing that through weakness her wearied body might fall. But we had no sooner done so and remounted ourselves than we were assailed from all sides.

Then, taking our swords in our hands, we began to defend ourselves in a manly way, and so well that at first each of us cut down his man, who afterward did not have the strength to rise again. But our assailants, taking confidence in their superior numbers, strove with great arrogance to injure us, so that both Quezinstra and I were slightly wounded, but our wounds served only to make us fight more ardently. Because of the enormous blows that our enemies continually received, their number began to diminish so much that there was not one of them who was not sorely afraid. Wherefore they resisted us only a little. After they had suffered a long time, they fled, and as they went away they all cursed the evil-tongued lady for having urged them to attack us.

After we had victoriously driven them off, we withdrew, giving thanks and praise to the sovereign divinity who had been so favorable to us, whereby we were overjoyed. It seemed to us that it remained only to console Madame Hélisenne and then joyously go on our way. Therefore I began to praise and extol Fortune, thinking she was at peace with us. But she clearly demonstrated that she was not yet finished wreaking her wrath on us, for as we tried to rejoin my lady, we could not do so because in pursuing our enemies we had gone a great distance away from the place where we had left her. And so we began to investigate and search for her. Meanwhile I cried out in a loud voice, calling milady's name. But no one but Echo answered us. Nonetheless, after having looked a long time, we found the place we were looking for, but alas! I saw milady in such an extremity that I had cause only for woe and heartache.

Hélisenne's repentance and her death.

Chapter 8

Apollo was abandoning the farthest part of Pisces and holding Aries' head in his right hand when we presented ourselves before milady. As soon as my sweet lady had seen me, she showed by her external behavior that the sight of me was inexpressibly pleasing to her. When I was sitting beside her, giving her pale face many kisses, she said to me in a weak voice: "O my only consoling refuge! O light of my eyes! O creature whom I love more than it is humanly possible to believe! I can truly say that with the delight I feel in seeing you, no kind of death can frighten me. O my sweet friend! In a short time you shall have certain proof of how grievous and full of bitterness your absence has been to me; for because I had no hope of ever seeing you, I was so afflicted and distressed that I am unable to express it to you. In addition, I have been so troubled by the winter cold that this bodily pain combined with the passions of the soul have so persecuted me that I feel myself approaching the three sisters who will prematurely cut my vital thread."[24]

When she had said this, she fell silent. Then, being deprived of all hope, what particularly distressed me was that there was nearby no habitable place. Wherefore, with continual sobs and sighs which rose from my breast in great multitudes, I said: "Dear Madame, I cannot find words by which I could express the extreme pain I suffer because of yours, for you must believe that seeing you infirm and languishing in this way is incredibly painful to me. So I assure you that the words you have uttered are so many arrows that wound my heart. Wherefore I am certain that your death will cause mine, for my life lives only through yours. Alas! Madame, would you ever have thought the incomprehensible affection I have for you would allow me to go on living when I see you die? Certainly if you were to think so, you would be very far from the truth. Alas! My life is beyond all hope, although when I returned to you, having won a victory over our enemies, a great happiness accompanied me. Not knowing about the misfortune and woe about to befall me, I thought that in the future my life would be sweet and tranquil. But these consoling thoughts were soon converted into bitter and harsh ones. O woeful and distressing mutation! O cruel time! O day full of misery! O accursed fortune, cruel, furious, detestable, execrable and abominable! Why do you want to exterminate me? Have I not suffered enough hardship and travail? If your wrath is not yet sated, why don't you vent it in some other way without wishing to deprive me of the lady whom I thought I had won through so many trials? O blind, spiteful, and vexatious one, see to what extremity and calamity your ingratitude has led me. Surely I have nothing that can comfort me, unless I hope that what the body cannot do, the soul can; for by means of my death, my soul, milady, will continually accompany you."

As soon as I had stopped speaking, although she was weak and near her end, she replied with these words: "O my sweet lord! I believe you when you say my pain causes you an extreme sorrow; but many reasons should induce you to endure it. Among others, you should recall that neither I nor others are engendered to be immortal, for it is manifest that all things that begin naturally, end naturally; for our matter, having its origin in four contrary qualities, cannot be perdurable, for it is created of matter and form, as the Philosopher teaches us in his *Physics*.[25] And so, considering this, I beg you, when I am dead, try not to be too mournful, but reflect that a prudent and wise man should not be exalted by joy or cast down by suffering. If being deprived of me through my absence distresses

---

[24]The three Fates, who spin the thread of life.
[25]Aristotle.

you, you should be more consoled to see me freed from the calamities which overcome us every day in this mortal world. You must also think of the expectation of the true immortality of the soul. O glorious death! Through you we live, and the whole human condition depends on you; for you make what is corruptible eternal. And so it should be deemed false and vulgar to think that dying and ending one's days in old age is more fortunate than dying in the flower of youth. How often people demonstrate in that way their ignorance and meager understanding! For they stop at transitory things, and do not follow the opinions of all wise minds, who do not fear death at all, as it appears in the words of Saint Paul, who cried out: 'I desire to die, in order to be with life, which one attains, o death, through you.'[26] The philosopher Socrates, having an indubitable faith in the immortality of the soul, was consoled as he drank the poison. The wise Cato would not have willingly died had he been in doubt of this. If you reflect on that of which I am reminding you, you will find it easy to mitigate your bitter pain, which grieves me far more than the approach of death. Therefore if you have no compassion for yourself, I beg you to have compassion for me, for I suffer your pains and mine. But if I thought after my departure you could acquire the fair virtue of patience, I should endure death without feeling much pain, about which the divine Plato wrote that it was of all woes the smallest." This said, she lifted her eyes to the heavens, and uttered these words:

"O eternal and sovereign God who sees our hearts and knows our sins! I pray that in your mercy you may turn into oblivion my continual iniquities through which I know I have committed a very grave offense against you, for I have always persevered in evil thoughts, following my sensuality, which has led me where reason, conscience, and honor refuse to go. But all the same I have such great faith in your divine clemency and infinite goodness that I hope my prayer will not be inefficacious but will be acceptable to you. For you never refuse a pardon to your creatures when they beg it of you with a devout heart; for you expressed yourself through Ezekiel your prophet in these words: 'Whenever the sinner shall return to God in true penitence, all the sins he may have committed shall not be imputed to him, nor shall they prevent him from having eternal life.'[27] For this reason, although my return is late, still we must have indubitable faith that we shall receive mercy. For as Saint Cyprian says: 'At the point where the soul is about to leave the body, your clemency and

---

[26]Our translation. Cf. Philippians 1.23: "I am in a strait betwixt two, having a desire to depart, and to be with Christ; which is far better."

[27]Our translation. Cf. Ezekiel 18.21-22: "If the wicked will turn from all his sins that he hath committed, and keep all my statutes, and do that which is lawful and right, he shall surely live, he shall not die. All his transgressions that he hath committed, they shall not be mentioned unto him; in his righteousness that he hath done he shall live."

benevolence, my most merciful God, does not refuse it if there is true penitence, which cannot be too late, though it must be true.' Nor is the sin then irremissible, if the will rejects it. Whatever necessity leads one to true penitence, one may readily obtain pardon for one's sin, despite the crime and the latter's enormity, the shortness of the time one has to live, the extremity of the hour, or the dissolution of the preceding life and association—provided one is moved to contrition and the rejection of the preceding sensuality and pleasure. For Your charity, my God, is like that of a mother who opens her arms to kindly receive those who willingly return to her. Therefore Saint Paul says: 'Moreover the law entered, that the offense might abound. But where sin abounded, grace did much more abound.'[28] And the prophet, exhorting sinners to return through true contrition and penitence, speaks to them in this manner: 'Return through worthy patience to the Creator, for he is most kind and merciful, and far more ready to forgive than you are to ask forgiveness.' For this reason I entrust myself to your mercy, sublime God, for I believe you shall see how I acknowledge my great sin, how I condemn my vituperation and turpitude, and detest my vices, which in your immense prudence and incomprehensible goodness you shall forgive, and grant my final prayer, by joining my soul to the company of the elect, where it may find consolation and joy." And as she had perceived by my external comportment that I was suffering an unspeakable pain without parallel, which forced me to tear my fair hair and to strike violent and enormous blows on my white breast, she promptly began to say these words to me:

"O Guenelic, because you continue your weeping, your tears and moans, you are depriving me of all the hope I had in your knowledge, which I believed sufficient to restrain your wrath and mitigate your passions, which are so excessive that you are not showing your virtue at all. Nevertheless, the time has come when you must show and endorse it, overcoming the pain you feel at my death. If you strive to do so, you will succeed; for there is no travail so great that it cannot be moderated by prudence, nor any pain so acute that it cannot be broken by patience. Therefore I beg you to put an end to your great suffering, and console yourself with the thought that the divine clemency has taken pity on us, since it has not wished to allow the sin of adultery to be committed by us, which would have caused me to die a more unfortunate death than the one I shall soon suffer, which I shall accept without fear. For I hope my soul will be transported to the place where it was first created. Thus do not offend me so much as to wish to deny me my beatitude. If up to now you have loved me with a sensual love, desiring the satisfaction of your useless desires, at present you must desist from all such vain thoughts. As

---

[28]Romans 5.20.

much as you have loved the body, henceforth be a lover of the soul in charitable delight. Correct your life so that the poison of concupiscence does not deprive you of the possession of the divine heritage we are promised. Hence I pray to our Maker that you and I may be consoled and led thereto."

The lover's regrets at the death of his lady.

Chapter 9

As soon as she had finished, because pain tortured her too much, it was obvious on looking at her face that her final end was near. For her fair eyes began to grow dim and dark because of the shadows of death, which she was near. Seeing there was no remedy, I suffered such acute pain that I was no less pale than she. When I tried to utter some words, the faculty of speech was not granted me because of the irruption of countless sighs accompanied by infinite tears, which completely prevented me from uttering them. Seeing this, Quezinstra, although his heart was greatly burdened by his compassion for us, nevertheless sought to console me. Meanwhile, I saw my lady begin to look at me again, and she opened her mouth, trying to say something. But because of the mortal pains that assailed her, her tongue and all her limbs were deprived of their powers. Then, lying in my arms, she remained as if dead. Immediately my woeful heart was agitated by such an extreme distress that for a long time I neither moved nor breathed. Then, when I was able to speak, in a broken and halting voice I said:

"O bitter death, cruel, furious, and worthy of every execration! Why have you so prematurely entered this body? Alas! You have disinherited me of the one in whom I deemed my eternal contentment to consist. But I see very well that mortal hearts are nourished on many errors, for what I thought was to be my solace has been converted into corruption. O frail and false human hope! O fragile condition of ours! How transitory are mundane things! Surely there is nothing in this terrestrial realm on which one can rely. Alas! I was well warned by that saintly and good person who so often remonstrated with me, that I should succumb to some extreme peril. I see very well that he knew this because he was aware of the unfortunate planet that shone over my birth, which lent me an unlucky influence from which I have never been able to escape. O accursed and detestable was the hour in which I was born! O how I desire that I had never been brought forth into this world! O how happy I should have been if at my sad and woeful birth the naked earth had been my bed, or had I lived no longer than the men who sprang up from the teeth Cadmus sowed.[29] Alas! If that had happened to me, I should not have been troubled by so many torments, misfortunes, tears, sighs, pains, tortures, and despairs, which evils have all taken up residence together in my heart. I shall never be free of them, unless by means of death, which I have blamed and depreciated. But if death were soon to separate my soul from my body, it would repair part of the harm it has done me. And so I beg death not to spare me, since I am ready and prepared to depart. When I have passed to the other shore, contemplating the sweet sight, I shall have everything I desire." So speaking, and expressing such laments and exclamations because of my cruel suffering, my voice failed in my mouth. Then Quezinstra said to me:

"Guenelic, I am greatly astonished at your continual complaints regarding the death of this lady. Aren't you afraid of offending God, who has decreed such a law for all creatures? Don't you know what is written, that there is no wisdom nor prudence, strength, or anything else which can resist the will of the sublime and powerful God; to His will you must yield, giving clear proof of your discretion. Do not detest and blame death, since it liberates us from all our travails. Hence the Psalmist calls it forth and requests it, that it might come quickly so as to put an end to his groans and tears. And Saint Paul (Philippians 1) deems it the portal through which we are delivered from prison. Now consider therefore what is most just, most holy and worthy of the greatest praise: by these means we reach the fruit of blessed life and we are raised to the loftiness of divine things, which because of their profundity are incomprehensible to human understanding, as we are taught by the glorious Saint Paul (1 Corinthians 12 and Acts 9), who tasted this mellow sweetness when he was ravished for three days into the third heaven. When he returned, he said (1 Corinthians 2) that the eye of mortal man could never see, nor the ears hear, nor the mind comprehend, what God has promised and prepared for those who love Him. Therefore how ardent should be the desire to attain this glorious felicity! Certainly for this reason we should not weep or lament for those whom we see dying with strong faith, which gives hope that it will give rise to perfect charity; and as it is written in Saint John (1 John 4), 'God is love; and he that dwelleth in love dwelleth in God, and God in him.' O great gift of faith from which such beatitude comes that it is not in our power to express it! Nonetheless, not to be negligent in consoling you, I have wished to remind you of the Holy Scriptures, thinking thereby to heal your pain. For if you are prudent, you will meditate and think often on the faith and true contrition with which Madame Hélisenne rendered up her spirit to God and her body to the earth. I

---

[29]Most of the soldiers who sprang up from the dragon teeth sown by Cadmus, the founder of Thebes, were quickly killed.

have no doubt that in reflecting on this you shall find some balm for your suffering, persuading yourself that she has truly joined the glorious company. For that reason you should put an end to your woeful complaints. And I also beg you to desist from that damnable and false opinion that consists in saying that we are controlled by means of the planets, for that is a terrible error.[30] Some heretics called Priscillianists say that every man is born under a constellation of stars and is ruled and governed by their influences, which they call *fatum* in Latin, that is to say, *destiny* in our language. They say moreover that according to the arrangement of the influences of these stars man is forced to do good or evil; the error of these heretics is condemned and clearly disproved by several arguments given by Saint Augustine in the first chapter of the fifth part of *The City of God*. This heresy is also condemned by Chrysostom, who says that it blasphemes against God in three ways. The first is that it would follow that God is and has been evil in creating the stars; wherefore concerning the Gospel according to Saint Matthew he says: 'If anyone is made a homicide or an adulterer by the stars, a great iniquity and injustice must therefore be attributed to the stars, but even more to their creator. For since God is aware and not at all ignorant of future things, and he knew that such iniquity must proceed from the stars, if he had not wished to amend them, he would not be good; if he had wished to do so and was not able to, he would be impotent, and not omnipotent.' The second blasphemy is that God would be cruel to make us suffer punishment for crimes that we might commit through the creations and constraint of these stars. Wherefore, says Chrysostom, 'Why should I endure punishment for something I might have done, not willingly, but necessarily?' The third blasphemy is that God would not be wise in his commandments. For who commands someone and forbids him to perpetrate an evil that through constraint he cannot avoid? Surely there is no one in the world who would be deemed wise in making such commandments. Therefore such an opinion is a great offense against God. It is also said in the eighth sermon on Saint John that the Lord and Creator of the stars is not under their control and disposition. We have for that a natural proof. For when a king or great lord is produced in the world, if this were done by the heavens, it would follow that [all] those who are born under this influence would be kings and great lords, which is not the case. One might ask if the impression made by the celestial luminaries is not the cause of the diversity of morals and conditions among men. To this we may reply that the question has two

---

[30]As Secor points out, most of the following discussion of predestination and free will is taken from a book on astrology, probably from an early, lost edition of David Final's *Epitome de la vraie astrologie et de la reprouvée, auquel est traité du franc arbitre, de predestination, prescience*, etc. See Secor, 468ff.

senses, according to different interpretations. If one wishes to say that these stars are causes determining necessarily the wills, fortunes, and conditions of men, this will be heresy; for it is against the faith insofar as it would follow that whatever one did, one could thereby earn neither merit nor glory. But if one wishes to say that the morals of men are dispositionally and contingently varied according to the disposition of the stars, that may be true and not be rejected by faith or reason; for it is manifest that the diverse disposition of the body produces much of the variation and mutation of the perturbations of morals and temperaments, as the author of the six principles says. Thus choleric people are naturally disposed and prompt to anger, sanguine people are kindly; melancholiacs are miserable, and phlegmatic people are lazy. But this is not at all necessary, since the mind has control over the body when it is aided by grace; as we see many cholerics who are sweet and amiable, and also many melancholiacs who are kindly. Because the power of celestial bodies affects and has some causal role in the composition and quality of temperaments, it follows that it can have some small dispositional and contingent effect on the morals and conditions of men, although the power of inferior nature has more effect on the quality of the temperament than the power of the stars. Thus Saint Augustine, in the second chapter of the fifth book of the *City*, in resolving a question concerning two brothers who fell sick and were cured at the same time, approves and praises more the physician Hippocras's reply when he was asked why they had fallen ill and were cured at the same time. He replied that it was because of the similarity of their temperaments; but the astrologer said that it was because of the identity and conjunction of their constellations. On these grounds is resolved the preceding question,[31] namely, whether the influence of the stars has some dispositional effect on the variation and diversity of morals, but not a necessary or sufficient effect, for we have a free will by means of which we may, with God's help, resist them. And so Ptolomeus says in his *Almagest*: 'The wise man will have power over the stars.' For these reasons it appears that the aforementioned Priscillianists err greatly, for as Saint Thomas says (in his first part, question 116, chapter 1), all natural and human acts may be traced back to a first cause, which is divine providence. Hence Saint Augustine once again says on this subject in the first chapter of the fifth part of the *City*: 'The man saying of the divine will that it is predetermined, holds back his judgment and corrects his tongue' as if he meant that such a man understands better than he says. For to speak directly, Destiny is nothing if not referred to the divine will and prescience. Saint Augustine says in his gloss on Psalm 101 that

---

[31]Secor notes that this is not in accord with the corresponding passage in Saint Augustine, which goes on to stress the role of purely natural causes. See Secor, 469.

divine predestination, through which God has eternally elected us, is the principal cause of all our merits, and that our will is only the concomitant and associative cause. Therefore it is said in the ninth chapter of Romans that it is not in the power of him who willeth or of him who runneth to predestine, but only in that of God, who has mercy on those who please him; and he allows the others to harden in their wickedness.[32] In this passage of the Apostle, says Saint Augustine's gloss, we find an ample explanation for men's obstinacy, but mercy is not accorded any cause or merit, for God, through his grace, grants men reward and remuneration without their having deserved it. However, that is not to say that God hardens the obstinate out of malice by withholding and depriving them of his grace, of which they are not in any way worthy, since they are not willing to bend their hearts and affections to the divine commandment. Therefore it is not written without reason in the fourth question of the twenty-second case that through equity and justice hidden from us and unknown to us, God does not confer on these his grace. Whence on this occasion the apostle cried out in the eleventh chapter of the Epistle to the Romans: 'O loftiness of the divine wisdom and knowledge, how inscrutable and unknown are your judgments, when through your grace you clothe the naked that it pleases you to be clothed, which is done for a reason known only to [you].'[33] Because speaking about this matter is too arduous, I shall abstain from doing so. Once again I beseech you not to persist in such errors, whose end result is nothing other than the travail of the body and the death of the soul." After Quezinstra had ended his speech, although I had such a great heartache that neither medicine nor comfort could remedy it, nevertheless, gathering all my strength, I answered him in this manner:

The death of Guenelic.

Chapter 10

"Dear companion and friend, your mellifluous and artful words might easily cure all woes, if they were curable, but mine, which is intolerable, cannot be tempered. Alas! The privation of such a lady is too grievous and unbearable for me. Wherefore I cannot find a remedy for my ultimate passions, for it is not in my power to show myself more tolerant than many of our predecessors, who, because of their friends' death, have not ceased to weep and cry. Phoenix and Chiron, who did not wish to sur-

---

[32] Cf. Romans 9.14-18.

[33] The text shifts from second to third person; in the interest of consistency we have given the second person throughout. Cf. Romans 11.33: "O the depth of the riches both of the wisdom and knowledge of God! how unsearchable are his judgments, and his ways past finding out!"

vive after the death of their pupil, offer us a manifest example.[34] Timoleon mourned his brother's death for twenty years.[35] Hagar wept perpetually because of her son's death.[36] Saint Augustine, with a great abundance of tears and moans, lamented his mother's death. Thus if so many famous and renowned men have wept, and some of them were so distressed as to abandon life, I could not avoid similarly succumbing. But as for the reproaches you made me concerning the influence of the heavens; I do not wish to be pertinacious on that head, but yield to all good judgments. Because I feel my wretched body weary of living, as if it were heavy with its natural years, I wish my sorrowing soul could be reunited with my dear lady Hélisenne, who seems to me to call me in a piteous voice, telling me that if my life is long, travail and woe will never cease to accompany me. And so it would benefit me more to die than to languish continually." After I had uttered such words, I remained silent for a rather long time; then, when I began to speak, raising my eyes toward the heavens, a great abundance and superfluity of tears flowed from my eyes, and with a humble heart I said:

"O Eternal Creator, who know[37] before the day of my birth what I would be, what I am and what I must be, I beseech and entreat you not to punish me according to my iniquitous sins, which are so great in number that to confess each of them would exceed my powers. But I hope to receive your mercy, for from you proceeds all good; in you consists all felicity; and from you come all gratitude and grace. I beg you therefore to make use of your great clemency toward me, your poor creature, by redeeming my multiple faults, which I believe you will not refuse to do. For you say, my creator, in the fifty-third chapter of Isaiah, that you have truly borne our griefs, sorrows, and infirmities. O source of infinite generosity, since you yourself pay our debts! O sweet redeemer, being yourself without sin, you bear our sins! O my sweet savior, although you may justly accuse me, I hope that you will excuse me; for you do not desire the death of the sinner. And so, provided with infallible hope, I am prepared and ready to render up to you my spirit, which I humbly commend to your divine providence."

End of The Torments of Love

---

[34]Phoenix was Achilles' tutor and accompanied him to Troy; Chiron was a centaur and also served as Achilles' tutor.

[35]Timoleon (ca. 365 B.C.) conspired to kill his brother when the latter attempted to make himself tyrant.

[36]Hagar believed her young son Ishmael was doomed, but God saved him. See Genesis 21.

[37]In the French text this verb is in the present tense. Although other sixteenth-century editions give it in the imperfect, we have elected to retain the present here, because it may be intended to reflect the Augustinian notion of the supratemporal nature of divine knowledge set forth in the preceding chapters.

There follows a full and ample narrative,
made by the magnanimous Quezinstra, describing the
premature death of his faithful companion the gentle Guenelic;
including what happened to the aforementioned Guenelic
and to his lady Hélisenne after their deplorable deaths,
which shall be set forth with the ornamentation
of the delightful poetical style.

Chapter 11

As soon as he had said these last words, I looked at his fair face, which, because of his bitter pain, took on diverse colors, and his pain augmented with such great violence that all of a sudden the separation of his body and his soul took place. On seeing that, I was so anguished and distressed that I was unable to utter a word. My weakened limbs were not even able to support me. Wherefore, having sat down beside them,[38] I contemplated them with an incredible compassion. But in looking at Hélisenne's face, I was greatly astonished, because I had thought her long dead, and I saw that she was still heaving a sigh, which was her last, dying sigh. And almost immediately thereafter I had reason to be still more amazed, for I perceived in the spacious and clear air a man flying on golden wings, holding in his hand a marvelously bright staff, and with such accoutrements he passed over and flew through the air more rapidly than the raging Boreas. Suddenly he descended to the earth. Seeing that he was near me, I began to look at him. But because he shone with such a brilliant and dazzling light, my eyes could scarcely endure it, which made me understand that this vision was not something human, but lofty, supernatural, and divine. And so my spirit was wholly transported. I was so ravished to see something so novel and unusual that I remained for some time without moving, not being able to take my eyes off this splendor.

While I was occupied in this contemplation, I could do nothing else, except prostrate myself on the ground, fearful and trembling, wishing to worship this celestial body. Then, in a mellifluous and gentle voice, he began to speak to me in this way:

"Noble knight, because I know your mind is occupied by diverse thoughts on account of my arrival here, I wish to explain it to you, for your valor surely deserves it. Therefore I declare to you that I am Mercury, the god of eloquence, the guide of souls and the messenger of the gods. I have come to this place in order to lead the souls of these lovers to the realm of Minos,[39] where their perpetual dwelling-place shall be de-

---

[38]Hélisenne and Guenelic.
[39]A mythical king of Crete who came to judge the dead in Hades; cf. *The Odyssey,* xi, 568.

cided." As soon as I heard these kind words, being somewhat reassured, I was so bold as to urgently beg him that I might not be denied what had already been granted to others, that is, to descend into Proserpina's realm. At these words he replied: "O knight, what greed goads and urges you to want to descend into these obscure and shadowy places? There you will see nothing but sad and odious things which will cause you painful anxieties. Nonetheless, since your desire is so great, I shall not frustrate it. Because it would not be right to leave these bodies here, I want to deal with them properly." Then he took a vessel full of ambrosia and nectar, which is the ointment of the gods, and began to anoint the two noble bodies so as to preserve them from corruption. But as he was busy with that, he perceived that near Hélisenne's body there was a small packet wrapped in white silk, which he picked up very promptly. Then he looked inside it and saw that it was a book. Immediately, having come a little closer to him, I knew by its title that in it were written down all our adventures and travels. Thereby I could easily guess that the poor dead lady had written it, after the account Guenelic might have given her. And so I told this to Mercury, who said with great joy that he would make a present of it to milady Pallas, who took special pleasure in reading. After he had said this, he did not delay in using divine power to make a golden cloud come over the bodies of the two lovers. He did so in order that they might not be seen until my return, when I could have them entombed.

That done, Mercury began to invoke the name of the triform goddess Hecate, who is the mistress of enchantments. He asked her for his sake to be so kind as to allow me to be transported through the air as far as the river Styx. These words had no sooner been uttered than his request was granted, for when Mercury began to soar up with his winged shoes and caduceus, I was also raised up, by what means I cannot say, and at first this gave me some fear. But we rapidly arrived at a river, in which flowed a obscure, deep, dark, and diaphanous water, so that looking at it made one terribly afraid. There was Charon, a vile old man, ugly and odious to look at, who was using his old boat to ferry across souls who had shed their bodies. There was as great a multitude of them as the leaves that fall in the autumn. I readied myself to cross over, but the cruel Charon refused me. With his voice full of horror, he told me that I must go back, and that he was resolved not to carry me across. Mercury came promptly to my aid, pressing and urging Charon so much that he yielded.

When we were on the other shore, I heard horrible cries and lamentable shrieks. Then Mercury said to me, "These frightful cries you have heard are the souls who have not yet been completely purged, and who still recall their bodily habits. Because they did not receive in the other life the divine wages of their[40] acts, they lament and suffer here until the ultimate purgation, when, having been washed in the river Lethe, they will forget everything." Conversing and walking along in this way, I saw a great dog, which had three horrible heads, and was baying viciously. Mercury threw him a bit of food, which he seized in his three maws. Then, while he was devouring and eating it, we passed safely by. Next we arrived at the river Cocytus, which flows out of the marshes of the Styx (and signifies weeping and moaning). Afterward, we saw the Phlegethon, which is the burning of wrath and cupidity; and from it the Lethe takes its origin.[41] When we had gone further, I saw the place where Minos resides; seated on his sublime throne, he is accompanied by Rhadamanthys. There everyone is examined regarding the ways in which he has ruled and governed his life. According to their merits or demerits a place is assigned them as their perpetual home. When we had seen these things, Mercury showed me the cruel daughters of the Acheron, who are named Tisiphone, Allecto, and Megaera,[42] who were combing their serpentine hair, from which flowed poison in great abundance. Clotho and Atropos were also there, and their sister Lachesis who endlessly spins thread. But I saw Tisiphone rise and take up a bloody torch, and she was all entwined by serpents and her gown soiled and stained with abominable blood, and in her eyes were tears and dread. Yet she was all blackened with wrath and furious ire. Then I saw her tear from her head a great and horrible serpent; afterward, this hideous creature left the underworld. This caused my mind to be occupied with various ideas. Therefore I asked Mercury what such a thing signified; he replied that this Fury was leaving at the request of Venus, to go torment the evil-tongued lady, who had so persecuted the two lovers. Then I inquired whether these Furies were thus accustomed to carry out the wishes of my lady Venus. To which he responded: "Certainly, they are always ready to do harm, for it is they who continually trouble the human race. Long ago Tisiphone, at the request of the goddess Juno, tormented Athamas[43] and his wife in the same way." After these words, he showed me those who have lived in an evil way, who shall always be troubled and agitated by the horrible judgment of Erebus[44] and dealt with in the dark region of Chaos, where there are countless cruel and evil spirits. There is Tantalus, amidst fair, clear water and an abundance of delicious fruits; yet he is continually hungry and insatiably

---

[40]Secor's text has "ses" here; we have assumed this is an error and have adopted the reading "leurs," which is given in some of the variants.

[41]These great rivers of Hades are mentioned by Homer and other classical writers.

[42]The Greek Furies.

[43]Juno was displeased with Athamas because he had hidden Dionysus from her; she thus drove him and his wife Ino mad and tricked them into killing their own children.

[44]One of the primeval deities that sprang from Chaos.

thirsty. Titius is also there, suffering great torments, for every day the vultures eat his liver, and every day his liver is reborn. There also Ixion suffers grievously, for he lies with his belly on a razor-sharp and red-hot iron wheel that turns incessantly. Sisyphus labors incredibly to hold up a great rock. The forty-nine daughters of Danaus are there, constantly working to draw up running water with sieves and vessels with holes in them, so that their effort is in vain.

Reflecting on these grievous torments, I felt a pitying compassion on hearing the lamentable groans of the souls that were in these gloomy prisons. And so I asked Mercury why these souls endured such extreme punishments, and he promptly answered: "Some of them are those who in life remained inveterate and hardened in their sins, without ever wishing to repent them; wherefore their offenses are not forgiven, and goaded by their internal conscience, they are, as you hear, troubled and persecuted. The others are those who ruled and governed their estates and demesnes with outrageous tyranny, and who were respected by their subjects more out of fear than out of love."

While Mercury was telling me these things, the souls of Guenelic and Hélisenne were being carefully examined. When Minos had heard everything, he judged them, and determined that without delay they should be taken to the Elysian Fields, where souls repose in sweetness and felicity. Then Mercury took us to the lake called Lethe, and had the two blessed souls drink the water of oblivion. That done, we went down a narrow path that was difficult and arduous to climb; but little by little the air cleared, and gave me reason to rejoice. Finally a bright and radiant light appeared. Soon afterward, we found ourselves at the gate, which was beautiful and very fine-looking. The guardians stood in great silence, like marble statues. When they had espied Mercury, they promptly opened the gate. Then we entered this field, which is so pleasant and delightful; for the place is always green and full of aromatic plants and fragrant violets of many colors; the springs there are clear and crystalline. There one can hear diverse kinds of birds, singing in great harmony and melodious resonance. A great many people, both men and women, were listening to them, comfortably resting on the beautiful green grass. Marvelling at such a vision, in order to discover the truth I asked Mercury who these people were who were there in such a great crowd. Then he answered in this way: "These shades and souls you see, whose bodies have not yet been restored to them, reside here, while they await them, in this place filled with sweet pleasure."

To these words I replied: "O my God, I cannot conceive, and cannot believe that these souls desire their bodies, for when I reflect thereon, it seems to me that the delight of this place ought to be enough to prevent them from wanting to aspire or pretend to any beatitude other than this."

As soon as I had said these words, Mercury said to me: "Quezinstra, you must believe that through the divine power these souls will put on their bodies again. And because they come from heaven, they will be associated with astral substances, and they shall be eternal dwellers in the divine consistory, where, enjoying the continual contemplation of the divine vision, they shall live." When Mercury had stopped speaking, several splendid and luminous souls approached him, all showing signs of joy, for they were flitting around the souls of Guenelic and Hélisenne. Greeting them kindly, they gave them an honorable welcome, all of them saying together that they could have no more complete pleasure than to be associated with such a noble company. They said this because these two souls shone with such radiance that they exceeded all the other souls in their illustrious brilliance.

When we had done these things, Mercury, having completed his office, wanted to leave that place. Not without weeping and sobbing, I said farewell to the two blessed souls. Then I heard Guenelic, who most urgently begged me to remember perpetually everything I had seen, in order that I might be able to manifest it to the world, which I promised him to do.

Immediately, without further delay, Mercury conducted me to the place whence he had taken me, and we arrived there in a short time. Then Mercury parted the golden cloud. We found a way to give these two noble bodies an honorable burial. So that there might be a perpetual memory of these two true lovers, on their tombs was described in writing the bitter and cruel treatment they had received in the service of love, and how in the end passion had led them both to a premature death. After doing all these things, I could no longer keep from beginning once again my tears and groans, lamenting this sad and painful event. I believe I should have made a sad end of my life, whose excessively long duration was already displeasing to me, had it not been for Mercury, who turned me away from this mortal intent through his sweet eloquence. Then, somewhat consoled, I began to reflect on the mutability of fortune, saying to myself that a man is worthy of being castigated who bases and fixes his thoughts on transitory things. For all mortal pleasures, if they are not governed by virtues, are not only useless, but very harmful to the soul. Wherefore it seemed to me that those are very happy, who, while they have on earth the power and government of their free will, put their supreme hope in something firm and stable, and so conduct their lives that the approach of death causes them no fear. Because one who avoids sin separates himself from that fear, I came to consider that a solitary life is more suitable for achieving a blessed life than continual intercourse with the world, and I decided to live in that way. Because of the desire I had for such a life, I found a way to lay the foundations of a small temple, which was constructed on the very spot where the bodies of Guenelic and Hélisenne were buried. I also began to build a small hut, with the intention of making this place my perpetual dwelling-place. But in order not to be prolix in my account, I shall put an end to it, for I wish to tell you what happened to the little book found by Mercury, who later told me the story.

Conclusion, in order to perpetuate the present story.

Chapter 12

After Mercury had left me, he flew off toward the heavens, and soon arrived in the celestial consistory, where he was graciously received by all the gods and goddesses. He found them assembled for a solemn banquet which was taking place in Vulcan's home. There was the Trojan Ganymede, who served Jupiter, giving him his cup of nectar. Then afterward served graciously the three sublime goddesses, Juno, Pallas and Venus, who were talking together on many pleasant and diverse subjects. The meal was marvelously sumptuous. When it was over, they began to engage in many relaxing amusements. But the god Mars, seeing Venus sitting down, went to sit next to her, which greatly displeased Vulcan; but because he could not prevent it, he had to be patient. To put this thought out of his mind, he walked about pensively, at which the other gods laughed, looking at his deformity, for Vulcan was crippled because he had long ago been thrown down from heaven onto the earth. Soon afterward came Apollo, who began to play a golden harp adorned with many jewels. And with him were the nine muses, who sang very melodiously. Seeing that, Mercury took pleasure in listening for a while to their harmonies; then, approaching the goddess Pallas, he said to her:

"O goddess born from the brain of thundering Jupiter, because I am well aware that you take sovereign delight in reading, I want to make you a present of a little book, which I found down there in that terrestrial region; and since I realized that it was very worthy of being heard, I kept it, hoping that it might be welcomed into your chaste hands." So saying, he drew it from his sleeve and gave it to her. The goddess, thanking him, kindly received it. Then she began immediately to read it. But as she was so occupied, Venus came up to her. Venus was very curious to see new things, and wanted to share in the reading. When she had heard it and had seen that it mentioned love, turning to Mercury she said to him:

"O Mercury, I see clearly that you have very little regard for me, since in order to please Pallas you have deprived me of this book which ought to be dedicated to my divinity, since you know it deals with matters of love and sensuality. And so, if Pallas does not hand it over to me, I may justly reproach her, saying that she has usurped what does not belong to her."

On hearing these words, the virgin Pallas said: "Venus, I am greatly astonished at these remarks of yours, which are so arrogant. It seems that your bold speech will have the power to take away from me what manifestly belongs to me, for if you consider well, you will find that it deals with warlike matters, which are supposed to be conducted under my protection. And for that reason, I ask you to cease to reproach me, for I assure you that your words will not make me yield to your will, but on the contrary they will be vain and useless."

When Venus saw that Pallas had finished speaking, it seemed to her that it was not a time to keep silent. And so she promptly replied: "Pallas, after everything is carefully considered, it is quite obvious that all your allegations are of no value. For if it is true that you have some domination over matters of war, you are not to be preferred to my friend Mars, under whose power warlike acts are conducted. And so if I am to be deprived of [this book], still you should not have it, for if it is determined by judgment with discretion, you shall present it to the one to whom it would far more rightly belong than to you."

Pallas and Venus engaged in a great argument, greater than one could say; but after Jupiter learned of their disagreement, he did not wish to permit such a debate to continue, but rather, as the sovereign and rightful judge, he proposed that he should be a friendly mediator between them. To this, with a single will, the goddesses gave their consent and consigned the point at issue to his hands. But while he was preparing himself to understand and discuss it, Mercury told him that because of something he had to do, it was very urgent that he immediately return to the world. Then he began to tell him why he had to do so. Jupiter promptly told him that he wanted him to make a copy of this book and have it immediately printed in order to show the world the anguish, travails, and painful torments that proceed from love.[45] Mercury obeyed Jupiter's command, and was happy to accept this charge. But before he left to carry out his mission, he asked where he wanted the book printed. Jupiter replied that to do so there was no place more suitable than the renowned and populous city of Paris.

Then Pallas said: "O, how I love that noble city, where I am so assiduously served, for there is found an infinite multitude of studious people. And so one can rightly call this noble city a true fount and source of wisdom and knowledge. And so, Mercury, since you are going to that place, I beg you to inquire of the noble orators, poets, and historiographers whether they have newly composed anything."

When Pallas had said these last words, Venus said what follows: "Certainly, Pallas, this city that you have so praised and extolled is

---

[45]This virtually repeats the title under which the book was published in 1538: *Les Angoysses douloureuses qui procedent d'amours.*

the place in which I am continually venerated and adored, and so is my son Cupid, who under his empire rules and governs the largest part of its habitants. And so, Mercury, I beg you not to forget to give my greetings to those whom you know to be among our most faithful servants. To those who are sometimes weary and woeful after long servitude and wish to abandon love you shall say that they must not give up their pursuits, for in the end Love gives victory to his faithful servants."

When Mercury had carefully listened to what Venus said, he replied: "I assure you, Venus, that I do not intend to deliver your amorous messages, for from what you say about rewarding so well your servants who persevere in servitude to you, it seems to me that you are worthy of great reproach, for as evidence demonstrates, you have poorly rewarded Guenelic and Hélisenne, who, for having continued in your service, have won no reward other than death."

So saying, Mercury departed, and left the goddesses still embroiled in their dissensions, awaiting the definitive decision of their judge (and I don't know what happened afterward). But when Mercury had flown long enough through the azure region, he arrived at the place where he had left me, and found that I had been very busy completing the edifices I had begun. Nevertheless, as soon as he had landed and recounted all the things previously mentioned, I was happy for two reasons to take on the task of having the book printed: first to satisfy Guenelic's desire which he had so insistently urged on me. And so, knowing that it is a perilous thing to incur the wrath of souls, I did not wish to fail to keep my promise, for the divine Plato warns us not to offend people so that the souls of their relatives may not become wrathful toward us. We read that the souls of Marius's family troubled and disturbed Sulla.[46] If one believes a tragedy, the shades and spirits goaded the mad Orestes.[47] When Polydorus was killed, out of domestic charity he warned [Aeneas] to quit that cruel and avaricious shore.[48] Achilles urgently prayed that to avenge him the virgin Polyxena might be sacrificed on his tomb.[49]

Therefore, considering these examples, I have desired to publish this work. The other reason that led me to do so is in order that all readers[50]

---

[46]Lucius Cornelius Sulla (ca.138-78 B.C.) was a Roman general and leader of the aristocratic faction in the civil war against the popular leader Marius.

[47]Probably an allusion to Aeschylus's *Eumenides*, in which Orestes is pursued by the Furies for having killed his mother Clytemnestra and her lover Aegisthus.

[48]Polydorus's ghost warned his countryman Aeneas to flee Troy. See Virgil, *Aeneid*, III:44.

[49]After the fall of Troy, Achilles' ghost claimed Polyxena, daughter of Priam, king of Troy, as his prize, and she was sacrificed on his tomb.

[50]The French here is "tous lecteurs," the unmarked masculine form that can refer to both male and female readers.

who busy themselves with reading these painful torments, may preserve themselves and not allow sensuality to dominate reason, for fear of succumbing to such lasciviousness, from which only intolerable pains and travails can result. In order preserve you from them I beseech the eternal divinity to grant you all the prudence of Cato, the subtlety of Laelius,[51] the reason of Socrates, the acute erudition of Aristotle, along with the precepts of the great Solon,[52] so that by this means you may have the will to leave behind transitory things in order to acquire perpetual things.

End of Quezinstra's narrative concerning the death of his companion Guenelic and his lady Hélisenne.

---

[51]Marcus Porcius Cato (234-149 B.C.), Roman politician, orator, and moralist. Gaius Laelius, Roman consul in 140 B.C., soldier, and orator. Cato is the main interlocutor in Cicero's dialogue *On Old Age*; Laelius is also an interlocutor in this dialogue, and the main figure in Cicero's *On Friendship*.

[52]Athenian statesman and poet (ca. 640-after 561 B.C.) who reformed his city's constitution.

Bibliography

Baker, M. J. "*Fiammetta* and the *Angoysses douloureuses qui procedent d'amours.*" *Symposium* 27 (1973): 303-8.

———. "France's First Sentimental Novel and Novels of Chivalry." *Bibliothèque d'Humanisme et Renaissance* 36 (1974): 33-45.

Bergal, Irene May. "Hélisenne de Crenne: A Sixteenth-Century French Novelist." Ph.D. diss., University of Minnesota, 1966.

Ching, Barbara. "French Feminist Theory, Literary History, and Hélisenne de Crenne's *Les Angoysses douloureuses qui procedent d'amours.*" *French Literature Series* 16 (1989): 17-26.

Conley, Tom. "Feminism, *écriture*, and the Closed Room: The *Angoysses douloureuses qui procedent d'amours.*" *Symposium* 27 (1973): 322-32.

Cottrell, Robert D. "Female Subjectivity and Libidinal Infractions: Hélisenne de Crenne's *Angoisses douloureuses qui procedent d'amours.*" *French Forum* 16 (1991): 5-19.

Coulet, Henri. *Le Roman jusqu'à la Révolution.* Paris: Colin, 1967.

Debaisieux, Martine. "Des dames du temps jadis": Fatalité culturelle et identité féminine dans *Les Angoysses douloureuses qui procedent d'amours.*" *Symposium* 41 (1987): 28-41.

Demats, Paule. Introduction to her critical edition of the first part of *Les Angoysses douloureuses qui procedent d'amours (1538)*, pt. 1. Paris: Les Belles Lettres, 1968.

Dulac, Liliane. "Christine de Pisan et le Malheur des *Vrais Amans.*" In *Melanges de Langue et de Littérature Médiéales Offerts à Pierre Le Gentil.* Paris: S.E.D.E.S., 1973: 223-33.

Guillerm, Luce. "La Prison des textes ou *Les Angoysses douloureuses qui procedent d'amours* d'Hélisenne de Crenne (1538)." *Revue des Sciences Humaines* 67 (1984): 9-23.

Jeanneret, Michel. "Modular Narrative and the Crisis of Interpretation." In *Critical Tales.* Ed. John D. Lyons and Mary McKinley. Philadelphia: University of Pennsylvania Press, 1993: 85-103.

Jordan, Constance. *Renaissance Feminism: Literary Texts and Political Models.* Ithaca, N.Y.: Cornell University Press, 1990.

Larsen, Anne R. "The Rhetoric of Self-Defense in *Les Angoysses dou-*

loureuses qui procedent d'amours (Part One.)" *Romance Quarterly* 29 (1983): 235-43.

Lejeune, Philippe. *Le Pacte autobiographique.* Paris: Seuil, 1975.

Loviot, Louis. "Helisenne de Crenne." *Revue des Livres Anciens* 2 (1917): 137-45.

Mustacchi, Marianna, and Paul Archambault. *A Renaissance Woman: Helisenne's Personal and Invective Letters.* Syracuse, N.Y.: Syracuse University Press, 1986.

Nash, Jerry C. " 'Exerçant oeuvres viriles': Feminine Anger and Feminist (Re)Writing in Hélisenne de Crenne." *L'Esprit Créateur* 30 (1990): 38-48.

———. "The Rhetoric of Scorn in Hélisenne de Crenne." *French Literature Series* 19 (1992): 1-9.

Pascal, Roy. *Design and Truth in Autobiography.* Cambridge, Mass.: Harvard University Press, 1960.

Raitt, Janet. *Madame de Lafayette and La Princesse de Clèves.* London: Harrap, 1971.

Reynier, Gustave. *Le Roman sentimental avant L'Astrée.* Paris: Colin, 1908.

Robbins-Herring, Kittye Delle. "Hélisenne de Crenne: Champion of Women's Rights." In *Women Writers of the Renaissance and Reformation.* Ed. Katharina Wilson. Athens: University of Georgia Press, 1987: 177-218.

Sasu, Voichita. "Tradition et modernité dans le roman autobiographique." *Zagadnienia Rodzajow Literackich: Woprosy Literaturnich Zanrov* 23 (1980): 33-43.

Saulnier, V.-L. "Quelques nouveautés sur Hélisenne de Crenne." *Bulletin de l'Association Guillaume Budé,* 4th ser. (1964): 459-63.

Secor, Harry R. "Helisenne de Crenne: *Les Angoysses douloureuses qui procedent d'amours (1538):* A Critical Edition Based on the Original Text, with Introduction, Notes, and Glossary." Ph.D. diss., Yale University, 1957.

Stone, Donald. "The Unity of *Les Angoysses douloureuses.*" In *From Tales to Truth: Essays on French Fiction in the Sixteenth Century, Analecta Romanica* 34. Frankfurt: Klostermann, 1973: 12-21.

Vercruysse, Jérôme. "Hélisenne de Crenne: Notes biographiques." *Studi Francesi* 31 (1967): 77-81.

Winn, Colette H. "Perception spatiale dans *Les Angoysses douloureuses qui procedent d'amours. Degré Second* 9 (1985): 1-13.

———. "La Symbolique du regard dans *Les Angoysses douloureuses qui procedent d'amours* d'Hélisenne de Crenne." *Orbis Litterarum* 40 (1985): 207-21.

Wood, Diane S. "The Evolution of Hélisenne de Crenne's Persona." *Symposium* 45 (1991): 140-51.

Lisa Neal teaches French language and literature at the University of Puget Sound. She has published articles and reviews on sixteenth-century French literature, and in 1993 she was a fellow at a National Endowment for the Humanities Institute on Translation Theory sponsored by the State University of New York at Binghamton.

Steven Rendall is a professor of Romance languages at the University of Oregon and editor of *Comparative Literature*. He has published many studies on early modern French literature, including *Distinguo: Reading Montaigne Differently* (1992). His previous translations include Michel de Certeau's *The Practice of Everyday Life* and the first volume of Honoré d'Urfé's pastoral novel, *L'Astrée*.

Marguerite Briet was a member of the minor nobility who published her works under the pseudonym Hélisenne de Crenne. She was born in northern France between 1510 and 1520, and died around 1550. In addition to *The Torments of Love* (1538), she wrote an epistolary novel (*Personal and Invective Letters*, 1539) and an allegorical fable (*Dream*, 1540). She also produced the first French translation of Virgil's *Aeneid* (Books I-IV).